D0019731

THE BEDFORD SERIES IN HISTORY AND CULTURE

Benjamin and William Franklin

Father and Son, Patriot and Loyalist

Related Titles in

THE BEDFORD SERIES IN HISTORY AND CULTURE

The World Turned Upside Down: Indian Voices from Early America
Edited with an introduction by Colin G. Calloway, *University of Wyoming*

The Autobiography of Benjamin Franklin
Edited with an introduction by Louis P. Masur, *City University of New York*

Benjamin and William Franklin: Father and Son, Patriot and Loyalist
Sheila L. Skemp, *University of Mississippi*

Narrative of the Life of Frederick Douglass, An American Slave, Written by Himself
Edited with an introduction by David W. Blight, *Amherst College*

Muckraking: Three Landmark Articles
Edited with an introduction by Ellen F. Fitzpatrick, *Harvard University*

Plunkitt of Tammany Hall by William L. Riordon
Edited with an introduction by Terrence J. McDonald, *University of Michigan*

American Cold War Strategy: Interpreting NSC 68
Edited with an introduction by Ernest R. May, *Harvard University*

The Age of McCarthyism: A Brief History with Documents
Ellen Schrecker, *Yeshiva University*

Postwar Immigrant America: A Social History
Reed Ueda, *Tufts University*

THE BEDFORD SERIES IN HISTORY AND CULTURE

Benjamin and William Franklin

Father and Son, Patriot and Loyalist

Sheila L. Skemp

University of Mississippi

BEDFORD/ST. MARTIN'S
Boston ♦ New York

For Bedford/St. Martin's
Publisher: Charles H. Christensen
Associate Publisher/General Manager: Joan E. Feinberg
History Editor: Niels Aaboe
Developmental Editor: Louise D. Townsend
Managing Editor: Elizabeth M. Schaaf
Copyeditor: Barbara G. Flanagan
Text Design: Claire Seng-Niemoeller
Cover Design: Richard Emery Design
Cover Art: Benjamin Franklin by Joseph Sifrede Duplessis, 1783. Pastel on paper. Collection of The New York Public Library. Astor, Lenox, and Tilden Foundations. *William Franklin* by Mather Brown. Private Collection. Print no. 31399. Collection of the Frick Art Reference Library.

Library of Congress Catalog Card Number: 92–75893

Manufactured in the United States of America.

9 8 7
l k j i

For Information, write: Bedford/St. Martin's, 75 Arlington Street, Boston, MA (617-399-4000)

ISBN-10: 0-312-08617-2 (paperback)
0-312-10283-6 (hardcover)
ISBN-13: 978-0-312-08617-6 (paperback)
978-0-312-10283-8 (hardcover)

Acknowledgments

William Franklin, letter to Benjamin Franklin, September 7, 1765, and Benjamin Franklin, letter to William Franklin, November 9, 1765. Leonard Labaree, ed., *The Papers of Benjamin Franklin*, vol. 12, Yale University Press. © 1968 American Philosphical Society Held at Philadelphia for Promoting Useful Knowledge and by Yale University.

Benjamin Franklin, "Causes of the American Discontents before 1768," January 1768. William B. Wilcox, ed., *The Papers of Benjamin Franklin*, vol. 15, Yale University Press. © 1972 American Philosophical Society Held at Philadelphia for Promoting Useful Knowledge and by Yale University.

Foreword

The Bedford Series in History and Culture is designed so that readers can study the past as historians do.

The historian's first task is finding the evidence. Documents, letters, memoirs, interviews, pictures, movies, novels, or poems can provide facts and clues. Then the historian questions and compares the sources. There is more to do than in a courtroom, for hearsay evidence is welcome, and the historian is usually looking for answers beyond act and motive. Different views of an event may be as important as a single verdict. How a story is told may yield as much information as what it says.

Along the way the historian seeks help from other historians and perhaps from specialists in other disciplines. Finally, it is time to write, to decide on an interpretation and how to arrange the evidence for readers.

Each book in this series contains an important historical document or group of documents, each document a witness from the past and open to interpretation in different ways. The documents are combined with some element of historical narrative—an introduction or a biographical essay, for example—that provides students with an analysis of the primary source material and important background information about the world in which it was produced.

Each book in the series focuses on a specific topic within a specific historical period. Each provides a basis for lively thought and discussion about several aspects of the topic and the historian's role. Each is short enough (and inexpensive enough) to be a reasonable one-week assignment in a college course. Whether as classroom or personal reading, each book in the series provides firsthand experience of the challenge—and fun—of discovering, re-creating, and interpreting the past.

Natalie Zemon Davis
Ernest R. May
Lynn Hunt
David W. Blight

Preface

In 1776, members of the Second Continental Congress met in Philadelphia to announce their intention to sever all ties with England. Today, Americans take for granted the successful conclusion of the colonial quest for independence. They assume, without thinking much about it, that the American Revolution was virtually inevitable, that events like passage of the Stamp Act, the Boston Massacre, and the Boston Tea Party led almost unavoidably to the Declaration of Independence. They do not understand the reluctance with which American patriots arrived at their decision to reject the authority of Crown and Parliament, for they fail to appreciate the deep emotional ties that bound English-Americans to the mother country. Nor do they fully realize that many ordinary colonists, men and women who loved America as much as the patriots did, opposed independence and remained loyal to the king.

The American Revolution was a civil war as well as a war for independence. Neighbor fought against neighbor, brother fought against brother, and father fought against son. The dramatic, and in some ways tragic, experience of Benjamin Franklin and his son, William, reveals something of America's internal struggle over the question of independence. It helps students understand why by 1776 some Americans, at least, felt that independence was essential to their very survival, while others—some twenty percent of the colonial population—were persuaded that independence was both unnecessary and wrong.

Benjamin Franklin, who perhaps more than any other American of his generation left his mark on the Western world, was a leading force in America's march toward independence. The son of a Boston candlemaker, he was not a rabble-rouser or a firebrand. He came to his decision to advocate independence cautiously, haltingly, and reluctantly. Until the 1770s he was proud of his English heritage, and he was determined to bring America—especially his adopted colony of Pennsylvania—ever more closely into the web of empire. His support for independence developed slowly. As king and Parliament grew increasingly intrusive, interfering in local colonial affairs, attempting to tax the colonies, and sending troops to America to enforce their unpopular mandates, Franklin, like many other Americans, became convinced that English rule meant that colonial rights and liberty were at risk. By 1776, he believed that Americans faced a choice between tyranny and independence. For him, the obvious choice—indeed the only choice—was independence.

Throughout the 1760s and 1770s, William Franklin often shared his father's unhappiness with British policy. He had spent his entire adult life serving the king, first as a captain in His Majesty's army and then as the royal governor of New Jersey. As governor, he was charged with the duty of upholding English authority in America, a duty he took very seriously. Still, as an American, he often understood the complaints of New Jersey inhabitants who believed that king and Parliament were exceeding their legitimate powers and destroying the traditional "rights of Englishmen." As the relationship between England and America deteriorated, however, William Franklin found that he had no desire to join his father's fight for independence. The colonies, he thought, were too weak, too disorganized, too poorly led to survive without England's help. Standing alone, they would divide along regional and factional lines and begin fighting among themselves. For Governor Franklin, the choice that faced America was one that promised order and stability on the one hand or anarchy and chaos on the other. For him, as for his father, there was only one real choice.

ACKNOWLEDGMENTS

My interpretation of the views of William Franklin, and to a lesser extent of the views of Benjamin Franklin, relies to a considerable degree on my *William Franklin: Son of a Patriot, Servant of a King* (New York: Oxford University Press, 1990). I would like to thank Oxford's senior vice-president, Sheldon Meyer, for allowing me to incorporate material from that earlier work into this volume. I would also like to thank Michael Landon and Fred Laurenzo of the University of Mississippi for helping me understand the vagaries of the governmental structure of eighteenth-century England. Thanks, too, to Marilyn Baseler, John B. Frantz, Monys A. Hagen, and Robert Middlekauff, all of whom read and made extensive comments on the entire first draft of this manuscript.

Many individuals at Bedford Books deserve special commendation. Chuck Christensen and history editor Sabra Scribner encouraged me to consider writing this book. Louise Townsend, Bedford's developmental editor in history, is a wonderful editor. Her suggestions have always been wise and useful, making my own work—even the rewrites—almost a pleasure. Elizabeth Schaaf, managing editor, guided the book through all stages of production.

Copyeditor Barbara Flanagan saved me from many infelicities of phrase and even helped me shorten an impossibly long manuscript. I also appreciate the help of Donna Dennison, Bedford's advertising and promotion manager, who designed the artwork for the cover, and editorial assistant Richard Keaveny, who was responsible for manuscript preparation.

Sheila L. Skemp

Contents

THE BEDFORD SERIES IN HISTORY AND CULTURE

Benjamin and William Franklin

Father and Son, Patriot and Loyalist

PART ONE

Benjamin and William Franklin

INTRODUCTION

Divided Loyalties

On July 4, 1776, William Franklin, governor of the colony of New Jersey, rode into Hartford, Connecticut. He was the prisoner of a heavily armed guard of men acting under the orders of General George Washington. He was tired, dirty, and suffering from a high fever, and his discomfiture was made even worse when he recalled the jeers and insults that had greeted him along the route from Burlington, New Jersey, to the Connecticut capital. Now he faced a meeting with Governor Jonathan Trumbull, who would decide his fate. If he signed an agreement promising not to attempt an escape, his captors would treat him like a gentleman, and his accommodations would be relatively comfortable. If he refused, they would incarcerate him like any common prisoner. By defying the Continental Congress and defending the king, William Franklin had become an enemy to his country.

The governor had no way of knowing that even as he rode toward Hartford, the very Continental Congress whose prisoner he had become was voting to adopt the document that would be known as the Declaration of Independence. Nor in all probability was he aware that his own father, Benjamin Franklin, was a member of the five-man committee that had begun to draft the document on June 11. He realized, of course, that Franklin was one of the leading exponents of American independence, while he himself, as a Crown servant, opposed any move to dismember the British Empire. The war that would divide America from England had already separated father and son.

It had not always been so. Until the 1770s, Benjamin and William Franklin had enjoyed a close personal and political relationship. They trusted one another with their intimate secrets, offering one another advice, encouragement, and support. The two men shared similar views. William may, as his father once complained, have been a "thorough government man,"[1] but he was also a defender of assembly rights, and he often chafed at the intransigence and exasperating insensitivity of London bureaucrats. The elder Franklin was a staunch advocate of American rights, but in the decade before independence he also supported a strong and united empire and had long hoped that nothing would ever diminish America's "Loyalty to our Sovereign or Affection for this Nation in general."[2] Both men had grown up believing that English and American interests were harmonious and that it was possible to serve king and colony simultaneously. Nevertheless, after 1770, father and son, colonies and empire, slowly, inexorably, drifted apart.

The story of Benjamin and William Franklin reveals a great deal about Anglo-American relations in the years before 1776 and about the nature of the conflict between the colonies and the mother country. Still, a word of caution is in order. The experiences of two individuals can never adequately encompass the wide range of motivations that impelled Americans either to support or to reject independence. Loyalists, who composed about 20 percent of the white American population, and patriots were found in every region and virtually every town. Each camp could legitimately claim to cut across class, racial, religious, and gender lines. People supported one side or the other for myriad reasons. Self-interest and principle, ideology and economic opportunity, hope and fear all played a role in helping each person arrive at one of the most important and difficult decisions he or she would ever make.

Nevertheless, in some ways the divisions between Benjamin and William Franklin did reflect the changing relationship between England and its North American colonies. On the one hand, the English colonists who dominated the political and cultural life of the provinces valued their ties with the mother country and strove valiantly to imitate its policies and institutions. They were proud of their English heritage and were generally willing to help England in its quest for international power. On the other hand, as the popular metaphor of the time indicated, if the colonies had always been children, they were now growing up, and they were ready to support themselves. Americans like Benjamin Franklin had come to see that the colonial population was booming, the provincial governments had become increasingly sophisticated, and provincial leaders were more self-confident. If they did not want to separate from England—and none in the beginning did—they realized that they could, at the very least, survive independence. Should the interests of England and America diverge, should the home government demand too many sacrifices, should their claims to English rights be threatened, many of them were ready to go their separate way.

The men and women who remained loyal to the king found it impossible to consider separation. Like William Franklin, they disliked many of the economic laws and regulations emanating from England after 1763, especially Parliament's attempts to tax the colonies. They valued their representative assemblies and their jury trials as much as the patriots did. They did not believe, however, that their disagreements with English policy constituted enough reason to declare independence. Nor did they think that the colonies were sufficiently mature to survive on their own. Without the beneficent care of king and empire, they feared that colonial order would disintegrate, that American society would descend into chaos. Their nightmare vision of a world gone mad led them to remain loyal to the king.

Benjamin and William were active participants in the major events of the day; neither was an ideologue or an extremist; at least until the mid-1770s, each could see the virtues of both sides of the increasingly acrimonious dispute between England and its North American possessions. The elder Franklin's gradual movement toward independence reflects the journey of many of America's reluctant revolutionaries. His very moderation and his love of England make his ultimate decision to support independence more complex, more deliberate, and more reflective of the American mood as a whole than do the actions of "radicals" like Samuel Adams or Patrick Henry. William Franklin, who ultimately opposed his father's cause, was a royal appointee who thought long and deeply about the course that his position as royal governor dictated he take. Virtually all Crown servants remained loyal, and William Franklin was no exception. Still, as a governor who had worked with his legislature as much as he had worked against it and who sought to do what was best for America as well as to honor his duty to the king, he found it difficult to oppose his father—and his native land.

The Franklins' experience reveals that the war with England was not simply a war for colonial independence, although it was surely that. Nor was it a war fought solely to alter the very structure of American society and politics, although in some respects it was that as well. It was also a civil war, in which Americans fought other Americans even as they fought with or against the British forces. Neighbor fought neighbor, brother fought brother, and as the experience of Benjamin and William Franklin attests, father fought son. The suffering of antagonists on both sides of this civil war should not be underestimated. Some 80,000 loyalists, including William Franklin, left America during or after the war to live in exile for the rest of their lives. Those loyalists who remained in America were subject to economic, political, and military persecution. Their lands were confiscated, their political rights abrogated, and many of them endured physical deprivation, or, like William Franklin, imprisonment at the hands of their patriot neighbors. In the deep South and in colonies like New Jersey and New York, where the loyalist population was relatively high, they gave as good as they got. Both sides were victims of shocking atrocities in a world where law and order often disappeared altogether.

The Franklins' story reminds us that independence was not inevitable, that all Americans faced serious and difficult choices in the years before the American Revolution. Perhaps no side was "right" or "wrong." There were only winners and losers in a war that most participants wished to have avoided altogether.

NOTES

Abbreviations used in the notes throughout:
BF: Benjamin Franklin
WF: William Franklin
PBF: Leonard W. Labaree et al., eds., *The Papers of Benjamin Franklin* (New Haven: Yale University Press, 1959–).
Autobiography: Benjamin Franklin, *The Autobiography of Benjamin Franklin*, ed. Leonard W. Labaree et al. (New Haven: Yale University Press, 1964).

[1]BF to WF, 6 Oct. 1773, *PBF* 20:437.
[2]BF to Samuel Cooper, 27 Apr. 1769, ibid., 16:118.

1

Self-Made Men

Even by American standards, neither Benjamin nor William Franklin could claim an auspicious beginning. Benjamin's childhood was spent in more humble circumstances than his son's, and his material advantages were fewer. Still, he did not grow up, as William did, an illegitimate child whose step-mother barely tolerated his presence. It all, more or less, evened out.

Both men were the sons of tradesmen, and while they were bright and ambitious, neither should have harbored any realistic hopes of joining the ranks of the colonial elite. This, after all, was the eighteenth century. Colonial society was more fluid than its English counterpart, but even in America few people advanced much beyond the position to which they were born. Indeed, opportunities for advancement were diminishing throughout the eighteenth century, as the colonies grew more cosmopolitan and distinctions in rank there were more rigidly defined. The accident of birth, not industry, merit, or even luck, was increasingly important. This trend was evident everywhere, but it was especially obvious in America's major cities. There, evidence that fewer and fewer people amassed more and more wealth was hard to ignore. In Boston and Philadelphia, the top 5 percent of taxpayers had about as much wealth as the rest of the taxpayers combined. In both cases the divergence between those at the top and those at the bottom had become more marked in the last fifty years.[1] In a society where wealth and power tended to go hand in hand, this concentration of wealth at the top levels of society had obvious implications. Benjamin and William Franklin might go far in this world, but eventually they could expect to encounter very real limits to their ability to transcend their inherited status.

Virtually every schoolchild is familiar with the broad outlines of Benjamin Franklin's early life. His *Autobiography* reads—as Franklin no doubt intended that it should—like an American success story. It is the tale of a poor, essentially self-educated apprentice who, though bred in "poverty and obscurity," through industry, determination, and the development of strong character, rose to "a State of Affluence and some Degree of Reputation in the World."[2]

Franklin was born on January 17, 1706, the tenth and youngest son of seventeen children. He came from humble but respectable stock. His father, Josiah, had left the English county of Oxford in 1683 and sailed for Boston, where he could worship as a Puritan in congenial surroundings. He was a silk dyer in the old country, but there was little market for his talents in provincial Massachusetts. Exhibiting an ability to adapt to his surroundings that would be a defining characteristic of his son, he learned the art of candlemaking, joining the ranks of Boston's artisan class. Franklin's mother, Abiah, was the daughter of Peter Folger, teacher, surveyor, weaver, miller, and writer of homespun verse. Her mother had been an indentured servant before her future husband bought the remainder of her term of service for twenty pounds.

Franklin grew up in the thriving seaport of Boston. In 1700, the town boasted six thousand inhabitants; by 1720, its population had nearly doubled. Even in the eighteenth century, Boston had not drifted far from its Puritan roots. While Franklin never exhibited much interest in a stern Calvinist God or the demanding doctrine of predestination, his values were nevertheless shaped by the theology he rejected. His moderation, industry, and frugality, his determination to succeed at his calling, his desire to improve the lives of his fellow human beings in concrete ways, all were a secularized reflection of the ideals espoused in 1630 by John Winthrop's little band of dissenters.

If Boston was a town shaped by its Puritan past, it was also a trading center most of whose inhabitants were not ashamed to strive for material success. Its society was stratified, but it was small, and, compared with its European counterparts, its social relations were fluid. For those who were industrious, thrifty, and blessed with a modicum of luck, some social advancement was a possibility. Benjamin Franklin believed in America's promise long before he began to portray himself as the best proof that his native country was the land of opportunity.

Franklin's beginnings were not promising. He received only two years of formal education—excelling at every subject but arithmetic—before his father decided that schooling was an expensive waste of time considering the "mean Living many so educated were afterwards able to obtain."[3] Thus, at the age of ten, Benjamin entered the world of trade. He worked for his father for two years but quickly developed a decided aversion to candlemaking. With Josiah's blessing, he finally agreed to serve for nine years as an apprentice to his older brother James, printer of the *Boston Gazette* and soon to become the owner of his own newspaper, *The New England Courant*. There he began to learn the printing trade, but he chafed under James's stern discipline, which he considered unduly harsh, especially as it came from a brother. The ever optimistic Franklin later claimed that James's "harsh and tyrannical Treatment" was a blessing, for it gave him the early "Aversion to arbitrary Power" that he carried with him for the rest of his life.[4] Be that as it may, he did not endure his brother's tyranny for long.[5] In the fall of 1723, the seventeen-year-old apprentice abandoned James's shop and ran away, first to New York and then to Philadelphia, to seek his fortune.

Franklin's first night in Philadelphia scarcely suggested the heights to which he would rise in his adopted home. Dressed in his old working clothes, his pockets "stuff'd with Shirts and Stockings," he bought "three puffy roles" from a local bakery for his evening meal and wandered alone up Market Street, past the house of Miss Deborah Read, who was standing in the doorway with her father. The future Mrs. Franklin later recalled that he made a "most awkward, ridiculous appearance."[6]

Benjamin Franklin's move to Philadelphia was fortuitous. A much younger town than his native Boston—it was less than half a century old when he arrived—it already nearly equaled Boston's population and would soon surpass it. Indeed, though Franklin obviously did not know it, Boston's economic fortunes were on a downward trajectory, while Philadelphia, which served a vast and fertile hinterland, was destined to be one of the colonies' most prosperous cities. Although its economy suffered occasional downward cycles, good wages and full employment for the city's burgeoning artisan community were the norm. Pennsylvania may not have been, as one historian has argued, "the best poor man's country in America," but its chief city surely offered considerable promise to the "middling sort" who moved there throughout the eighteenth century.[7] Philadelphia impressed even foreign visitors with its vitality as well as with its ethnic and religious heterogeneity. Its inhabitants were, they claimed, "the most enterprising on the continent."[8] Virtually every observer commented on the city's "very flourishing state" and the "very mixed company of different nations and religions" that clogged its major thoroughfares.[9]

Philadelphia was the capital of the "proprietary colony" of Pennsylvania. In 1681, Charles II had granted Quaker leader William Penn the right to govern the province and to extract a profit from its land. As the colony's proprietor, Penn hoped that the colony—which he saw in part as a refuge for members of his pacifist sect—would be a "Holy Experiment" where people of different nationalities and religions would prosper in harmony. His experiment was only partially successful. Penn's efforts to govern the colony ran into immediate trouble as settlers demanded a more representative government, especially the right to levy taxes and make laws for themselves. By the time Benjamin Franklin arrived, the colony had passed to the hands of Penn's sons, Thomas and Richard, both of whom had abandoned their father's faith in favor of the more prestigious Anglican religion. Nevertheless, Pennsylvania's government, especially its elected assembly, remained in the hands of the Quakers. Opposition to the new proprietors and to the governors they appointed to administer the colony in their place characterized the assembly's operations throughout the mid-eighteenth century.

Philadelphia, like every other American city, had its own social hierarchy, and Franklin had little chance of being welcomed into the inner circles of either of the city's two exclusive oligarchies. While the Quakers accepted anyone who joined their perennial battles with the proprietors, their religious beliefs precluded them from embracing a free thinker such as Franklin as one of their own. The other ruling elite was dominated by an insular group of interrelated families, tied by blood, land, merchant activities, and politics, that had grown ever more powerful in recent years and generally supported the proprietary interest. Wealthy and genteel—at least by American standards—its members valued their inherited status and welcomed few outsiders into their midst. Still, it was a prosperous, vital, growing commercial center that Franklin decided to make his own. Philadelphia rewarded its talented and industrious inhabitants, even though the uppermost reaches of its society were generally closed to them. If Benjamin Franklin aspired to fortune and power, he had selected, no doubt accidentally, an excellent base from which to launch his career.

Surprisingly, Franklin's first years in Philadelphia were marked by a series of unqualified failures. He floundered; he wandered aimlessly. He was ambitious, even driven, but had no specific goals. He grabbed any opportunity that came his way, but most of those opportunities led to dead ends. He secured a job with printer Samuel Keimer when he first arrived in Philadelphia, but the two men never got along. Consequently, Franklin eagerly accepted Governor William Keith's offer to set him up in the printer's trade. In 1724, when he was just eighteen, Franklin set sail for London, secure in the knowledge that Keith had promised to entrust the ship's captain with letters of credit that he could use to purchase the press and other printing materials he would need to start his business. But when the ship docked in England, the young man was shocked to find that no letters existed. Only then did Franklin discover what most Philadelphians already knew: Keith was "liberal of Promises which he never meant to keep."[10] Once more he found himself in a strange city with no money, no prospects, and no connections.

Franklin managed to gain employment as a printer, carelessly spending his paltry earnings on "Plays and other Places of Amusement" and living from "hand to mouth."[11] For a time he considered traveling throughout England as a swimming teacher, but decided in the end to return to Philadelphia to serve as a clerk in a friend's general store. When his new boss died, however, Franklin was jobless once more. Financially, he was no better off than he had been two years earlier when he had left for London with such high hopes. Despite his obvious humiliation, he turned again to Samuel Keimer, who agreed to take him on as the manager of his printing establishment.

Unfortunately, Franklin was no happier with Keimer now than he had been earlier. The two men quarreled, and Franklin threatened to resign his position and return to Boston, admitting that all his efforts to improve himself had resulted in ignominious failure. One of Keimer's apprentices, Hugh Meredith, persuaded Franklin to remain in Philadelphia. Meredith's father promised to advance the two men enough money to set up their own printing establishment as soon as his son completed the terms of his apprenticeship. Meredith begged Franklin to bide his time—and bite his tongue—in the meantime. Thus Franklin grudgingly remained in Keimer's employ, not bothering to mention that he intended to open a rival printing shop that would, he hoped, drive his boss out of business.

By 1728, Franklin and Meredith's partnership was official. As political and religious passions heated up throughout the mid-eighteenth century, urban Americans became voracious consumers of newspapers and pamphlets. Consequently, talented printers were well positioned to augment their fortunes. Franklin and Meredith had good reason to hope that their establishment would thrive. Meredith, however, was not much of a printer, and he was rarely sober. Even worse, his father suffered severe financial reverses, and he could not pay even his own creditors, much less those of his son. The partners were in danger of losing their business altogether when two of Franklin's friends rescued him. If he promised to get rid of the useless Meredith, they said, they would lend him enough money to become the sole proprietor of his business. With his friends' support and his shrewd ability to anticipate the needs of his customers, Franklin quickly turned his operation into a successful concern. By 1730, he had his own shop, a newspaper, *The Pennsylvania Gazette*, and a stationery store.

Poised to embark on his career as Philadelphia's most eminent printer, Franklin still had to settle one matter: He wanted to get married. Marriage would provide him with the accoutrements of respectability and would free him from that "hard-to-be-govern'd Passion of Youth" that often led him into seedy "Intrigues with low women."[12] A woman who would bring a sizable dowry to the marriage would be ideal. Franklin soon discovered, however, that no one viewed an unknown, debt-ridden printer as a likely prospect, so he turned his attentions to Deborah Read. Before he left for London in 1724, he had been indifferently courting the young woman and had "interchang'd some promises" with her.[13] Once in London, however, he forgot his fiancée, sending her only one letter, and that was to let her know that he was not likely to return. By the time Franklin made his way back to Philadelphia in 1726, Deborah had married a "worthless Fellow," who may have already been married to a woman in the West Indies.[14] The couple soon separated, and Deborah's husband fled the country, leaving her penniless and humiliated. Franklin felt guilty about the way he had treated Deborah. She was a good woman, worked hard, and would be an excellent partner for an ambitious tradesman of uncertain prospects. Perhaps most important, she would be a suitable stepmother for his child.

Benjamin and Deborah entered into an informal, common-law marriage on September 1, 1730, and William Franklin was born shortly thereafter.[15] The identity of William's mother remains a mystery, but the evidence indicates that she was probably one of those "low women" with whom Franklin consorted prior to his marriage. One of Benjamin's closest friends insisted that she was "not in good Circumstances," but he claimed that Franklin provided his son's mother with some money.[16] William never fully escaped the cloud cast by the circumstances of his birth. His stepmother, while she agreed to raise "Billy" as her own child, often treated him with "a coldness bordering on hostility."[17] Moreover, the Franklins' enemies never missed an opportunity to use William's illegitimacy to undermine both father and son. The snickers and knowing winks of his detractors were a constant reminder to William that he was a "base-born Brat."[18]

If William did not enjoy a perfect childhood, his circumstances were superior to those his own father experienced as a boy. He was born after Franklin had finally embarked on a steady and lucrative career. For nearly twenty years, Benjamin lived the life of a successful businessman. *The Pennsylvania Gazette* was popular, for Franklin knew his clientele and he made sure that the paper offended no one. In 1732, the first issue of *Poor Richard's Almanac* appeared. This compendium of witticisms and information—most of which were culled from other sources and rewritten in Franklin's homespun style—was a huge success. Benjamin's stationery shop, thanks largely to Deborah's unflagging work, was also a thriving concern.

Franklin claimed to be an indulgent father—and no doubt he was. Like many self-made men, he gave his son the advantages he had never enjoyed. William had his own pony. When the boy was only four, Benjamin advertised for a tutor for his son. And when William was eight, he started school in earnest, first under the able tutelage of Theopholis Grew and then at Alexander Annand's classical academy, where he remained until 1743. The sons of some of Philadelphia's most genteel inhabitants studied with Annand. If the elder Franklin would always be tarred with the reputation of an upstart tradesman, perhaps William, despite his illegitimate birth, would manage to open doors that were closed to his father. At the very least, William knew that he would never be pulled out of school and obliged to learn a trade from a tyrannical master.

If Benjamin Franklin was indulgent, he was also distracted, and there must have been many times when William felt ignored. The Franklins' house and shop were located on Market Street in the busiest part of town. The little establishment was always overflowing with relatives who lived with the family for long stretches of time as well as with friends and visitors from home and abroad who gravitated to Benjamin's shop to discuss religion and science, politics and business. In 1732, with the birth of Francis Folger Franklin, a potential competitor for his father's affections appeared. Franky took his grandmother's maiden name, giving him a legitimate connection to the Franklin family that William could never claim. Although the child died of smallpox when he was only four, his presence continued to haunt the household. Deborah kept his portrait prominently displayed in her parlor, and nearly forty years after his son's death, Benjamin continued to mourn Franky's loss, claiming that he never thought of him "without a sigh."[19] In 1743, William's half-sister Sarah was born, but while Deborah lavished attention on her only living child, as a girl Sally did not threaten to supplant William in his father's eyes.

William's most formidable rival for his father's affection was Benjamin's voracious appetite for public affairs. As early as 1727, Franklin had formed his famous Junto, a secret organization composed of ambitious tradesmen like himself, designed with the lofty—and as it turned out not totally unrealistic—goal of improving both its members and the city of Philadelphia. By 1731 he and his friends had begun their circulating library; they organized the Union Fire Company in 1736; and in 1744 they founded the American Philosophical Society, by which time Franklin had already begun plans for the Pennsylvania Academy (later the University of Pennsylvania). In 1736, Franklin was appointed clerk of the Pennsylvania Assembly. It was not an especially important job, nor did it pay very well. But Benjamin, always on the lookout for new opportunities, accepted it "as a Means of securing the Publick Business to our Printing House."[20] By 1737, Franklin had also become Philadelphia's postmaster. He ran the post office out of his shop, thus drawing more potential customers to his already prospering establishment. By 1743, Franklin owned three printing houses located in three separate colonies and he was considering further expansions. Benjamin Franklin had taken a long time to settle on a career, but now there was no stopping him.

If Franklin's prospects were expanding almost daily, his son had reached a dead end. William left Annand's academy in 1743, at the age of thirteen. After that he drifted. He helped his father around the shop, but he was no more interested in the printing business than his father had been in candlemaking. His situation must have been frustrating. Benjamin was preoccupied. It was not easy to ignore Deborah's hostility. Like his father, William was ambitious and yearned for adventure. He never tired of hearing Benjamin's story of his own successful flight, and he doubtlessly felt that Philadelphia promised him no more opportunities than Boston had offered his father.

As a youth, Benjamin had exhibited an "inclination for the sea," and William apparently shared that proclivity.[21] When he was about fifteen, he tried to run away from home, boarding a privateer resting in Philadelphia's harbor. Benjamin quickly "fetched him," loudly protesting that "no one imagined it was hard use at home that made him do this."[22] But while Benjamin tried to make light of William's escapade, for once the boy clearly had his complete attention. Franklin knew that he had to give his son some guidance, or William might well try to do the same thing again.

Remembering how he had once reacted to his brother's harsh discipline, Franklin recognized that stern measures would be counterproductive. He had no intention of becoming a tyrant. Instead he channeled his son's desire for adventure into more appropriate avenues, encouraging William to enlist as an ensign in the king's army. England and France, aided by their respective allies, were locked in combat throughout much of the first half of the eighteenth century. In the mid-1740s, the War of Austrian Succession (or, as the colonists would have it, King George's War) was being waged on North American soil as well as in Europe. Relatively few Pennsylvanians gave more than lip service to the war effort, but much to his father's surprise, William embraced the opportunity for military adventure. He was soon on his way to Albany, a member of one of four Philadelphia companies raised to participate in an anticipated expedition against the French forces in Canada.

William spent the winter of 1746 under wretched conditions. The raid on Canada never materialized. As a result of bureaucratic bungling and colonial penny-pinching, the unit's members were supplied with nothing but "stinking beef" and defective weapons. The whole operation, said one disgruntled observer, was riddled with "criminal negligence" and "corruption."[23] Not surprisingly, desertions were virtually an everyday occurrence. William Franklin, however, did not join the deserters. Instead, he performed admirably, earning a promotion and volunteering to join a dangerous march on the French forces at Saratoga, New York. That expedition, too, never got off the ground.

Benjamin Franklin hoped that William would tire of military life. He did not object to having his son enlisted as a defender of king and empire. He knew, however, that a successful career in the royal army was not a realistic possibility for most colonials. Commissions in the British army cost money, and the chance to rise above the rank of captain depended on wealth and connections, not on merit. Still, when Benjamin realized that William refused to be discouraged by his experience and actually thrived on military life, he acquiesced to his son's wishes, even attempting to promote his prospects. The end of the war, not Benjamin Franklin, finally forced William to admit that there was no "Prospect of Advancement in that Way," and in 1748 he vaguely decided to "apply himself to other Business."[24] Still, his military career, brief as it was, remained one of his fondest memories and one of his greatest sources of pride.

William did not return immediately to Philadelphia at war's end. Instead he joined an expedition to Logtown, in the Ohio territory, traveling with Conrad Weiser, the leader of a group of Indian traders commissioned by the colonies of Virginia and Pennsylvania to negotiate a treaty with members of the Miami confederacy. The expedition, the first of many official colonial efforts to make inroads into territory claimed simultaneously by England, France, and Native Americans, was only one indication that the end of King George's War would be little more than a temporary truce. The hostilities between England and France were deep and far reaching, and they were never confined to quarrels over the disposition of power and land on the North American continent. Still, until the warring parties could settle their conflicting claims over the vast and fertile western lands, peace in America would be impossible to maintain. Many Americans, especially young men like William Franklin, saw the West as their best chance to improve their fortunes. Opportunities were drying up for small farmers everywhere. In New England, where the soil was poor and families were large, fathers found it especially difficult to provide their sons with a chance to eke out a bare subsistence. Elsewhere, too, the pressure on the land was becoming more noticeable. Men with capital to spare also responded to the lure of potential profits in the West. It seemed almost too easy to buy up huge tracts of cheap land and to sell them to settlers eager to penetrate the continent's interior. Only the French and their troublesome Indian allies were keeping the colonists from realizing their fondest dreams. Consequently, American support for the English wars against the French was based on self-interest as well as patriotism.

William Franklin's journey to the trans-Allegheny West made a deep and lasting impact on the impressionable young man. It was an arduous journey, but he was young and had inherited his father's physical stamina. He was enchanted by the beauties of the wilderness and convinced that the future of the British Empire—as well as his own prospects for fortune, if not fame—lay in the American West. His father may have found his niche in the cobbled streets of Philadelphia, but his own prospects surely lay in the untilled land and abundant resources of the continent's hinterland.

The younger Franklin hoped to be a speculator, not a farmer. Unfortunately, it took capital to make the fortune he envisioned. His father would not supply it, and William himself certainly did not have it. Thus at the age of eighteen, he returned to Philadelphia, once more at loose ends. He refused to live at home, and while he helped his father on occasion, his life was aimless, if not unpleasant. He was handsome and well educated. His experiences in the war, not to mention his expedition across the Alleghenies, enveloped him with an aura of glamour. Philadelphia's elite seemed ready to accept him. William joined the Annual Assembly, an exclusive social club formed in 1749 by some of the city's most prominent young gentlemen. He also began keeping company with Elizabeth Graeme, the pretty and intelligent daughter of Dr. Thomas Graeme, director of the Pennsylvania Hospital, a provincial councilor, and an ally of the Pennsylvania proprietors. He was, his father half-complained, becoming "much of a Beau." He seemed to have acquired a "Habit of Idleness" and was apparently content to live indefinitely off his father's largesse.[25]

At first Franklin let his son relax and have a good time. He was hardly in a position to criticize. He had enjoyed many aimless days in his own youth before settling down to the discipline required of Philadelphia's leading printer. Moreover, he was experiencing a bit of an identity crisis himself and needed to get his own priorities in order before he could think seriously about his son's future. In 1748, when he was just forty-two, he moved the family away from the house on Market Street, finding quarters in a quieter part of town. The move signaled his intention to quit the world of business altogether. Franklin retired, he told a friend, "to enjoy Life and my Friends." He planned to "read, study, make Experiments, and converse at large with such ingenious and worthy Men as are pleas'd to honour me with their Friendship or Acquaintance."[26] His interest in science, especially in electricity, consumed him in these years, and his list of correspondents grew, as he shared the results of his experiments with men of similar bent in America and England. Soon his house was so filled with crowds who came to watch him at work—they were, Benjamin explained, attracted by "the novelty of the thing"—that he soon had "little leisure for any thing else."[27]

Franklin's friends were not convinced that he was as busy as he claimed to be. Consequently, they had no compunction about luring him away from his parlor and into the Philadelphia State House.[28] To be fair, they needed no great powers of persuasion to nudge him into the political arena. Franklin was not suited to a life of leisure, and despite his protestations that he had no interest in "Publick affairs," he turned down no opportunity that came his way.[29] At first he served all political factions with ease. He was as comfortable with the proprietary governor as he was with the Quaker leaders in the assembly. He sat on the Governor's Commission for Peace at the same time that he won a seat as Philadelphia's representative to the colonial legislature. Nor did he disdain royal preferment. In May 1751, when he learned that the deputy postmaster general of America was on his deathbed, he began lobbying for the soon-to-be-vacated position. The job paid only 150 pounds a year, but Franklin appreciated its value. If he could manage to turn a haphazard and inefficient postal system into a well-regulated concern, he could improve communications in the king's vast North American empire and turn a profit for himself as well. Consequently he wrote Quaker botanist Peter Collinson, one of his many scientific contacts in England, soliciting his support and indicating that he was willing to "advance a considerable Sum," as much as 300 pounds, to obtain the job although he knew that his predecessor had paid only 200 pounds.[30] Franklin was not a naive colonial; he knew that connections and hard cash were the way to preferment in England, and he exhibited no reluctance to play what moralists might consider an unseemly game.

Despite his successes, and there were many, the elder Franklin was as unsure of his own prospects as his son seemed to be of his. He was, as one historian has asserted, "an obscure provincial Philadelphian," respected, even admired by many, but giving no indication that he would one day dine with kings or be venerated by generations of Americans.[31] Indeed, in 1750 Franklin was forced to confront his own limitations when he "try'd a little" to fill the office of justice of the peace. To his chagrin, he discovered that his charm and intelligence were not sufficient to the task. There were some jobs, even in provincial America, that required special training. Franklin quit his post in favor of "the higher Dutys of a Legislator in the Assembly."[32] But the experience rankled. It was no accident that Benjamin decided at this juncture to pay more attention to his son's fortunes.

Franklin knew that he was too old to begin training for a legal career himself. But it was not too late for William. With the proper training, his son could embark on a successful career, helping both men rise even further in Philadelphia society. Father and son were intelligent, charming, and ambitious. With luck, they could become real partners in their ongoing efforts to erase all vestiges of their humble births.

Once Ben embarked on any project, he proceeded with efficiency and thoroughness. He set William to studying law under the tutelage of Joseph Galloway, a young man about his son's age, of sound mind and impeccable social credentials. The three men began a long and fruitful relationship. Galloway proved to be one of Benjamin's staunchest political allies, helping him wage his many battles against the Pennsylvania proprietors and supporting his efforts to further his own and his colony's prospects. He was William's good friend as well as his tutor, introducing him to some of the most important men in Philadelphia. Only the coming of the American Revolution would drive the men apart, when William Franklin and Joseph Galloway remained loyal to a king whose authority the elder statesman did not recognize.

All that, however, lay in the future. In 1750, Benjamin was determined to set William's life in order. He asked London printer William Strahan to enter William's name in one of London's Inns of Court, so that at some point he could complete his legal studies in England's capital. Most American lawyers got their training by serving as an apprentice to or "reading law" with an established local attorney. But a select few—future patriots as well as future loyalists—topped off their education in London, where they studied the finer points of English law under the tutelage of England's eminent legal scholars. Franklin's decision to accord his son a sojourn at the Inns of Court is a reflection of the distance he had traveled from his humble roots as a Boston apprentice. It is an indication, as well, of his determination to continue advancing his own and his son's prospects.

Franklin's devotion to his son's career was unremitting. When Benjamin won election to the Pennsylvania assembly, he arranged for William to occupy the clerk's position he had vacated. In 1753, when he, along with printer William Hunter, finally obtained the long-coveted post of co-deputy postmaster general of North America, he appointed William as postmaster of Philadelphia and the following year promoted him to a position as controller of the North American postal system. Franklin's determination to distribute political plums to a member of his immediate family would be characterized as crass nepotism in the twentieth century. But in the eighteenth century, grants of patronage to friends and family were perfectly acceptable. Indeed, had Franklin refused to use his own power on his son's behalf, William would have been shocked and disappointed.

Father and son grew increasingly close throughout the 1750s as their interests converged and their paths crossed frequently. They joined the same clubs, contributed to the same charities, and genuinely enjoyed one another's company. Benjamin began to appreciate his son's ability, while William was unabashedly proud of his father's political skill. Perhaps nothing reflects the closeness of the two men more than the spectacular experience they shared some time before the fall of 1752, when they conducted the famous kite experiment. They contrived, said scientist Joseph Priestley, "actually to bring lightning from the heavens" when they flew a kite with a metal key attached to its string during an electrical storm.[33] The consequences of this experiment to Benjamin Franklin's reputation cannot be underestimated. His successful effort to harness the power of lightning earned him an international reputation in scientific circles, raising him overnight above the level of an ordinary provincial and placing him in the eyes of some on a par with Galileo and Copernicus. Thus it was Franklin the scientist, not Franklin the politician or statesman, who first captured the fancy of the learned world.

William shared in his father's achievement. Benjamin feared ridicule if his bold experiment failed; consequently, he trusted only his son with his plans. The two kept the secret, put Benjamin's plan to the test, and celebrated their success together. In the years following the kite experiment, electricity continued to fascinate both men. Typically, Benjamin found a practical use for his newfound knowledge by inventing the lightning rod. And while William's interest in electricity was more pedestrian than his father's, he helped Benjamin with his experiments and provided him with useful data.

It was politics, especially the affairs of empire, not the taming of lightning, that ultimately forged the real bond between father and son, as the two men worked in tandem to improve the position of Crown and country throughout the 1750s. They did not imagine that the interests of England and its colonies were divergent. "Britain and her Colonies," the elder Franklin argued, "should be considered as one Whole, and not as different States with separate Interests."[34] William did not disagree. The colonial "system," such as it was, had evolved haphazardly over the years and, despite its obvious inefficiencies, had worked relatively well most of the time. No colonist in the mid-eighteenth century believed that London's interests fundamentally threatened America's prospects.

The colonies all obtained their legitimacy from the king and did most of their business with the king's government, or ministry. In the eighteenth century, the ministry, often referred to by contemporaries as "Whitehall" (from the street in which the government's offices were located), was ill-defined and constantly changing. Essentially, it was the administrative and bureaucratic arm of the Crown, and as such it was appointed by and responsible to the king, not to Parliament. For the colonists, its most important components were the Privy Council and the Board of Trade. The Privy Council was the chief advisory body appointed by and responsible to the Crown. It helped the king exercise his considerable power over American affairs in such areas as making appointments, disallowing colonial laws, and ruling on appeals from colonial courts. Some members of the Privy Council were particularly important to Americans. Until 1768, the secretary of state of the Southern Department assumed responsibility for all colonial affairs. After that time, the Crown appointed a new secretary who devoted most of his attention to American issues. The customs commissioner and the head of the admiralty were responsible for regulating colonial trade. The second major body dealing with colonial affairs was the Board of Trade. Created in 1696, it was also responsible to the king, although it included some members of the House of Commons in its membership. It recommended legislation to Parliament, drafted instructions to royal governors, recommended colonial appointments to the Privy Council, and examined colonial laws, all in an effort to keep the distant colonies under control.

While the colonists owed their very existence to the Crown, Parliament gained more influence in imperial affairs with the passage of time. In the seventeenth century, Parliament began its efforts to regulate colonial trade, demanding that American merchants organize their operations with an eye to the empire's needs. The colonists, for instance, had to conduct all trade on English ships using predominantly English crews. Colonists could not sell some valuable items, such as tobacco, rice, and indigo, to foreign buyers. And all European goods had to pass through England before proceeding to any colonial port. These Navigation Acts, as the various trade regulations were collectively known, never operated very efficiently, and the colonists generally found it easy to ignore their most onerous provisions. Still, throughout the eighteenth century, Parliament expanded its authority in all directions, and it began to act as the Crown's partner in colonial matters.

England's efforts to control its colonies were often met with quiet resistance or sheer indifference. The distance separating the mother country from its colonial possessions made communications difficult. Moreover, the colonies were a diverse lot. By the mid-eighteenth century, all but four were royal colonies, owned and operated by the Crown. Two, Rhode Island and Connecticut, still held charters from the king, which gave them more autonomy than their counterparts. They chose their own governors and other officials, for instance, and did not have to send their laws to England for approval. Pennsylvania and Maryland were proprietary colonies whose private owners acted at the will of the king.

Colonial governments of whatever type were composed of three tiers. The governors, who in the royal and proprietary colonies held their appointments from the Crown and the proprietor respectively, claimed significant power on paper. They could convene and dissolve assemblies, veto legislation, and recommend or appoint a variety of colonial officials. The governors' theoretical powers were limited in practice. Increasingly restrictive—often secret—instructions from England, the invasion by the Crown or the proprietor of their prerogatives, and the general lack of support that the home government accorded them restricted their maneuverability and made most governors increasingly vulnerable to attack from above and below.[35]

The governors nominated the council or upper house in all but three colonies. In Rhode Island, Connecticut, and Massachusetts, the lower house elected council members. Councilors, who were generally drawn from the colonial elite, acted as more than the governors' advisers. They also served as a legislative upper house and sometimes exercised judicial functions as well.

Every American colony boasted an elected assembly. Their legislative duties, as well as their control of the purse strings, gave assembly members considerable leverage. As they attempted to widen their sphere of influence, often without exploring the ramifications of their actions, they began increasingly to see themselves as mini-parliaments whose rights and privileges approximated those enjoyed by the House of Commons. The English, of course, did not share the colonists' exalted view of their own powers. They saw the colonial assemblies as little more than administrative units operating at the convenience of the Crown. Such differences of opinion did not matter very much so long as no one addressed them directly. But when the home government began its efforts to tighten up and rationalize the imperial system, colonial leaders were bound to resist. The exigencies of war provided the context in which the growing struggle between English power and colonial rights first took place.

In 1754, the French and British were once again gearing up for war, and any war with the French was sure to involve the American colonies. The French and Indian War, as the colonists called it, was one of a series of global conflicts involving the English, the French, and their respective allies. A war for imperial dominance in the Western world, it eventually forced both major protagonists to enlist all their resources in a struggle that promised untold wealth and power for the victor. Americans had their own reasons for supporting the English war effort. Patriotism played a part. So, especially in New England, did the colonists' detestation of the "papist" religion of the French enemy. But by the 1750s, the desire to expand unmolested into the trans-Allegheny West made many colonists long for the removal of French influence in North America.

Everyone realized that any war on American soil would be fought not merely by the French Canadians and the American colonists but by the various Native American tribes who occupied the land that both belligerents wanted for themselves. The Board of Trade believed that a united American policy was needed to secure the support of the powerful members of the Iroquois nation in particular. Thus it ordered each colony to send representatives to Albany, New York, to develop such a policy and to negotiate a defensive alliance with the Indian delegates who agreed to attend the meeting. Benjamin Franklin was one of Pennsylvania's representatives to the conference.

In June, William traveled with his father to Albany. He surely knew that Benjamin hoped that much more than a treaty with the Iroquois would result from the conference. The elder Franklin was already outgrowing the provincial insularity characterizing most Americans. His duties as deputy postmaster allowed him to travel along the eastern seaboard and into the South, and he could fairly call two colonies—Massachusetts and Pennsylvania—home. As a result, he had developed a continental view of the British colonies that relatively few of his contemporaries shared. At Albany, he persuaded a majority of like-minded convention delegates to embrace his dream of colonial unity and to adopt the basic principles contained in the Albany Plan. The plan called for a single American government with the power to pass laws and raise money to manage Indian affairs and the colonial defense. Headed by a

Crown-appointed president general, the continental government would also have a Grand Council composed of delegates from each colony. The plan was too daring, however, for the American assemblies, who did not want to share their authority with anyone. Not one assembly—even Franklin's own Pennsylvania legislature—adopted the Albany Plan. To be fair, Benjamin's hope that Parliament would impose some version of the proposal on the recalcitrant colonies also came to nothing. Franklin believed that colonial unity would serve the needs of England and America alike, for it would help those who lived on both sides of the water to see themselves "not as belonging to different Communities with different Interests, but to one Community with one Interest." This, he argued, "would contribute to strengthen the whole, and greatly lessen the danger of future separations."[36] But in 1754, everyone ignored the Albany Plan, proving to both Franklins that colonial selfishness and English myopia could destroy the plans of more prescient observers.[37]

If everyone soon forgot the Albany conference, no one in Pennsylvania could ignore the perils to the colony that came in the wake of the French and Indian War. Previous Anglo-French conflicts had left Pennsylvania relatively unscathed. The colony had not spent much money on earlier war efforts, and very few of its inhabitants had joined military expeditions against the French enemy. In Massachusetts, where war fever was higher and opportunities for peacetime advancement lower, this had not been the case. Consequently, the Bay Colony had endured high taxes and had sustained heavy battle casualties throughout the eighteenth century. Now Pennsylvania was about to experience the consequences of war for itself: This time, much of the war would be fought in the colony's hinterland. The resulting economic and political dislocations would be devastating. For Benjamin and William Franklin, however, the disruption of politics-as-usual opened up tantalizing opportunities.

As the French and their Indian allies threatened the settlers scattered throughout rural Pennsylvania, Benjamin Franklin, with the enthusiastic support of his son, seized the chance to become one of the major players on the local political scene. The elder Franklin had long since become disgusted by the policies of Thomas and Richard Penn. Perhaps in part because they resided in England, they tended to see Pennsylvania primarily as a source of prestige and potential profit. Absentee owners of much of the colony's unimproved land, they appointed deputy governors to run the colony and protect their interests. By the 1750s, the proprietary faction—whose adherents could be found in the Governor's council as well as among the Scots-Irish who lived along the sparsely settled and poorly defended frontier—was at loggerheads with the Quaker-dominated popular party.

The issues dividing the assembly and the proprietors were complex, but they ultimately boiled down to a struggle between incompatible views of proprietary prerogatives and assembly rights. Two issues, in particular, were at stake. First, the Penns habitually tried to bind their appointed governors with detailed sets of secret instructions, making it virtually impossible for them to negotiate any workable compromise with a suspicious assembly whose members insisted that they, and not the proprietors, had the right to make all laws governing the province. The king, of course, was doing the same thing in the royal colonies, and inhabitants there were as incensed by the threat to their control of local affairs as were their counterparts in Pennsylvania. Pennsylvanians, however, had another, even greater reason to resent the proprietors.

The second issue involved the difficult question of taxation. The members of the Pennsylvania assembly, like the English everywhere, insisted that only the people, through their representatives, had the right to raise money for the government and to determine how that money was spent. This issue became especially troublesome during time of war. All colonial governors had difficulty persuading their legislatures to raise money for the empire's defense. In Pennsylvania the problem was exacerbated because the Quaker-dominated assembly was reluctant to raise any money for military purposes. Over the years, the Quaker faction had occasionally agreed to appropriate funds "for the king's use," knowing full well that the money would help supply the British army. Many assembly members, however, were uncomfortable with such compromises. Their discomfiture was made even worse because the proprietors refused to allow the assembly to tax the proprietors' own vast estates, even though the money raised was being used, at least in part, to protect the Penns' own property. They had, insisted Speaker Isaac Norris, "a large Interest to defend."[38] Yet they insisted that because they were not represented in the assembly, that body had no right to pick their pockets.

When Benjamin Franklin began serving in the Pennsylvania Assembly, he cast himself in the role he always professed to relish, seeing himself as an advocate of compromise and sweet reason. "I like neither the Governor's Conduct nor the Assembly's," he told Peter Collinson, "and having some Share in the Confidence of both, I have endeavour'd to reconcile 'em, but in vain, and between 'em they make me very uneasy."[39] It was not long, however, before he became a leader of the antiproprietary faction and a firm defender of assembly rights. He thought the Penns acted from "petty private Considerations."[40] Their governors, he said, brought "Disgrace" on themselves and deserved the "Curses of all the Continent."[41] Each time a new governor appeared on the scene, Franklin entertained brief hopes that this one might prove more amenable to the assembly's perspective. Nothing ever changed, and he became convinced that the proprietors were solely to blame for the colony's difficulties.

William Franklin, who would himself one day be a colonial governor appointed by the Crown, shared his father's views. He sat as a clerk in the assembly, watching Benjamin and his cronies maneuver behind the scenes, observing the stalemate that resulted when neither assembly nor governor would budge from a firmly held position. He was as disgusted with the "incredible Meanness" of the Penns and their hangers-on as his father was, and, at least where the proprietors were concerned, he was an advocate of assembly rights.[42]

If the Franklins opposed proprietary policy, they were not altogether comfortable with the position of the assembly's Quaker leaders. As zealous supporters of the British cause, the Franklins wanted Pennsylvania to be an active participant in Britain's war for empire. The Quakers, however, only reluctantly defended their colony from enemy attack and found offensive war anathema. Benjamin, in particular, would have to tread carefully to promote England's interests in America without alienating his Quaker allies. He was more than equal to the task.

Franklin's chance to promote himself, Pennsylvania, and the empire came when General Edward Braddock arrived in America with two regiments and orders to defend the colonies from a combined French and Indian attack. In 1755, Braddock was in Maryland, and Pennsylvania sent Franklin to his headquarters to confer with the general—ostensibly to discuss post office affairs, but in fact to remove some of the prejudices the general harbored toward the colony because of its pacifist reputation. As was so often the case, William traveled at his father's side.

From the Franklins' perspective, the trip was a huge success. They arrived at Braddock's headquarters to find his affairs in disarray. The general could not obtain adequate wagons or supplies, and he was facing the demise of his entire campaign. Benjamin knew an opportunity when he saw one and quickly worked out an agreement that called for Braddock to hire horses and wagons from Pennsylvania farmers. William set to work amassing necessary supplies.

Braddock heaped praise on the Franklins' efforts, but his campaign was a disaster. A small enemy contingent ambushed the general's forces, and he himself was fatally wounded in the debacle. More important, his defeat left the Pennsylvania frontier completely undefended. Rumors of attacks on settlers filtered into Philadelphia by October 1755, and in late November word came that enemy forces had leveled the Moravian settlement at Gnadenhütten, a mere seventy-five miles northwest of Philadelphia. Even many Quakers recognized the need to take swift military action. Two events forced Governor Robert Morris and the assembly to reach a compromise on the issue of defending the colony. First, Thomas Penn granted the colony a "gift" of five thousand pounds for Pennsylvania's defense. He pointedly refused, however, to concede that the assembly could tax his own estates. Second, streams of refugees—some seven hundred in all—began flowing into Philadelphia. Every refugee had a horror story to tell, and they all demanded protection.

Benjamin Franklin used the occasion to his own advantage, pushing his hastily contrived Militia Act through the legislature. The act called for the creation of a voluntary militia with the right to elect its own officers. By making membership in the militia voluntary, Franklin was, of course, assuring the Quakers that they could avoid military service. The assembly approved Franklin's bill on November 22, 1755, just three days after Franklin introduced it. Governor Morris acceded to the legislature's wishes, although he knew that the Penns would disapprove of many of the bill's provisions. The proprietors wanted the power to draft soldiers into the army, and they favored appointed, not elected, officers. With the frontier in flames, however, Morris had little choice. Still, he was clearly worried. As the architect of the colony's defense program, Franklin had elevated himself to a position of considerable importance. He appeared to be on the brink of creating a new and powerful antiproprietary party that would repudiate Quaker pacifism while continuing to advocate assembly rights.

Despite his distrust of the Franklins, Morris needed their help. In December, he appointed Benjamin one of three commissioners to organize the defense of rural Pennsylvania. William accompanied his father, first to Easton and then to Gnadenhütten where they supervised the erection of forts, bolstered the spirits of the nearly hysterical survivors of Indian raids, and stayed the tide of settlers fleeing their war-torn settlements.

Benjamin Franklin celebrated his fiftieth birthday on the frontier. It was a physically demanding and dangerous adventure, even for someone his son's age. Yet both men made light of the hardships they endured, as they marched through cold winter rain, camped in drafty barns, and forded swollen creeks and rivers. William's military expertise was indispensable. Benjamin, as usual, proved to be a superb organizer and leader, and he was proud of his ability to keep up with men half his age.

As the Franklins rushed back to Philadelphia at the beginning of February to attend a special session of the assembly, they both had reason to be pleased. They had temporarily stabilized conditions on the frontier, even winning the grudging respect of their political enemies in the process. Working together under adverse conditions, they had strengthened the bonds between them, forming the basis of a partnership that would endure for nearly twenty years. His experiences on the Pennsylvania frontier helped Benjamin Franklin appreciate his son's enchantment with the American West. He, too, began to imagine that Britain's future strength lay in the continent's interior. And he dreamed of organizing a western colony under the auspices of the Crown. Seeing his life as a "dramatic Piece," he thought he was now "in the last Act." He wanted "something fit to end with," for he hoped to conclude his short time on earth "with a bright Point."[43] It would be many years before he began what were destined to be futile efforts to act on his vague dreams of a western empire. In 1756, however, with a record of achievement of which any American would be justifiably proud, anything seemed possible.

NOTES

[1]See James Kirby Martin, *In The Course of Human Events* (Arlington Heights, Ill: Harlan Davidson, 1979), 9, 10; Gary B. Nash, *The Urban Crucible: Social Change, Political Consciousness, and the Origins of the American Revolution* (Cambridge: Harvard University Press, 1979), 257. For an opposing view, see G. B. Warden, "Inequality and Instability in Eighteenth-Century Boston: A Reappraisal," *Journal of Interdisciplinary History* 6 (1976), 586–620.

[2]Benjamin Franklin, *The Autobiography of Benjamin Franklin,* ed. Leonard W. Labaree et al. (New Haven: Yale University Press, 1964), 43. (Hereafter *Autobiography.*)

[3]Ibid., 53.

[4]Ibid., 69. Ironically, when Franklin later employed apprentices, his attitude changed rather dramatically. Apprentices, he said, were "always dissatisfied and grumbling," and he thought "the correction very light, and not likely to be effectual, if the stroke left no marks." To Jane Mecom, [?] June 1748, *PBF* 3:303–4.

[5]*Autobiography,* 69.

[6]Ibid., 76.

[7]James T. Lemon, *The Best Poor Man's Country: A Geographical Study of Early Southeastern Pennsylvania* (Baltimore: Johns Hopkins University Press, 1972); Gary Nash, *The Urban Crucible: Social Change, Political Consciousness, and the Origins of the American Revolution* (Cambridge: Harvard University Press, 1979).

[8]Andrew Burnaby, *Travels through North America,* ed. Rufus R. Wilson (New York: A. Wessels Co., 1904), 97.

[9]Ibid., 90; Alexander Hamilton, *Gentleman's Progress: The Itinerarium of Dr. Alexander Hamilton,* ed. Carl Bridenbaugh (Chapel Hill: University of North Carolina Press, 1948), 20.

[10]*Autobiography*, 87.

[11]Ibid., 96.

[12]Ibid., 128.

[13]Ibid., 92.

[14]Ibid., 107.

[15]It had been rumored that Deborah Franklin's former husband, John Rogers, had already been married when he and Deborah wed; but there was no proof that this was the case, and thus she could not annul her marriage. While she thought that Rogers had since died, she could not prove this either. If Rogers had reappeared, Benjamin and Deborah would have been guilty of bigamy. Thus they resorted to a common-law marriage.

[16]George Roberts to Robert Crofton, 9 Oct. 1763, Charles Morton Smith MSS, vol. 2, Historical Society of Pennsylvania, Philadelphia.

[17]"Extracts from the Diary of Daniel Fisher, 1755," *Pennsylvania Magazine of History and Biography* 17 (1893): 276.

[18]John Adams, *Diary and Autobiography*, ed. L. H. Butterfield, 4 vols. (Cambridge: Harvard University Press, 1961), 4:151.

[19]BF to Jane Mecom, 13 Jan. 1772, *PBF* 19:29.

[20]BF to William Strahan, 29 April 1749, ibid. 3:377.

[21]*Autobiography*, 53.

[22]BF to Jane Mecom, [June? 1748], *PBF* 3:303.

[23]Joseph F. Folsom, "Colonel Peter Schuyler at Albany," New Jersey Historical Society, *Proceedings*, new ser. 1 (1916): 161; Carl R. Woodward, *Ploughs and Politics: Charles Read on New Jersey and His Notes on Agriculture, 1715–1774* (New Brunswick, N.J.: Rutgers University Press, 1941), 65.

[24]BF to WS, 19 Oct. 1748, *PBF* 3:321.

[25]BF to Abiah Franklin, 12 Apr. 1750, ibid., 474, 475.

[26]BF to Cadwallader Colden, 29 Sept. 1748, ibid., 318.

[27]BF to Peter Collinson, 28 Mar. 1747, ibid., 119.

[28]*Autobiography*, 196.

[29]*Autobiography*, 196; BF to Cadwallader Colden, 29 Sept. 1748, *PBF* 3:318.

[30]BF to Peter Collinson, 21 May 1751, ibid. 4:134.

[31]Willaim Hanna, *Benjamin Franklin and Pennsylvania Politics* (Stanford: Stanford University Press, 1964), 23.

[32]*Autobiography*, 197.

[33]*PBF* 4:367.

[34]BF to Peter Collinson, 28 May 1754, ibid. 5:332.

[35]See especially Bernard Bailyn, *The Origins of American Politics* (New York: Knopf, 1967).

[36]BF to William Shirley, 22 Dec. 1754, ibid. 5:450.

[37]BF had actually begun to develop his plan as early as 1751. For an account of the Albany conference and copies of the various versions of the Albany plan, see ibid. 5:276ff.

[38]Isaac Norris to BF, 15 June 1758, ibid. 8:101.

[39]BF to Peter Collinson, 26 June 1755, ibid. 6:86.

[40]BF to William Johnson, 11 Aug. 1755, ibid., 140.

[41]BF to Richard Partridge, 27 Nov. 1755, ibid., 274.

[42]*Autobiography,* 214.

[43]BF to George Whitefield, 2 July 1756, *PBF* 6:469.

2

Forging a Partnership

In 1757, Benjamin and William Franklin were about to leave America's shores to embark on an adventure that would, at least in the short run, bring them closer together than ever before. They were headed to London. The Pennsylvania Assembly had asked Benjamin to present its case to the Penns concerning the taxation of the proprietor's lands. William accompanied his father, serving as his secretary.

While the Franklins' discussions with the Penns went nowhere, both men savored their experiences in England's capital. William, especially, used the trip to his advantage. He completed his legal studies at the Inns of Court, launched his career as a Crown servant, and married Elizabeth Downes, a woman of impeccable social credentials. Benjamin was equally enchanted with England's possibilities and even considered moving to London permanently. Instead, he returned to America in 1762 to lead a single-minded crusade to destroy proprietary influence in Pennsylvania.

In the 1760s, both Franklins were proud of their English heritage and valued their opportunity to serve the Crown. Significantly, they shared a conviction that loyalty to the king would invariably redound to their personal benefit as well as to the well-being of Pennsylvania.

By the mid-1750s it had become clear that the conflict between the Penns and the assembly over the issue of taxing the proprietary estates would not be resolved. Moreover, the personal enmity between Governor Robert Morris and Benjamin Franklin had grown so bitter that it was unlikely that the two men would ever reach an accommodation. In February 1756, Franklin won election as colonel of the Philadelphia city regiment, and Morris searched desperately—but in the end futilely—for a way to avoid granting him his commission. In March, when Benjamin, with his son's able assistance, paraded his troops before the State House in a grand review, Morris was pointedly absent. Franklin's military position, coupled with his growing influence in the assembly, made him appear as a formidable power and a dangerous man. There were many, even among Benjamin's supporters, who feared that the

Franklins were plotting a military coup against the proprietary government. Franklin shrugged off all complaints. He was embarrassed by the adulation of his admirers, but, he explained, "the People happen to love me." And he refused to listen to the carping of his critics.[1]

In August 1756, William Denny replaced Robert Morris as the Penns' deputy governor. Hard-drinking, avaricious, and personally corrupt, he was just as determined to protect proprietary prerogatives as his predecessors had been. Clearly, no governor the Penns chose would ever serve the interests of the assembly. Governor Denny, like every governor before him, refused to sign any bill that taxed the proprietary estates, even if that meant that the colony would contribute no money toward the British defense of North America. From the standpoint of the Franklins and their allies, the policies of the proprietors and their minions were characterized by selfishness and miserliness, and they obstructed the interests of Crown and colony alike.

By the beginning of 1757, governor and assembly were on a collision course. In desperation, the assembly decided to send two envoys—Isaac Norris, the aging speaker of the house, and Benjamin Franklin—to London to plead its case to the proprietors in person. Norris resigned his position, but Franklin eagerly accepted the assignment. He had both personal and political reasons for wanting to go to England. He knew that former governor Morris was in London criticizing him to anyone who would listen and trying to get him fired from his post office position. Franklin wanted to be in London to defend himself should Morris's campaign prove successful. In addition, the trip provided an excellent opportunity for William to accompany him to London to complete his legal studies. Franklin was also concerned about William's private life. His son's romance with Betsy Graeme had grown serious. While Betsy's mother encouraged the match, her father did not. Dr. Graeme despised the Franklins' politics and no doubt imagined that his daughter could do better for herself than to marry the bastard child of an upstart printer from Market Street. While Benjamin was ambitious for his son, he saw nothing but trouble should William and Betsy continue their relationship. Either William would be humiliated or, even worse, he might join the proprietary camp in order to win Thomas Graeme's blessing. Thus Franklin persuaded his son to accompany him to England, where William could serve as his clerk, finish his legal training, and improve himself by seeing a bit of the world under the care of a loving parent. Benjamin surely remembered the cooling effect that England had once had on his own relations with Deborah. Perhaps the diversion would work the same magic for his son.[2]

The Franklins left Philadelphia in April 1757, heading for New York where they planned to embark for England. Once there they were met by interminable delays. Benjamin, never happy when he was at loose ends, grew increasingly irritable. William divided his time between the new friends he met, a social life replete with parties that included a "mixed Company of both sexes," and writing romantic letters to his "dear Betsy."[3] They both enjoyed an excursion to Woodbridge, New Jersey, organized by Benjamin, who was never happy simply marking time. Deborah and Sally—but not Betsy—traveled from Philadelphia to join them, and together they explored a part of a colony that would one day be William's home. The young man was taken by the beauty of the region and the "Variety of romantic Prospects" that characterized this bucolic paradise. It "afforded me," he rhapsodized, "far greater Pleasure than any Thing I had ever seen before."[4]

On the 20th of June, the Franklins left for England on the *General Wall.* They were tossed about on the high seas for nearly a month, barely avoiding capture by enemy privateers. And they were almost smashed against the rocky shore when they tried to land. The elder Franklin shrugged off the dangers of ocean travel, but his son did not. "Few are the inducements," William wrote Betsy as his feet touched solid ground, "that will tempt me to pass the Ocean again, if ever I am so happy to return to my native Country."[5]

In London, Franklin's Quaker connections and his reputation in scientific circles smoothed the way for the weary travelers. Benjamin viewed his own reception as a pleasant contrast to his first trip to England. He immediately struck up a warm friendship with printer William Strahan, with whom he had corresponded for years. He just as quickly found comfortable lodgings with Mrs. Margaret Stevenson and her daughter Polly on Craven Street, just off the Strand and within easy walking distance of the houses of Parliament and ministerial headquarters at Whitehall. His quarters were also close to the magnificent Northumberland House, center of the London social scene and a mecca for the fashionable denizens of English society.

Father and son settled easily into their routines. Benjamin attended meetings of the Royal Society, the Monday Club—a group of affluent businessmen who met regularly at a tavern called the Crown and Vulture—and the Club of Honest Whigs, which met each Thursday at St. Paul's Coffee House. He was most comfortable with men like himself—writers, scientists, and political dissenters, whose conversation never failed to stimulate him. Franklin always liked to cast himself in the role of an honest, down-to-earth tradesman who valued simple pleasures and disdained the luxuries that an increasingly corrupt England prized. Still, whenever he was in London, he welcomed the opportunity to indulge in frivolous pleasures. He enjoyed the theater and other "Entertainments or Amusements," as he flitted from engagement to engagement in his newly hired private coach.[6] He lived, he later admitted, "in a Fashion and Expence suitable to the Publick Character I sustain'd."[7]

William also found the capital city to his liking. He dutifully began his legal training and was called to the bar in November 1758. He was pleasantly surprised to discover that his studies never took much time, and from the start he was able to explore London, dine with his father's friends, and find companions of his own. Dressed in London's latest fashions, he often attended parties at Northumberland House, where he mixed easily with the beaus and belles of English society. He was enchanted by the "great Metropolis," never tiring of the "publick Diversions and Entertainments" offered by the "betwitching Country."[8] Philadelphia looked dowdy and provincial compared to London, and before long, even the image of his "dear Betsy" began to fade.

If both Franklins derived considerable pleasure from the London scene, they enjoyed their trips away from the city even more. Beginning in 1758, the two men fled London's soot and heat every summer, partly, as Benjamin always explained, for his health, but mostly for the sheer pleasure they derived from their little jaunts. They visited the fashionable spas at Bath and Tunbridge Wells. They traveled to Scotland, where in 1759 the University at St. Andrews made Benjamin a doctor of laws. The trip to Edinburgh was especially pleasing to both men, as they were wined and dined, flattered and amused by some of Scotland's foremost philosophers.[9] The sojourn in Scotland was, remarked Benjamin, "Six Weeks of the *densest* Happiness I have met with in any Part of my Life."[10] There were other excursions as well. They journeyed to northern England and Wales and crossed the channel for a trip to Belgium and the Netherlands. In 1762, they traveled to Oxford, where Benjamin received his second honorary doctorate and William was accorded a master of arts. For father and son alike, these were heady times indeed.

Perhaps no trip meant so much to either man as the sentimental journey they took to the British Midlands in the summer of 1758. They went first to Northamptonshire, the Franklins' ancestral home, where they located Mary Fisher, the only child of Benjamin's Uncle Thomas. The frail old woman remembered Franklin's father and his first wife and chatted amiably about the old days, before Josiah had decided to leave his homeland for America. They moved on to Ecton, just a few miles away, where Benjamin's father had been born. There they prowled around the grounds of the old Franklin house and studied the ancient church register where the names of generation upon generation of Franklins could be found, going back at least two hundred years. The experience was a moving one for father and son alike. Benjamin still remembered it in 1771 when he began his famous *Autobiography*, the first part of which he dedicated to William. It gave both men a palpable link not only with each other but with their English roots, a link that William, even more than his father, valued. If he needed a sense of his connections with the past, the trip to Ecton gave him a framework within which he could begin to shape his identity. For Benjamin, the excursion strengthened his already abiding love for England, making him more determined than ever to promote Anglo-American unity.

Unfortunately, most of the English sojourn was not spent in idyllic side trips in the English countryside. William managed to escape the congested London streets more often than his father did, but the Pennsylvania assembly expected both men to represent its interests in the nation's capital. While their successes were negligible, their efforts were prodigious.

When he first arrived in London, Benjamin paid his respects to Lord Granville, the head of the Privy Council, from whom he received a startling lesson on the English view of colonial rights. Granville, who was related to the Penns by marriage, assured his amazed audience of one that both royal and proprietary instructions to colonial governors had the force of law, and as such the provincial legislatures could neither reject nor alter them. Franklin spiritedly disagreed. This, he said, was "new Doctrine to me," and he insisted that the various colonial charters gave the assemblies, not the governors, the proprietors, or even the king, the right to make their own laws.[11] Franklin was no doubt correct, but the argument was disquieting, and Franklin was uneasy when he left Granville's presence.

His first meeting with Thomas Penn, just a few days later, was even more disturbing. Each man already blamed the other for the quarrels between the proprietors and the assembly. Neither was willing to concede a single point. Franklin's demands were simple. He wanted a governor who could work with the assembly unhampered by rigid proprietary instructions. He insisted on the assembly's right to control the mode of raising money for the colony's own defense. And he was determined to make the Penns allow the assembly to tax their estates. In fact, the whole argument between Franklin and the proprietors centered on one issue, an issue that would plague the relationship between the colonial assemblies and the English government in the near future. The Penns believed that the Pennsylvania assembly was "not a parliament, nor had any thing near so much power as the House of Commons," while Franklin insisted that the assembly was, in essence, a mini-parliament, with "as full powers as the House of Commons."[12] Benjamin Franklin's remark that his differences with the proprietors were "very wide" was surely an understatement.[13]

Franklin met only once more with Thomas Penn, in January 1758. Their discussion promptly degenerated into a disastrous disagreement. Franklin reminded the proprietor that William Penn had promised full governing powers to Pennsylvania's first settlers, but Thomas, "with a Kind of triumphing laughing Insolence," repudiated his own father's guarantee. Franklin choked back an angry retort, but when he recounted the conversation to Isaac Norris, he was uncharacteristically bitter. I "conceived that Moment," he said, "a more cordial and thorough Contempt for him than I ever before felt for any Man living."[14] Benjamin Franklin's quarrel with the proprietors was no longer simply a political disagreement. It had taken on the dimensions of a personal crusade.

Throughout the fall of 1757, Benjamin was seriously ill. He was virtually incapacitated for nearly eight weeks, during which time William took his father's place at court, meeting daily with Benjamin's friends and advisers and impressing everyone but the Penns with his charm, ability, and good judgment. The experience gave William a chance to be evaluated on his own merits without risking comparisons with his father, and it went a long way toward equalizing the relationship between father and son. William became less a willing foot soldier and more Benjamin's "friend, his brother, his intimate and easy companion."[15]

Even after his father recuperated, William continued to be invaluable. As an agent who, at least ostensibly, was still involved in negotiations with the proprietors, the elder Franklin could not publicly attack the Penns. But William, merely his father's clerk, operated under no such constraints. In September 1757, he wrote—and signed—a letter to a London newspaper, *The Citizen or General Advertiser*, attacking the proprietors as the "Clogs or Obstructions" to Pennsylvania's military defenses.[16] By the winter of 1757 William was hard at work with Richard Jackson, a lawyer at the Inns of Court and a devoted friend of America, gathering material for a political history of Pennsylvania to be written from the assembly's perspective.[17]

Despite the Franklins' prodigious efforts, it was obvious by the middle of 1758 that the Penns were, and would remain, obdurate. They had no intention of allowing their far-flung estates to be taxed. Nor did they intend to share their power with Pennsylvania's assembly. In September, Benjamin Franklin proclaimed that he harbored "no longer any Hopes of an Accomodation," and he suggested in a letter to Joseph Galloway that Pennsylvania's only chance for salvation lay in the revocation of the proprietors' charter, coupled with a Crown takeover of the colony.[18] William, who like his father had become disgusted with the Penns' "little dirty Aspersions they were continually publishing" and their "low contemptible" attacks on the assembly, agreed.[19]

The Franklins' faith in the advantages of royal government over proprietary rule was not as curious as it seems in hindsight. Both men firmly believed that the Crown would support the assembly rights they cherished. They had come to England as defenders of the Pennsylvania legislature, which, from their perspective, had been held hostage to the claims of a stubborn and selfish proprietary interest. They knew that the Penns held the assembly in contempt, and they saw no chance that those views would ever change. Still, both men were proud of their English heritage and grew ever more fond of the mother country the longer they remained in London. They saw the English government as the best and freest in human history, and they relied on that government to guarantee the hard-won rights of English subjects in the colonies as well as at home. Neither the future patriot nor the future loyalist saw any conflict between their support of the Crown and the preservation of colonial rights. To them, the proprietors, not the king, represented the greatest threat to Pennsylvania's liberties.

In the short run, their perspective seemed justified. In April 1759, when Governor Denny bowed to the wishes of the Pennsylvania assembly and agreed to a defense bill taxing the proprietary estates, the Penns asked the ministry to declare the bill unconstitutional. The Board of Trade held hearings on the issue, which both Franklins attended, before deciding in favor of the proprietors. Benjamin appealed the decision to the Privy Council and, much to everyone's surprise, won at least a mixed victory. The council ruled that the Pennsylvania assembly could tax the proprietary estates if it agreed to assess them at the lowest rate at which it taxed other land in the colony. The decision contained enough loopholes to continue the controversy between the proprietors and the assembly for decades. Still, it was more than anyone had expected and surely confirmed the Franklins' belief that the king's men, not the proprietors, were more likely to be persuaded by the rational arguments of colonial leaders.[20]

For all practical purposes, the Franklins had no reason to remain in London after 1760. William had his law degree and Benjamin had won as much as he could from the proprietors. Yet, despite the elder Franklin's constant assurances to Deborah that he, at least, would soon be returning home, it was not until August 1762 that he sailed for Philadelphia. William did not leave England until November. Both men had compelling reasons for extending their sojourn.

The longer Benjamin remained in London, the more he dreaded returning home. Rumors abounded, spread with obvious glee by his enemies, that he was no longer viewed with favor in Philadelphia. Moreover, he thrived in the bracing intellectual atmosphere that England provided, and he frequently entertained thoughts of remaining there permanently if only he could persuade Deborah and Sally to join him. He even enlisted the services of William Strahan to try to convince Deborah to move to London. But the good lady—who harbored a deep fear of ocean travel—refused to budge. Still Franklin delayed his departure, enjoying the occasional trips he took with William and attending to whatever services he could render on behalf of the assembly.

William, too, had good reason to remain in London. By the fall of 1758, he and Elizabeth Graeme had broken their engagement, and thus he had no special desire to rush home. While Betsy actually ended the relationship, William had sent her unmistakable signals indicating that he welcomed the denouement. He seldom wrote to her, and when he did manage to scribble a few lines, his letters were filled with rapturous accounts of the social whirl that he clearly enjoyed. The final blow came in December 1759, when he wrote to Betsy bragging of the reception his little article in *The Citizen* had received and repeating his fulminations against the "Obstinacy and Wickedness of the

Proprietors."[21] Betsy, whose family supported the proprietors, assumed that William's letter was nothing more than his cowardly way of ending their engagement, and responding with fury, she insisted that it would be "*Folly*, nay Madness" to risk attachment to a man who was so lacking in morals and judgment.[22]

William claimed to be desolated by Betsy's letter, but he managed to recover from his loss rather quickly. London's brilliant society beckoned. Money, thanks to the largesse of his father and his father's friends, was no problem. He even managed to follow in Benjamin's footsteps by becoming, some time after 1759, the father of an illegitimate son, William Temple, whose existence remained a secret from all but the Franklins' closest friends. He discreetly placed Temple, as the boy would be called, in a foster home, his expenses guaranteed by Benjamin Franklin.

William had more socially acceptable diversions as well. Not long after Betsy Graeme broke their engagement, he began courting Elizabeth Downes, the wealthy daughter of a Barbadian planter whose connections were impeccable. Quiet, dignified, a little frail, she was a "Favourite" with all who knew her.[23] Benjamin was disappointed when the two young people married in 1762, for he had hoped that his son would be attracted to Polly Stevenson, Margaret Stevenson's daughter. Still, although he did not attend the wedding ceremony—he had sailed for home before it took place—he gave the couple his "Consent & Approbation," praised Elizabeth's "amiable" character, and claimed to be even happier about the marriage than he was with the news that his son had secured an appointment as the royal governor of New Jersey.[24]

For William Franklin did not gain merely a son and a wife in London. He also launched a career that would shape every facet of his political and personal life. William used his time in London wisely. Taking advantage of the connections he secured through his father, he managed to charm nearly everyone—with the obvious exception of the Penns and their supporters—with his intelligence and ability. After he had been called to the bar and his work for the assembly was virtually finished, he began to use his influence to secure a post in the imperial bureaucracy: a job in the customs service, perhaps, or a minor position in the Admiralty Court. Anything would do for a start. Like his father, he relished his London life, but he could not remain there forever. It was time to plan seriously for his future.

A combination of good luck and the right connections vaulted him into a position that no young and inexperienced colonial had any right to expect. In 1762, the king precipitously removed New Jersey Governor Josiah Hardy from office, and Hardy's intended replacement, Thomas Pownall, refused the offer of the job. Franklin, surely with his father's connivance, began a series of furtive negotiations to obtain the position for himself. He faced many obstacles. The governorship of even so poor and insignificant a colony as New

Jersey was a choice political plum. Moreover, Franklin's lack of experience, coupled with the fact that he was an American and a bastard to boot, surely gave the king's advisers some pause. Moreover, he did have his enemies. If the Penns had known that the ministry was considering William for the post, they would have made every effort to keep him from obtaining the governorship. Thus the negotiations had to be kept secret. Even the usually loquacious Benjamin Franklin was tight-lipped about the proceedings. "My Son stays a little longer in England," he told his friends, whenever they asked about William's plans.[25]

If William operated under some disadvantages, he had a few cards to play. The Franklins' friendship with Dr. John Pringle, King George III's personal physician, and Lord Bute, the king's tutor and confidant, were essential. In an environment where knowing the right people meant everything, both Benjamin and William could, at least on occasion, manipulate affairs to their advantage. To be fair, William impressed most observers with his ability. His appointment came only after Lord Halifax, head of the Board of Trade, submitted him to a "severe personal examination," which evidently convinced him that the young man, not yet thirty-five, was suited for the job.[26] On August 20, the Board of Trade submitted Franklin's name to the Privy Council. Shortly thereafter, William Franklin and Elizabeth Downes embarked to "the land of matrimony."[27]

It is tempting to argue that the division between father and son, patriot and loyalist, began with William Franklin's appointment as New Jersey's royal governor. In the long run, this may have been the case. But in 1762, neither Franklin would have predicted the destruction of the ties that bound England and America, father and son. Benjamin Franklin endorsed his son's decision to seek the New Jersey governorship. William's success was a tribute to his father, one more indication of how far he had traveled from his beginnings as a printer's apprentice. Moreover, while he always railed at royal governors who came to the colonies "merely to make Fortunes," Franklin surely did not see his own son as a governor of no "Abilities" or "Integrity," who had no "natural Connections" with the colonies.[28] William, unlike the parasitic sycophants the Penns regularly sent to Pennsylvania, had colonial interests at heart. Indeed, his son's appointment confirmed what Benjamin already believed—that the Crown, not the proprietors, was the best guarantor of colonial liberty.

Even more important in the months and years ahead, Benjamin and William Franklin shared a political philosophy, forged from their experiences together in Pennsylvania and England. Like Americans everywhere, both men valued their English heritage. Both thought that England and America gained untold mutual benefit from a close relationship, and Benjamin, at least, imagined that as the colonies became more prosperous and their contributions to the empire more obvious, the relationship between England and its colonies would grow more equal. "The Foundations of the future Grandeur and Stability of the British Empire," said Benjamin, "lie in America." Together, England and America could develop a government and society that would "awe the World."[29]

If neither Benjamin nor William envisioned a time when the interests of England and the colonies would not be the same, they did not have any illusions about the men who ran the British government. William agreed with his father's boast that England "never had a better Prince" than George III and joined in his hearty wishes that the young monarch's reign would be "happy and truly glorious."[30] But he fulminated against the corrupt practices of England's Board of Trade, that "Pack of d[amne]d R[ascal]s" whose demands for bribes and servile obedience made it impossible to "attain common Justice at their Hands."[31] William always jumped to America's defense whenever the honor or ability of the colonists was questioned. His heart remained, he said, with the "Gentlemen of America," and he was impatient with the "Prejudices" of Englishmen who had "little Knowledge of (or indeed Inclination to know) American affairs."[32]

Both Benjamin and William Franklin readily conceded that English attitudes toward the colonies left much to be desired. Both were Americans through and through. They were also *British* Americans. In 1762 they believed that English prejudices were the result of ignorance, not ill will, and they had supreme confidence in their own abilities to educate good-hearted but misinformed leaders from across the sea. Benjamin, as a leader of the Pennsylvania assembly, and William, as the royal governor of New Jersey, would continue to work together in their efforts to secure and enhance the strength of the empire and the prosperity of America.

NOTES

[1]BF to Peter Collinson, 5 Nov. 1756, *PBF* 7:13.

[2]In fact, before William left Philadelphia, he and Elizabeth Graeme considered a secret marriage but prudently decided against it, settling for a secret engagement instead.

[3]WF to Elizabeth Graeme, 11 Apr. 1757, William Franklin Papers, Simon Gratz Autograph Collection, Historical Society of Pennsylvania, Philadelphia.

[4]WF to Elizabeth Graeme, 16 May 1757, Simon Gratz, "Some Material for a Biography of Mrs. Elizabeth Fergusson, née Graeme," *Pennsylvania Magazine of History and Biography* 39 (1915): 262.

[5]WF to Elizabeth Graeme, 17 July 1757, *PBF* 7:244.

[6]BF to David Hall, 8 Apr. 1759, ibid. 8:317. See Esmond Wright, *Franklin of Philadelphia* (Cambridge: Harvard University Press, 1986), 114, 115, and Verner W. Crane, "The Club of Honest Whigs," *William and Mary Quarterly*, 3d ser., 23 (1966): 210–33 for details on BF's social life at this juncture.

[7]BF to Isaac Norris, 9 Feb. 1763, *PBF* 10:194.

[8]WF to Elizabeth Graeme, 9 Dec. 1757, ibid. 7:289.

[9]Their hosts, thanks to introductions by Dr. John Pringle and William Strahan, included David Hume, Adam Smith, and Alexander Carlyle.

[10]BF to Lord Kames, 3 Jan. 1760, *PBF* 9:9.

[11]*Autobiography*, 261, 262.

[12]Ferdinado John Paris to William Allen, 13 May 1758, *PBF* 8:63n.

[13]*Autobiography*, 262.

[14]BF to [Issac Norris], 14 Jan. 1758, *PBF* 7:362.

[15]William Strahan to Deborah Franklin, 13 Dec. 1757, ibid., 297.

[16]WF to the *Citizen*, ibid., 261.

[17]Jackson actually wrote the *Historical Review of the Constitution and Government of Pennsylvania*, but WF "afforded great Assistance and furnish'd most of the Materials." BF to Isaac Norris, 9 June 1759, ibid. 8:402. No one denies, however, that BF's sentiments shaped the document.

[18]BF to Joseph Galloway, 16 Sept. 1758, ibid., 150.

[19]WF to Mrs. Abercrombie, 24 Oct. 1758, Gratz, "Elizabeth Fergusson," 265.

[20]See *PBF* 9:125ff for a detailed account of the deliberations of the Board of Trade and the Privy Council.

[21]WF to Elizabeth Graeme, 9 Dec. 1757, ibid. 7:290.

[22]WF to Mrs. Abercrombie, 24 Oct. 1758, Gratz, "Elizabeth Fergusson," 263–67.

[23]Thomas Bridges to Jared Ingersoll, 30 Sept. 1762, *PBF* 10:155n.

[24]BF to Jane Mecom, 25 Nov. 1762, ibid., 154; BF to Lord Kames, 2 June 1765, ibid. 12:159.

[25]BF to John Morgan, 16 Aug. 1762, ibid. 10:146.

[26]William A. Whitehead, "Biographical Sketch of Governor William Franklin," *Proceedings of the New Jersey Historical Society* 3 (1849): 141.

[27]WF to William Strahan, 4 Sept. 1762, C. H. Hart, "Letters from William Franklin to William Strahan," *Pennsylvania Magazine of History and Biography* 35 (1911): 421.

[28]BF to William Shirley, 4 Dec. 1754, *PBF* 5:444.

[29]BF to Lord Kames, 3 Jan. 1760, ibid. 9:7.

[30]BF to John Whitehurst, 27 June 1763; to William Strahan, 19 Dec. 1763, ibid. 10:302, 407.

[31]WF to Joseph Galloway, 26 Aug. 1760, ibid. 9:189.

[32]WF to Elizabeth Graeme, 9 Dec. 1757, ibid. 7:290; WF to Peter Schuyler, 19 June 1759, ibid. 8:407.

3

Government Men

Benjamin and William Franklin, like England and America, would never again be as close as they were in the years immediately following the Franklins' English sojourn. In London, the Franklin men had developed a close personal and political relationship. Proud of their English heritage, convinced that the proprietors were subverting their rights, they left for home determined to bring Pennsylvania into the royal orbit. Benjamin hoped to persuade the assembly to support his plan to destroy the Penns' power. William, now a royal governor, would serve as an example of the benefits that closer ties to the Crown might bring. Neither man questioned the basic precepts that bound the empire together. Both assumed that the liberties of all Americans would be safe under the benevolent protection of the mother country.

Benjamin and William Franklin shared an intellectual tradition accepted by educated Englishmen on both sides of the Atlantic. That tradition was by no means monolithic. It was composed of a number of discrete, at times even competing, strains of thought. Religious attitudes, economic self-interest, and personal experience all played a role in determining which aspect of the English heritage any individual might emphasize. Still, there were some beliefs to which virtually everyone adhered. Ironically, while in the short run their common perspective drew Americans and the English together, in the long run that same shared perspective would help destroy the empire that everyone claimed to venerate.

The world of educated Americans was shaped by a belief in the instructive value of historical precedent. The colonists used history selectively. Some, especially in New England, looked with pride to the seventeenth century and the English Civil War, when their Puritan forebears had fought to protect Parliament from the tyrannical designs of King Charles I. Others, more secular in orientation, found the experience of the Roman republic to be especially relevant to their own concerns. They read historians such as Tacitus, Cicero, and Sallust for their depiction of a virtuous and free people who had lost their liberty and succumbed to a society that reeked of corruption and decay. They hoped to avoid the mistakes of their predecessors and to protect the liberty that the Romans had lost.

Many Americans were drawn to the work of a group of opposition politicans and writers in the early eighteenth century. To them, the arguments of men like John Trenchard and Thomas Gordon, whose influential *Cato's Letters*, published in book form in 1721, were especially attractive. Trenchard and Gordon celebrated Parliament's victories over the Stuart kings in the seventeenth century, and they agreed with most enlightened observers that England's unique form of "mixed government" was particularly suited to protect the fruits of those victories. All interests in England were represented in that government: The king represented the monarchy; the House of Lords, the aristocracy; and the House of Commons, the democracy. To maintain both liberty and order in such a near-perfect system, the three orders had to maintain a precarious balance, and each had to remain strictly independent of the other two. If the king or his ministers "invaded" the province of the Lords or the Commons, then tyranny would inevitably result. If the balance tipped too far in the direction of the House of Commons, liberty would automatically dengenerate into anarchy. The trick was to maintain an equilibrium.

Most Americans agreed that the greatest danger to political stability came from the Crown's tendency to aggrandize itself at the expense of the Commons. "Power," they argued, which was the monarch's province, was inherently grasping and expansive, while "liberty" was naturally weak and passive. Thus the people's representatives had to be ever vigilant, ever on the lookout for signs that the king's men were overstepping their bounds. Throughout the eighteenth century, a handful of people in England, and many more in America, became convinced that the king and his ministers had already destroyed parliamentary independence, that it had corrupted too many members of Parliament with offers of money, power, and position. If that was true, then the assemblies in America were England's, and indeed the world's, last hope for the preservation of liberty. Thus it was more important than ever that the colonists be aware of threats to their rights emanating from the ministry or from a corrupt Parliament.[1]

English history seemed to justify the fears of those who saw a sinister plot behind every monarchical effort to encroach on Parliament's sphere. The Stuart kings had twice attempted to destroy parliamentary liberty. A Puritan-dominated House of Commons had barely thwarted Charles I's efforts to raise both taxes and an army without Parliament's consent. In 1688, James II had to flee the country during the Glorious Revolution when he, like his father, threatened Parliament's rights. In defense of that revolution, John Locke had written his famous *Second Treatise on Government,* in which he argued that government was created by and responsible to the people and that no government could legitimately destroy its inhabitants' "natural rights" of life, liberty, or property. Should it attempt to do so, the people had the right to rebel against that government and to constitute a new one. Both future patriots and future loyalists were heirs to a revolutionary tradition.

The English believed that in addition to their "natural rights" as humans, they also shared what they loosely termed the "rights of Englishmen." They generally traced those rights as far back as 1215 and the Magna Carta. They included the rights to representative government, jury trials, and some form of religious toleration. Perhaps most important, the English claimed that no king could tax them without obtaining the consent of their representatives. To secure their rights, opposition leaders insisted that the king's subjects had to preserve their mixed and balanced government, maintaining the tradition of a limited monarchy and an increasingly influential Parliament. They had to be constantly on guard against signs that power was destroying liberty. If the king tried to tax his subjects without their consent, if he raised an army in time of peace, if he used bribery to influence the House of Commons, then liberty was in danger. A free press and broadly based voting rights were useful weapons in the ongoing effort to protect liberty. Above all, English people and Americans alike had to be virtuous, independent, and ever vigilant. They had to use petitions, pamphlets, speeches, and in the last resort violence to defend liberty from the depradations of power. In this context, riots were signs of a healthy society; the absence of crowd action might mean that liberty was already dead.

Most Americans assumed that they possessed the rights of English subjects. They did not imagine for a moment that they had surrendered those rights when they crossed the ocean to settle the American "wilderness." Beginning in the 1760s, however, they confronted the limits of their ability to protect their rights, as imperial priorities impelled both king and Parliament to take another look at the relationship between England and its North American possessions. English attempts to rationalize that relationship would eventually draw the colonies into the vortex of empire and to the brink of independence. The events surrounding Parliament's decision to levy a stamp tax on the colonies were the opening round in a series of events that in one decade would tear the empire apart.

When Benjamin Franklin arrived in the colonies in November 1762, he did not know what kind of welcome to anticipate, for he had been unable to ignore persistent rumors that he had lost all influence in Philadelphia during his extended stay in London. Thus it was with undisguised relief that he wrote to assure his London well-wishers that he was as popular as ever, his house "fill'd with a Succession [of friends] from Morning to Night."[2] He had just won reelection to the assembly, and he immediately set to work persuading friends in and out of the legislature that royal government was the only attractive alternative to proprietary rule.

By February 1763, William and his bride had followed Benjamin to America, enduring a stormy passage across the icy Atlantic and an almost equally hazardous trip overland to Philadelphia. As she rode more than one hundred miles in an open carriage, blasted by the wind and cold, Elizabeth must have wondered why she had abandoned the comforts of England for this alien land. William did his best to bolster her spirits, praising her courage and fortitude. Still, both were relieved when Benjamin, Sally, and a small contingent of the Franklins' friends met them near Philadelphia and escorted them into town.

William did not dally in Pennsylvania. Leaving Elizabeth with Deborah and Sally, the two Franklin men immediately set out for New Jersey. Benjamin was determined to attend his son's inauguration as New Jersey's royal governor. Moreover, he had friends in the colony—he had done some printing for the government, and his post office duties had occasionally taken him there. If William needed anyone to ease his way as he made his first impression on those whose support he would soon need, his father was ready to oblige.

While he surely did not know it, William Franklin became governor of New Jersey at the worst possible moment. The powers of all colonial governors had been considerably diminished throughout the eighteenth century. As the Board of Trade tried to exert more authority in North America, it demanded strict compliance with its increasingly explicit instructions. Governors found, for instance, that they could no longer wink at colonial evasions of the Navigation Acts. They also had to persuade their assemblies to comply with demands that they help finance what appeared to be a permanent military presence in America.

For the governors, the English determination to tighten up the imperial system came at an inopportune moment. Over the years, the colonial assemblies had become more aggressive, more likely to view themselves as mini-parliaments whose duty it was to defend their rights against real and imagined encroachments of their governors. While the colonial assemblies seemed content to allow the English government to regulate trade for the good of the empire, they demanded virtual autonomy in internal affairs. They jealously guarded their right to raise taxes, pay the governors' salaries, and make laws. Caught between aggressive assemblies and an activist ministry, many governors felt virtually helpless.

After 1763, the situation grew worse. England emerged from its last war with France victorious but broke. The national debt had nearly doubled by the end of the conflict, and Parliament was reluctant to raise taxes on an already overburdened and restive population. Moreover, the British Empire now included all of Canada as well as the land between the thirteen original colonies and the Mississippi River. The expense of governing this massive territory and maintaining peace among the English, former French subjects, and Native Americans promised to be enormous. The home government had long believed that colonial contributions to the empire were insufficient. The war in America, which the English claimed they had waged solely for the colonies' benefit, provided further evidence that this was the case. American assemblies were often reluctant to raise sufficient funds for British military needs. Merchants seemed to evade trade laws with impunity. Many English believed that it was time to exert more control over the colonies. Americans always talked about their rights as Englishmen. They had to realize that duties accompanied those rights.

The colonists did not share England's view of their contributions to the empire in general and to the war effort in particular. They provided raw materials for the mother country's manufacturers and served as markets for manufactured goods. Moreover, many colonies had donated men, money, and supplies to the king's army. Taxes had skyrocketed during the war years, and a severe postwar depression made Americans everywhere reluctant to come to England's aid.

Americans had one reason to be optimistic about their economic future. The end of the French and Indian War also meant the end of the French presence in America. In the past, the colonists had relied on the British army to protect them from the expansionist designs of their neighbors to the north. With France out of the picture and English troops soon departing for home, Americans would be left alone to enjoy the fruits of victory. Obviously, the postwar expectations of England and its colonies were divergent. In fact, England and America were on a collision course.

In 1763, William Franklin's concerns were immediate and concrete. He was not worried about the role of the colonies in the British Empire. He thought only of how well he would be able to perform his duties as the royal governor of New Jersey. He had been at least as nervous about his own welcome in the colony as his father had been concerning his reception in Philadelphia. For if the Franklins had friends in the governor's new home, they also had enemies. Moreover, New Jersey was in some ways a difficult colony to govern. It was a colony divided against itself. It even had two capitals: Burlington was in the Quaker-dominated West Jersey, while Perth Amboy was in East Jersey. Each section was determined to have the governor, his council, and the assembly serve its interests. Each demanded that the assembly convene in its own capital in alternating years. Ominously, former Pennsylvania Governor Robert Morris, the Franklins' old nemesis, was an influential resident of East Jersey, and he promised to be a thorn in the governor's side. Even before William arrived in the colony, the Franklins' enemies were moaning that his "shameful" appointment was a "Burlesque on all Government," and they clearly viewed his governorship as an "insult" to the colony.[3]

Despite the Franklins' fears, however, William's reception was friendly. He took his oath of office, first at Perth Amboy and then at Burlington. As he traveled from one capital to the other, he was greeted with the "greatest Demonstrations of Joy," and "all Ranks of People" seemed ready to accord him their "Respect and even Affection."[4]

In fact, while New Jersey's affairs were unsettled and Franklin would have to watch his step to avoid offending either the East or West Jersey faction, the colony was in some ways a haven of tranquility. To be sure, it was not a wealthy province, and it depended on New York to the east and Philadelphia to the west for trade, news, and culture. Still, it had no major cities, harbored no discontented group of sailors or artisans, no well-organized political factions, and no local newspapers to whip the populace into a frenzy. While many bemoaned the lack of a direct trade route with London or the West Indies, this meant that New Jersey was not significantly affected by many of the trade regulations emanating from London throughout the 1760s. Its provinciality, while often frustrating, could be counted as a blessing.

William's first job as governor was to decide which of New Jersey's two capitals he would call home. Neither site had much to offer. Perth Amboy was a little country village, and Burlington was hardly more cosmopolitan. East Jersey tried to tempt him with its new governor's mansion, but in the end, after more anguish than the decision merited, William opted for the western capital. He wanted no one to imagine that the leaders of East Jersey had succeeded in "byassing the Governor to their interest."[5] More important, Burlington and Philadelphia were only seventeen miles apart. If they stayed in the western capital, William and Elizabeth could make frequent excursions to Philadelphia where they could enjoy a day at the horse races or an evening dancing at the Annual Assembly. Proximity to Philadelphia also meant that Benjamin and William could continue the political partnership they both had so enjoyed in London.

William and Elizabeth settled quickly into their new life. By June they anticipated moving into a permanent residence and began planning the decor of their new home. William agonized over every detail. As an American, he could not count on the automatic respect that an English governor would take for granted, and he was determined to live in a fashion that did not reflect poorly on his new status. He also began to cultivate the friendship of some of New Jersey's political leaders. His most important conquest was East Jersey leader William Alexander, or Lord Stirling as he preferred to call himself, one of the wealthiest men in the colony, a member of the governor's council, and a close friend of the Penns.

In May, the governor traveled to Perth Amboy to preside over his first session of the New Jersey assembly. His maiden speech was calculated to please the lower house. Showing a laudable knowledge of the colony, he emphasized his desire to work with house members and to encourage agriculture and transportation in New Jersey. Although he promised to honor his oath to the king, he carefully avoided any challenge to assembly rights. His experience as a clerk in the Pennsylvania assembly had not been wasted. Franklin did not intend to make the kind of tactical blunders that so often put the proprietary governors at odds with Pennsylvania's lawmakers. So successful was the session that the normally tight-fisted assembly even agreed to raise the governor's salary by two hundred pounds, a concession, Franklin could not refrain from noting, that had "been fruitlessly attempted by other Governors."[6]

Franklin had every reason to be pleased. His first contact with the New Jersey assembly had been so agreeable that he felt vindicated in his belief that the interests of king and colony were identical. The Pennsylvania proprietors were grasping, selfish, and unreasonable. They exploited their colony without offering it anything in return. The king, however, ruled benevolently, thinking of the good of the empire as a whole. A royal governor who was sincerely interested in the well-being of king and colony alike would earn everyone's respect and gratitude. In the spring of 1763, Franklin anticipated "an easy agreeable administration."[7]

If his son's affairs were progressing smoothly, Benjamin Franklin found himself involved almost immediately in political controversy in Philadelphia. In 1763, a coalition of Ohio Valley tribes organized by Ottawa chief Pontiac began an extensive campaign to secure their land from further American incursions. In the seventeenth century, Pennsylvania had enjoyed relatively good relations with Native Americans, as William Penn had tried to pursue a reasonably enlightened Indian policy. By the mid-eighteenth century, this was no longer the case, and Pennsylvania, like most other colonies, found coexistence with American natives increasingly problematic. Indeed, Pontiac's Rebellion, as the colonists called this latest campaign, hit the colony's frontier with particular ferocity. Pennsylvania's farmers demanded protection, but the Quaker-dominated assembly dragged its feet. Consequently, the settlers took matters into their own hands. The entire frontier was ready to explode. Settlers slaughtered members of friendly and enemy tribes with equal abandon. The natives responded with depradations of their own. In December 1763, a group of settlers from the town of Paxton murdered twenty friendly Indians. When the assembly demanded the settlers' arrest and, even worse, appeared willing to offer safe haven to still other frightened Indians, the Paxton Boys, some five hundred strong, marched on the capital. On the night of February 5, 1764, they were in nearby Germantown threatening to storm the city. They blamed the Quakers for an Indian policy they felt was unconscionably weak; they also demanded more representation in the assembly. The settlers were convinced that unless they obtained a stronger voice in the colony government, they would remain at the mercy of Indian attack.

When he heard the news that the Paxton Boys were almost at his doorstep, Governor John Penn, nephew of the proprietor, swallowed his pride and ran frantically to Benjamin Franklin's house. He banged on the door, waking the entire household, and begged his erstwhile adversary for assistance. Two days later, a delegation of prominent Philadelphians, led by Benjamin Franklin and Joseph Galloway, traveled to Germantown to negotiate with the rebel leaders. By now the demonstrators knew that even the peaceful Quakers were preparing to defend the city. Realizing that brute force would serve no useful purpose, they grudgingly agreed to return to their homes in exchange for a chance to air their grievances formally.

If Benjamin Franklin expected the Penns to reward him for his service to the colony, he was mistaken. The assembly and the governor agreed that with the frontier at risk, the colony needed a new Militia Bill. Unanimity quickly collapsed, however, over the form such a bill would take. The assembly insisted that the militia should elect its own officers, while John Penn demanded the right to appoint militia leaders. Negotiations also broke down over the terms of the new supply bill. Once again the Penns resisted any attempt to tax their estates, while the assembly refused to proceed until the proprietors recognized its right to tax the proprietors' holdings. Franklin used the impasse over the supply bill to advance his project for a royal takeover of Pennsylvania, as he tried to blame the proprietors for the continued stalemate. In May 1764, the Quaker-dominated assembly approved a petition to King George III, begging him to assume control of Pennsylvania's government. But a new "Presbyterian" party, led by John Dickinson, objected. Its supporters, a curious mix of Anglicans, Presbyterians, and western settlers, blamed the Quakers, not the proprietors, for Pennsylvania's failure to defend the frontier. The stage was set for the next assembly election, which took place in the fall of 1764.

It was, as one historian has aptly called it, a "scurrilous campaign."[8] Two issues—the question of the petition for royal government and the character of Benjamin Franklin—dominated the race. Many Pennsylvanians were genuinely concerned that the colony might lose more rights, especially its tradition of religious freedom, under the Crown than it would under the proprietors. But they did not rely on reason alone to advance what was surely a legitimate case. They also tried to discredit the project by leveling a personal attack on Benjamin Franklin. They reminded German voters that he had once referred to them as "Palatine boors." They emphasized William's illegitimacy. They accused both Franklins of high living in London at taxpayers' expense. And they suggested that the elder Franklin's motives for advocating royal government were personal and selfish, not public-spirited. He had, they claimed, already secured the governorship of New Jersey for his undeserving son. Now, they predicted, he intended to wangle the royal governorship of Pennsylvania for himself.[9]

The Franklins fought back. William traveled to Germantown to work for his father, "propagating," claimed John Penn, "the most infamous lies he could invent."[10] At least some of the charges against Benjamin Franklin must have stuck, for in the end both he and his closest political ally, Joseph Galloway, lost their bids for reelection to the assembly. Still, there was room for optimism. While Franklin suffered a personal defeat, the Quaker party clung to its majority in the new assembly. Thus the plan for a royal government could go forward.

His usefulness at home temporarily diminished, Franklin saw no reason to remain in Pennsylvania. On October 26, 1764, the assembly made him its London agent, asking him to recross the Atlantic to lobby for a change of government. In little over a month he was back in his old rooms on Craven Street. He returned to England with relief. Temporarily rejected by Pennsylvania voters, bitter over his treatment at the hands of his enemies, he was, as one biographer points out, a "London man" at this stage of his career, and he was more comfortable in the English capital than he was in the city he had once made his home.[11]

The ability of Benjamin and William Franklin to work effectively with the royal government was about to be tested. In 1763, the king had signed the Proclamation of 1763, dividing British America in two parts and prohibiting settlement in the land west of the Appalachians. To secure the boundary between east and west, England planned to maintain some ten thousand troops in forts along the "Proclamation Line." The following year, at the behest of the king's first minister, George Grenville, Parliament passed the Sugar Act. The bill was intended to raise revenue in the colonies by renewing, with modifications, the Molasses Act of 1733, raising new duties on a variety of English imports in America, introducing new trade restrictions, and tightening up the customs service. Grenville planned to use the revenue to maintain the English soldiers remaining in America. Pontiac's Rebellion convinced him that those soldiers were needed not only to enforce the Proclamation of 1763 but to keep the peace in England's new inland empire. From the ministry's perspective, it was reasonable to ask the colonists to contribute to the upkeep of the soldiers.

Most colonial leaders disagreed. The economies of the major seaport towns were already in the doldrums. Any attempt to raise revenue or to restrict trade would only make matters worse. Moreover, they opposed the Sugar Act—or the Revenue Act, as the colonists preferred to call it—on constitutional grounds. They claimed that it was a tax, not a regulation, and hence violated the traditional right of all English subjects to tax themselves. Finally, at least some Americans were troubled by the presence of troops in the colonies. The English all knew that standing armies in time of peace were a sign of tyranny. Was this, they wondered, evidence that the ministers were part of a conspiracy to destroy colonial liberty?

At first, neither Benjamin nor William Franklin appeared much concerned about the new legislation. New Jersey traded through ports in New York and Philadelphia and hence was affected only indirectly by the Sugar Act. Benjamin was too involved in his campaign for royal government to give the legislation more than a passing thought. He even imagined that it might do some good, for if imports became too expensive, the law would promote "greater Frugality" in America.[12] Franklin even suggested that a "Duty not only on Tea, but on all East India Goods might perhaps not be amiss, as they are generally rather Luxuries than Necessaries."[13]

Grenville intended to follow the Sugar Act with the Stamp Act, an internal tax that required colonists to purchase stamps to be affixed to newspapers, merchant and legal documents, and even playing cards and dice. Grenville first proposed the Stamp Act in 1764, and Parliament easily passed the measure in February 1765. It was slated to go into effect on November 1. The delay, as William Franklin later pointed out, gave colonial leaders plenty of time to organize a challenge to the act. Future loyalists as well as future patriots opposed the Stamp Act. It hit some inhabitants—lawyers, merchants, and newspaper owners, for instance—particularly hard. But the colonists objected to the legislation not simply on economic grounds but because they believed it violated their rights as Englishmen. As most Americans saw it, the Stamp Act was a new and dangerous policy that, even more clearly than the Sugar Act, threatened colonial liberty. Everyone knew that no Englishman's property could be taxed without his consent. To argue otherwise was to open the way for the enslavement of the entire populace, for a man whose property lay at the mercy of another had lost his independence.

The colonists insisted that Parliament could not legally tax their property because they had no representatives in the House of Commons. They preferred to continue a practice that seemed to have worked in the past. When the king needed colonial contributions to the empire's defense, he submitted a requisition for funds to each assembly. Each legislature, in turn, decided how to raise the money. Thus the assemblies, not Parliament, taxed the colonists, supporting the king as Parliament did, with a voluntary "gift."

Grenville and his supporters disagreed with the colonial position for both practical and principled reasons. They believed that the requisition system simply did not work. The colonial assemblies virtually never gave the king everything he requested, and what they did contribute was slow in coming and often hamstrung by instructions devised by men whose interests were essentially parochial. Moreover, Grenville recognized, if the colonists did not, that since the Glorious Revolution in 1688, England had been moving inexorably toward the recognition of parliamentary supremacy. Parliament, not the king, was the supreme lawmaker, and Parliament, not the king, had the power to tax. If the king could request money from the assemblies, bypassing Parliament altogether, then the very nature of England's government was in jeopardy. Parliament could not imagine sharing power with the various local assemblies, nor would it grant the king the power to obtain money directly from England's colonial possessions.

The issues first introduced by the policies of the Grenville ministry were complicated—and ultimately they would prove impossible to resolve. But in the beginning neither Benjamin nor William Franklin realized their implications. William readily complied with the Board of Trade's request for a list of public documents that might be taxable. He even instructed his attorney general to point out those items that would "bear the highest Stamp Duty."[14] Benjamin was equally cavalier. He thought that England should grant Americans representation in Parliament if the house intended to tax the colonies. But he spent more time exploring ways to make the tax less onerous than he did worrying about constitutional principles.

Franklin, along with the other colonial agents, did his best to persuade Grenville to change his mind. Still, once he realized that the minister could not be budged, Franklin accepted the inevitable with grace. "We might as well have hinder'd the Suns setting," he told his friend Charles Thomson, than to have averted the passage of the Stamp Act. "But since 'tis down, my Friend, and it may be long before it rises again, let us make as good a Night of it as we can."[15]

For once in his life, Franklin was caught off guard. His obsessive desire to end proprietary government in Pennsylvania virtually blinded him to all other issues. He was determined to win royal favor by representing Pennsylvania as a law-abiding colony. If this meant that Pennsylvanians had to obey an unpopular, perhaps even an unconstitutional act of Parliament, so be it. No sacrifice of principle was too great when so desirable a goal was at stake.

When Benjamin Franklin first learned of the colonial protests against the Stamp Act, he was stunned. The colonial assemblies seemed to be trying to outdo one another in the various anti–Stamp Act resolutions they sent to the king and Parliament. More ominously, in August 1765, Stamp Act protesters in Boston took to the streets. They destroyed the residences of Andrew Oliver, the stamp distributor for Massachusetts, and Thomas Hutchinson, the colony's lieutenant governor. Similar action quickly followed in New York and Rhode Island. By fall, stamp distibutors everywhere were rushing to resign their posts. If this trend continued, it would be impossible to enforce the Stamp Act. No one wanted to distribute the stamps, and with no stamps there would be no Stamp Act. Popular action, not petitions and resolutions, appeared to be the most effective way to protect American liberty.

Philadelphia was the only major colonial city that managed to avoid anti–Stamp Act riots. Elsewhere, assembly leaders were united in their opposition, and rioters went unpunished. But Pennsylvania's leaders were divided, thanks to the antiproprietary crusade. Joseph Galloway, Franklin's closest adviser, urged Pennsylvanians to obey the Stamp Act and to avoid any activity that might incur the displeasure of the Crown. Franklin himself wrote to John Hughes, Pennsylvania's stamp distributor, begging him not to resign his post despite Hughes's fears for his life and property. "A firm loyalty to the Crown," Franklin said, "and faithful Adherence to the Government of this Nation, which it is the Safety as well as the Honour of the Colonies to be connected with, will always be the wisest Course for you and I to take."[16] Ironically, it was the proprietary party that led the opposition to the Stamp Act in Pennsylvania, as it cynically exploited the issue to discredit Franklin's supporters and to win the temporary allegiance of John Dickinson's Presbyterian party.

While he deplored what he termed the excesses of American protests against the Stamp Act, Benjamin Franklin was safely tucked away in London where he did not have to suffer their consequences. His friends and family in the colonies were not so fortunate. David Hall, Franklin's partner and the editor of *The Pennsylvania Gazette,* complained that his subscriptions were plummeting because his paper refused to condemn the Stamp Act. William had to divide his time between New Jersey and Philadelphia, as he defended his father from rumors accusing the elder Franklin of supporting the Stamp Act and even of having been one of its authors. In mid-September, word spread through town that a mob was preparing to march on the homes of both Franklin and Hughes. William rushed to Philadelphia begging Deborah and Sally to return with him to Burlington; Sally accepted her brother's hospitality, but Deborah refused to leave. Instead, she boarded herself up in the house and prepared to fire on anyone who crossed her doorstep. Fortunately, Galloway managed to round up about eight hundred of Franklin's faithful supporters, who roamed the streets on the night of the threatened attack, successfully thwarting the protesters' plans. Still, the experience was unnerving. In other colonies rioters had temporarily gained the upper hand, and Galloway did not know how long he would be able to count on his adherents to protect men like Benjamin Franklin and John Hughes.

In October 1765, the situation grew still more tense, as the fall elections gave the proprietary interest an excuse to step up its rhetoric against the Franklins. At one meeting, a proprietary supporter accused William of meddling in Pennsylvania politics and of making "*strong efforts* to subdue the *spirit of liberty*" in his own colony.[17] Such incidents endangered Deborah and Sally. Moreover, William worried that attacks on him might spread to neighboring New Jersey, diminishing his ability to govern his own colony. He feared, he said later, that he might have "[his] House pull'd down about [his] Ears and all [his] Effects destroy'd" unless he moved to "nip in the Bud" all the accusations that might destroy his "Character or Interest."[18] Indeed, William Franklin had a "difficult part to manage" throughout his first crisis as New Jersey's governor, as he tried to "steer clear of giving any Umbrage to the People here, and of embarrassing myself with the Ministry in England."[19]

Like his father, William was not prepared for the ferocity of the opposition to the Stamp Act. Only New Jersey's relative moderation saved him from the embarrassments that leaders in New York, Massachusetts, and Rhode Island endured. Even so, the Stamp Act was no more popular in New Jersey than it was elsewhere, and while Franklin understood and even sympathized with the colonial position, he, like all royal governors, had to enforce the law so long as it remained in place. His tenure depended on his ability to defend the Crown's interests in the colony. Moreover, his father expected him to maintain peace in New Jersey so that he could point to the colony as a shining example of the virtues of royal government. If William Franklin lost control of New Jersey, he would disappoint both his father and his London superiors. For him, the Stamp Act controversy was a political and a personal crisis.

Until the late summer of 1765, the governor had been confident that New Jersey would remain untouched by the protests that engulfed so many colonies. In May, the assembly had rejected the invitation of the Massachusetts legislature to send delegates to a Stamp Act Congress to be held in New York that fall. By September, however, Franklin's position had begun to erode. With the news of Stamp Act riots in Massachusetts and Rhode Island, William Coxe, New Jersey's stamp distributor, summarily resigned his post (see Part Two, Document 1). Franklin was furious at the decision, especially since he believed that Coxe's anxieties were baseless. William feared that the resignation might cause ignorant London officials to conclude that New Jersey was "as culpable as the N. England Governments."[20]

By October 1765 the governor had still more reason to be worried, when Robert Ogden, the speaker of the New Jersey house, succumbed to popular pressure and convened a rump session of the assembly. The extralegal meeting reversed the legislature's earlier decision, and appointed Ogden and two other men as delegates to the Stamp Act Congress. Moreover, New Jersey had no stamp distributor; Franklin did not know how he could enforce the Stamp Act when no one was authorized to distribute the stamps. The governor's increasingly frantic letters to London begging for guidance went unanswered. His own council thought he had no authority to appoint an interim distributor, but when Franklin asked its members if he should allow the colony's courts to function without using the hated stamps, the councilors, afraid to "displease the Ministry" or to "irritate the People," prudently declined to offer an opinion.[21]

Franklin continued to flounder. Significantly, the royal governor and future loyalist blamed Parliament and the ministry, not the people of New Jersey, for most of his difficulties. He thought the government should have known that nearly all Americans would object to the Stamp Act. In New Jersey, most people were content to fight the obnoxious legislation with "Proper application for redress." Unfortunately, there were others, especially in New England, who advocated "Riot & Violence."[22] While William Franklin deplored the methods of the latter, he refused to condemn the approach of the former.

At the end of November, Franklin convened his assembly. He did his best to avoid a confrontation with the lawmakers. "For any Man to set himself up as an Advocate for the S—— Act in the Colonies," he assured his father, "is a meer Piece of Quixotism, and can answer no good Purpose."[23] William Franklin was a practical man; he was no crusader, no ideological purist. Even so, everyone was on edge, tempers flared, and he temporarily lost the support of his assembly. Obviously, the "Infection" emanating from colonial radicals elsewhere had spread to the tranquil colony of New Jersey.[24]

Fortunately for William Franklin, some members of Parliament were beginning to have second thoughts about the Stamp Act. The Grenville ministry fell in the spring of 1765, and George III asked the Marquis of Rockingham to form a new government. While Rockingham's supporters had no doubt that the Stamp Act was constitutional, they did question its expediency. To protest the Stamp Act, American merchants had agreed to boycott British goods. The boycott was harmful, if not devastating, to English trading interests. Under the circumstances, the Stamp Act was counterproductive.

Benjamin Franklin took advantage of the change in the ministry. Previously he had avoided taking a strong public stand against the Stamp Act for fear that it would endanger his project for royal government. Now opposition to the act was safe. By November 1765, Franklin was immersed in a vigorous campaign to secure the repeal of the Stamp Act. He was, he said, "extreamly busy, attending Members of both Houses, informing, explaining, consulting, disputing, in a continual Hurry from Morning to Night."[25] Franklin advised Rockingham to proceed with caution. He thought the government should suspend the Stamp Act and promise not to revive it until the colonial economy had improved. Then, he thought, when tempers had cooled, Parliament could simply "drop it on some other decent Pretence, without ever bringing the Question of Right to a Decision."[26] Like his son, Benjamin had a predilection for compromise (see Part Two, Document 2).

The Rockingham ministry was clearly looking for a graceful way out of the mess that Grenville had created. On January 28, 1766, the House of Commons discussed the effects of the colonial boycott on English merchants. In February, the house heard testimony from individuals who had views on the Stamp Act. Benjamin Franklin testified on Thursday, February 13.

William Strahan credited Franklin with singlehandedly securing the repeal of the Stamp Act. While such praise made too much of the impact of the Pennsylvanian's testimony, his performance was masterful. Whenever he could, Benjamin stressed the practical rather than the constitutional problems that the Stamp Act created. The colonists could not afford to pay the tax, and England could not afford to enforce it. The Americans would never pay the tax "unless compelled by force of arms."[27] He reminded Parliament that until the present crisis the colonists had always been "zealous for the honour and prosperity" of the mother country.[28] Now their attitude was changing, and England risked alienating the colonies permanently if it insisted on enforcing a universally unpopular law.

Benjamin Franklin was less forthright when he discussed constitutional issues. He did call for a return to the old requisition system, insisting that the colonists would not submit to any tax to which they had not consented. Grenville's supporters shrewdly pointed out that the requisition system gave inordinate power to the Crown, while it cut Parliament out of the picture entirely. Would the colonists, asked one interrogator, grant money to the king even if Parliament objected to such a grant? Franklin answered in the affirmative. In his mind, the colonists owed their loyalty to the king, not to Parliament.

On other issues Franklin was more conciliatory than most other Americans would have been. He explicitly granted Parliament the right to regulate trade and to levy any duty that would serve that end. Americans might object to such duties as a burden, he said, but they would never question their constitutionality. This was a concession that the Stamp Act Congress had refused to make. It was, all in all, a dextrous if often disingenuous performance.

A little over a week after Franklin's testimony, following a long and acrimonious debate, the House of Commons voted to repeal the Stamp Act; on March 18 the Lords followed suit. Benjamin Franklin was elated. He knew that Parliament had also passed the Declaratory Act, which asserted that Parliament had the right to legislate for the colonies "in all cases whatsoever," but he assured his friends that this was "merely to save Appearances," and he insisted that "no future Ministry will ever attempt to tax us."[29] As Franklin saw it, Parliament's willingness to back down in the face of colonial opposition proved that the government was essentially beneficent. Given the right information, the English government would always be willing to grant Americans their rights. It now behooved the colonists to express their gratitude to members of a ministry that had "hazarded themselves greatly in our Behalf," to punish the rioters, to compensate those who had suffered damage in the riots, and to "behave decently and respectfully" in the future.[30] With imperial affairs settled in the colonies' favor, he could return to the issue that had brought him to England in the first place: securing a royal charter for Pennsylvania.

No one was happier than William Franklin when news of the Stamp Act's repeal trickled into the colonies throughout April 1766. He was especially pleased to learn about his father's appearance before the House of Commons. This surely would take the wind out of the sails of Franklin's detractors. It indicated, moreover, what an influential man Benjamin Franklin had become. William was angry when his father did not get all the credit he deserved—especially in Pennsylvania, where the proprietary party refused even to mention Franklin's name when the city celebrated the repeal of the Stamp Act. Thus he made sure that Benjamin received due recognition when he and Elizabeth hosted an "elegant entertainment" at Burlington in honor of the Stamp Act repeal.[31]

By the end of 1766, both Franklin men were guardedly optimistic. William had been shaken by the events of the previous winter. The Stamp Act crisis had clearly revealed the limits of any royal governor's ability to control events. William Franklin had no hand in forming the Stamp Act—indeed he quickly realized that the legislation was extremely ill advised—yet he was stuck with the obligation to enforce that legislation, even while the home government gave him no guidance or support. Just as he could not control the ministry, neither could he stop New Jersey's popular leaders from sending representatives to the Stamp Act Congress or from boycotting British goods. All his understanding and goodwill were not enough when he was caught between an increasingly intrusive ministry and an assembly that was becoming more and more protective of its rights.

Still, like his father, Franklin believed that Parliament's repeal of the Stamp Act proved that England and America were united in spirit, interest, and goals. He welcomed a future that promised an "indissoluable Union of the Hearts of all the king's Subjects in the Bonds of mutual Affection."[32] And he was confident that, with the exception of a few "pretended Patriots," who were motivated by a desire for temporary popularity or a "mere Propensity to Mischief," most inhabitants of New Jersey agreed with him.[33] He had, he thought, come through the entire affair "with Flying Colours."[34] He had not offended the ministry nor had he lost the support of most people in New Jersey. There had been no riots to speak of in the colony, no efforts to tear down his house or even to burn him in effigy. Now that the new ministry seemed so sympathetic to the colonies—and with his father's help it would surely remain so—the future looked exceedingly bright.

NOTES

[1]See Bernard Bailyn, *The Ideological Origins of the American Revolution* (Cambridge, Mass.: Harvard University Press, 1967), for the fullest treatment of what historians have come to call the philosophy of the Commonwealthmen.

[2]BF to Richard Jackson, BF to William Strahan, 2 Dec. 1762, *PBF* 10:160, 161.

[3]John Penn to William Alexander, 3 Sept. 1762, William Alexander Duer, ed., *Life of William Alexander, Earl of Stirling* (New York: Wiley and Putnam, 1847), 70, 71; John Watt to Sir Charles Hardy, 1 Dec. 1762, *Letterbook of John Watts, 1762–1765,* New York Historical Society, *Collections* 61 (1928): 102, 103.

[4]*New York Gazette*, 14 Mar. 1763; BF to William Strahan, 28 Mar. 1763, *PBF* 10:236.

[5]WF to William Strahan, 25 Apr. 1763, C. H. Hart, "Letters from William Franklin to William Strahan," *Pennsylvania Magazine of History and Biography* 35 (1911): 426.

[6]WF to Lords of Trade, 27 June 1763, F. W. Ricord and William Nelson, eds., *Documents Relating to the Colonial History of the State of New Jersey* (1757–67), 9:389.

[7]WF to William Strahan, 25 Apr. 1763, Hart, "Letters," 425.

[8]J. Philip Gleason, "A Scurrilous Colonial Election and Franklin's Reputation," *William and Man Quartely,* 3d ser., 18 (1961): 68–84.

[9]See ibid. and *PBF* 11:332, 369, 370.

[10]John Penn to Thomas Penn, 19 Oct. 1764, Penn Papers, Historical Society of Pennsylvania, Philadelphia.

[11]Esmond Wright, *Franklin of Philadelphia* (Cambridge: Harvard University Press, 1986), 151.

[12]BF to Richard Jackson, 14 Mar. 1764, *PBF* 11:108.

[13]BF to Richard Jackson, 11 Feb. 1764, ibid., 76.

[14]WF to Earl of Halifax, 28 Oct. 1764, Ricord and Nelson, *Documents* 9:480.

[15]BF to Charles Thomson, 11 July 1765, *PBF* 12:207.

[16]BF to John Hughes, 9 Aug. 1765, ibid., 235.

[17]Samuel Wharton to WF, 29 Sept. 1765, Franklin Papers 1:159, American Philosophical Society, Philadelphia, *Pennsylvania Journal*, 3 Oct. 1765.

[18]WF to BF, 30 April 1766, *PBF* 13:256.

[19]WF to BF, 13 Nov. 1765, ibid. 12:367.

[20]WF to BF, 7 Sept. 1765, ibid., 261.

[21]WF to BF, 13 Nov. 1765, ibid., 369.

[22]WF to Grey Cooper, 15 Jan. 1766, PRO Treas. 1 Bundle 452, fol. 65, Library of Congress, Washington, D.C.; WF to Secretary Conway, 30 Nov. 1765, Ricord and Nelson, *Documents* 9:508.

[23]WF to BF, 13 Nov. 1765, *PBF* 12:369.

[24]WF to Secretary Conway, 30 Nov. 1765, Ricord and Nelson, *Documents* 9:508.

[25]BF to Lord Kames, 25 Feb. 1767, *PBF* 14:64.

[26]BF to WF, 9 Nov. 1765, ibid. 12:363.

[27]"Examination before the Commitee of the Whole of the House of Commons," ibid. 13:134.

[28]Ibid., 150.

[29]BF to Joseph Fox, 1 Mar. 1766, ibid., 186, 187.

[30]BF to Joseph Fox, 24 Feb. 1766; BF to David Hall, 24 Feb. 1766, ibid., 169, 170.

[31]*Pennsylvania Gazette,* 29 May 1766.

[32]*Votes and Proceedings of the General Assembly of the Province of New Jersey* 66:5.

[33]WF to BF, [Dec. 1766], *PBF* 13:539.

[34]WF to BF, [13 July 1766], ibid., 334.

4

Men in the Middle

After the repeal of the Stamp Act, William Franklin settled into his role as New Jersey's royal governor, convinced that no more storm clouds loomed in the distance. He grew increasingly corpulent, his worries were few, and he looked forward to the return of harmony in a colony that he happily called home. He had learned a few lessons from the Stamp Act controversy. He knew that he had to be more aggressive and to avoid even the appearance of merely reacting to events. He could not afford to be caught off guard by either the ministry or the assembly. His position was precarious, but he was confident that he could handle any challenge.

Benjamin Franklin, too, was relieved by the repeal of the Stamp Act. Like most colonials, he saw the legislation as a temporary aberration, and he did not hesitate to remain in England and to return with renewed vigor to his project for making Pennsylvania a royal colony. His appearance before Parliament had given him visibility, and his London social calendar was filled with so many invitations that he could scarcely respond favorably to them all. The Franklins had survived the Stamp Act crisis with their relationship intact. Personally and politically they had reason to value one another. William assumed many of his father's private and public responsibilities and continued to defend him against all partisan attacks. Benjamin tended to the needs of his grandson Temple and ran interference for William whenever the ministry erected roadblocks to his success. Each man relied on the other for news and inside information. They each also served as a political sounding board for the other, as they shared their observations on the rapidly changing political scene.

No doubt the views of father and son were beginning to diverge during these years. Had they spent much time together they might well have discovered that they agreed on less and less. William's office was appointive. He owed his allegiance—and his livelihood—to the king. Though he was more sympathetic to the colonial assemblies than many royal governors were, and he was never reluctant to criticize his superiors, he had sworn an oath to uphold the king's prerogatives in New Jersey, and he had every intention of fulfilling his obligations. He shrank almost instinctively from confusion and "anarchy," and he fought any attempt to disturb the natural order of things. Moreover, his military experience and his training as a lawyer intensified his natural tendency to uphold law and order.

Benjamin Franklin was no radical firebrand. If he enjoyed his role as London agent for the Pennsylvania assembly (and later for the assemblies of Georgia, New Jersey, and Massachusetts), he also served as co-deputy postmaster at the king's pleasure. Moreover, like his son, he always preferred compromise to ideological purity. A strong empire man, a proud Englishman, he did not yet object to William's determination to represent the king's interests in America. Still, while William's position led him almost unavoidably to identify with the Crown perspective, Benjamin's years in London, where he remained for more than a decade, gradually led him to sympathize with those who defended colonial rights against the encroachments of king and Parliament. If familiarity breeds contempt, Benjamin Franklin's long sojourn in London ultimately led him to be contemptuous of the king's men.

The differences that would one day divide father and son, England and America, although they appear obvious with hindsight, should not be exaggerated. Benjamin was proud of his son, a soldier, a lawyer, and a royal governor. William was grateful to a father who had voluntarily taken an illegitimate son into his home and given him all the advantages at his disposal. "I shall ever," he once told Benjamin, "have a grateful Sense of . . . the numberless Indulgencies I have receiv'd from your paternal Affection."[1]

Politically, too, father and son remained close. They were partners in a number of interrelated schemes to exploit the promise of the American West, even dreaming of creating their own colony in the Illinois country. They both disliked English attempts to tax the colonies, even while they deplored what they saw as the excesses of American protesters. They chafed at the increasingly intrusive and rigid policies of the Board of Trade. Yet they tried doggedly to operate within the spirit of the law, always seeking compromises to the divisive issues that characterized imperial relations in these difficult years. If, like many Americans, they were often frustrated with the ministry and thought parliamentary policy ill advised, they remained proud servants of the king.

During the years immediately following the repeal of the Stamp Act in 1766, father and son were optimistic. Each suffered a setback or two, but neither thought his disappointments would be permanent. Benjamin Franklin's plan for a royal government did not proceed as smoothly as he had expected. The project had had "to sleep a little" while the issue of colonial taxation remained uppermost in everyone's mind.[2] With the collapse of Grenville's ministry, Franklin had been convinced that he would soon secure a royal charter for

Pennsylvania. But in November 1765, when he presented the assembly's petition to the Privy Council, the council refused to act on it, deferring a decision to some unspecified future date. For all practical purposes, the ministry had rejected the assembly request. When he learned about the hearing, Joseph Galloway was "not a little alarmed," and he thought the ministry was extremely unfair. During the Stamp Act controversy, he pointed out, the proprietary party had stirred up the populace, fomenting a "Spirit of Riot and Rebellion, which will be hereafter Quelled with great Difficulty, if ever Quelled at all."[3] Conversely, the Quaker party had been the only voice representing law and order in the colony. At the very least, the Privy Council owed its most loyal subjects a proper hearing.

Franklin, however, was strangely unconcerned by the government's decision. Usually so practical, in this instance he was not moved at all by political reality. When his friend Richard Jackson had first tried to discourage his efforts to destroy proprietary rule, reminding him that royal government, like its proprietary counterpart, might one day rest in the hands of "Profligate Men" who would establish "the Doctrines that have by degrees enslav'd almost every part of Europe but this Island," Franklin did not even acknowledge Jackson's argument.[4] His vendetta against the Penns was so obsessive that it colored his entire perspective. Thus, even after the Privy Council's ruling he continued to assure the Pennsylvania assembly that victory was in his grasp. It was not until the summer of 1768 that Franklin contemplated abandoning his crusade. Even then, he refused to admit that Crown rule might be a bad, even dangerous policy.

Benjamin Franklin's sense of personal and political well-being soared in the days after the Stamp Act's repeal. Buoyed by the plaudits he earned in the wake of his testimony before the House of Commons, he airily dismissed all unpleasant news. Friends like Joseph Galloway fumed when the Penns' supporters attacked Franklin in the American press. Deborah grew reclusive and sent her daughter to Burlington as often as possible so that neither of them would have to listen to the vicious barbs of Benjamin's enemies. William, too, rushed to defend his father's name at every opportunity, as he worried about the effects that partisan politics in Pennsylvania might have in New Jersey. But Benjamin Franklin did not have to deal with American affairs on a daily basis, and when both friends and family repeated the ugly rumors about him that floated through the colonies, he responded with lofty equanimity. So long as the "Wise and Good" recognized his worth, he claimed not really to care "what the rest think and say."[5] Indeed, he numbered the "Abuses" that he suffered "among my Honours."[6]

It appeared, in those heady days, as though the "Wise and Good"—not to mention the powerful—were listening to Benjamin Franklin. Throughout the spring and summer of 1766, he busily devised proposals for the benefit of the colonies and presented them to various ministers for their approval. He also began lobbying for a project designed by his son and a group of their mutual speculator friends that would create a new British colony in the Illinois country. To be sure, Franklin achieved nothing but empty words of praise for his efforts, but he remained confident. The problem was not with the king or with the men who ran the government, nearly all of whom, he insisted, looked favorably on Pennsylvania. Rather, he attributed his lack of concrete progress to the "unsettled" nature of the ministry. The Rockingham government fell in July 1766, to be replaced by an even more unstable ministry headed by William Pitt. No one seemed to bear any ill will toward the colonists, but no one wanted to take a stand on any issue until government affairs had sorted themselves out.[7] The turmoil, Franklin explained, "disposed People generally to lie awhile upon their Oars."[8]

Franklin's faith in the ability of England and America to work out their differences did not appreciably diminish throughout the late 1760s. He worried when he heard that many members of the House of Lords accused the colonies in general and Massachusetts in particular of hankering after "*Rebellion*," and he was troubled by his sense that everyone in power agreed that measures had to be taken "to enforce the Authority of Parliament."[9] Still, he was convinced that England's leaders were misinformed about colonial attitudes, and he gladly assumed the burden of educating them. He flooded the London press with letters and pamphlets, explaining and defending American views on every issue. Significantly, he maintained a conciliatory position. He shrugged off tales of colonial intransigence, claiming that they were either greatly exaggerated or that they represented the views of an insignificant minority.

Franklin's role as moderate and educator was soon put to the test. Almost immediately after George III asked William Pitt to form a new government, he made Pitt the Earl of Chatham, thus moving him from the House of Commons to the House of Lords. More or less by default, leadership in the Commons fell to Charles Townshend, chancellor of the exchequer. Townshend had the unenviable task of balancing England's budget. In February 1767, he stood before Parliament to propose what became known as the Townshend Acts, which laid duties in the colonies on such English imports as paper, lead, paint, and tea. Townshend intended to use the revenue from the duties to defray the expenses of soldiers stationed in the colonies and to pay the salaries of royal officials in America. Once again, Parliament was trying to tax the colonies.

Franklin's initial response to the Townshend Acts was low-key. While he knew the new duties were burdensome, if he thought that they constituted a dangerous attack on colonial liberty he did not say so publicly. He appeared most concerned about the possibility of a violent American reaction to the legislation, and he urged his compatriots to avoid all "rash Proceedings" and to do what they could to "lessen the present Unpopularity of the American Cause."[10] At the same time, he made every effort to find a way to soften the position of hardliners on both sides of the water.

At first, colonial leaders reacted to the Townshend Acts with what Franklin thought was admirable caution. In December 1767, his old adversary John Dickinson published the first of twelve "Letters from a Farmer in Pennsylvania to the Inhabitants of the British Colonies" (see Part Two, Document 3). Dickinson's letters merely plowed old ground, rejecting parliamentary taxation while admitting England's right to regulate colonial trade. Various assemblies, including Pennsylvania's, devised resolutions denying Parliament's right to tax the colonies, but the resolutions were remarkably mild. Most colonial leaders hoped to avoid the violence that had accompanied the Stamp Act protests. Moreover, American merchants were understandably reluctant to support a boycott of British goods, for they knew that their businesses would be hurt by any effort to curtail trade with London. Consequently, it was not until 1769 that the colonists adopted loosely enforced nonconsumption and nonimportation agreements.

The calm did not last forever. Townshend died in September 1767, to be replaced by Lord North, a staunch defender of parliamentary authority. More troublesome, in January 1768 the king appointed Lord Hillsborough as secretary of a newly created American Department. Six months later, Hillsborough also became president of the Board of Trade. An unbending defender of Crown prerogative, he was a stickler for detail who intended to make Americans obey the letter as well as the spirit of the law. As the English government ignored colonial protests against the Townshend Acts, tempers began to fray, and customs commissioners along the Atlantic seaboard frequently became the targets of angry mobs. Assaults on customs officials in New London and New Haven, Connecticut, were especially brutal, and by February 1768 commissioners in Boston were convinced that they could not collect the Townshend duties without military support.

Throughout 1768 and 1769, Benjamin Franklin remained hopeful that Parliament would repeal the Townshend Acts. While there were many who agreed with former minister Grenville that Parliament needed to deal forcefully with the colonies, Franklin thought that most House members realized the "Folly of the late Measures."[11] The problem, as it had been in 1766, lay in helping the government find an exit from a self-imposed dilemma. Once Parliament had passed the Townshend Acts, its members felt that "the National Honour [was] concern'd in supporting them."[12] Reports of anticustoms riots and the challenge to Parliament's power emanating from many American assemblies merely stiffened the government's resolve. No one wanted to appear weak; no one wanted to back down. Thus Franklin encouraged Americans to keep the peace, to be cautious in their public statements, and to continue to boycott British goods, exerting economic pressure on those in a position to convince Parliament to alter its course.

Franklin thought his strategy would eventually succeed. In June 1769, the ministry promised that it would not levy any new taxes on the colonies. Everywhere there were signs that the government was "growing more moderate with regard to America."[13] If this was the case, then as far as Benjamin Franklin was concerned the Townshend Acts, like the Stamp Act before them, would be a temporary inconvenience and nothing more.

Despite the furor over the Townshend Acts, his inability to secure a royal charter for Pennsylvania, and his failure to make any progress on the plan for an Illinois colony, these were pleasant times for Benjamin Franklin. He traveled to Germany, to France, and to various watering holes in England and Scotland. He made the rounds of the London coffeehouses and relished his meetings at the Royal Society. While he continued to promise Deborah that he would soon return home, his letters to his wife became shorter and more perfunctory.

For William, too, the years immediately following the repeal of the Stamp Act were a pleasant interlude. He grew comfortable in his role as governor and put down roots in his adopted colony. He acquired land near Burlington, "entered far into the Spirit of Farming," and began to build a magnificant three-story house on the Delaware River.[14] He was so content that, despite his occasional efforts to wangle a promotion out of Whitehall, he could truthfully tell his assembly that "it is here, if I return to a private station, that I propose to spend the Remainder of my Days."[15]

His days were full not only with his official duties but with his many private responsibilities and a constant round of visiting and entertaining that both he and Elizabeth enjoyed. They hobnobbed with Crown officials from New York, Pennsylvania, and New Hampshire. Sally was a constant visitor in Burlington, and even Deborah made an occasional trip to the West Jersey capital. The Franklins often traveled to Philadelphia, where William combined business with pleasure, tending to his father's affairs, catching up on Pennsylvania politics, attending the horse races, and embarking on a steady "Course of Eating and Drinking" that left everyone pleasantly exhausted.[16]

What made these years agreeable was the relatively smooth course of New Jersey politics. William had learned how to work with his council and assembly. He was adept at making compromises whenever the British government allowed him to do so. In fact, most of his quarrels in the late 1760s were not with the colony's lawmakers but with the ministry. For the most part, when the assembly chafed at the rigid and intrusive demands of London bureaucrats, William Franklin nodded in agreement. This was especially true after 1768, when the punctilious Earl of Hillsborough became secretary of the American Department.

As William Franklin worked with the members of his assembly, he often sympathized with their position even as he clung stubbornly to his belief that the interests of Crown and province were identical. Unfortunately, the king's ministers, who grew increasingly disenchanted with colonial rebelliousness, seemed intent on proving him wrong. Yet Franklin persisted, trying to explain the Crown's position to the assembly and putting the best face on assembly affairs whenever he wrote to England.

William Franklin's problems reflected the difficulties that all royal governors faced in these years. Ideally, governors served the interests of the king, the empire, and the particular colony to which they had been assigned. They arrived in America with a public commission authorizing them to govern the colony and with private instructions drawn up by the Board of Trade demanding that they enforce all trade laws and uphold the king's prerogatives. Throughout the eighteenth century, the board's instructions became more numerous and more detailed and, consequently, more of an irritant to colonial assemblies. While governors enjoyed many powers—they could veto legislation, refuse to convene assemblies, prorogue, or suspend legislative sessions, and issue calls for new elections—they also suffered from serious disadvantages. The assemblies in most colonies controlled the purse strings. They appropriated funds for military ventures and for government expenses and decided how to raise money. Perhaps most important, they paid the salaries of the governor and the other Crown officers. Thus, despite their frequent complaints, the assemblies had considerable bargaining power. Even in times of relative calm the relationship between governor and assembly could be prickly. After 1763, as the interests of England and America diverged, the governors' ability to work with their legislatures eroded.

William Franklin labored valiantly to narrow the gap between England and America, and in the 1760s he frequently blamed an insensitive ministry for many of the disputes that disrupted what he was convinced should have been an amicable relationship. The governor had many quarrels with the ministry in these years, but none was so troubling as the one precipitated by the Crown's continued demands for funds to supply the king's troops.

The troops were part of the contingent of soldiers that had remained in America at the end of the French and Indian War. Most of them were stationed along the frontier, but a few were quartered in New York, Pennsylvania, and New Jersey, where they developed supply lines to the West. Imbued with the nearly universal colonial suspicion of standing armies, suffering from a prolonged recession, and frustrated because the expense of maintaining unwanted troops fell more heavily on their colony than it did on most others, the New Jersey legislators balked at parliamentary demands that they bear an increasingly onerous financial burden. They became even more obdurate with the passage of the Mutiny Act (sometimes known as the Quartering Act) of 1765. The act required the colony to furnish suitable quarters for the king's troops. More troublesome, it insisted that the soldiers be supplied with specific items—bedding, firewood and candles, and beer, cider, or rum.

The Mutiny Act reintroduced many of the constitutional issues that had plagued imperial relations during the Stamp Act controversy. The colonists believed that the legislation was simply a tax by other means. While they claimed to be willing to contribute to the colonial defense, they insisted that the assembly, not Parliament, should decide what items it would furnish the troops quartered in their midst.[17] Beginning in 1766, the New Jersey assembly voted to allocate funds for the army, but its members ignored Franklin's pleas "to insert the very Words of the Act of Parliament" in their bill. Thus they maintained the fiction that they provided supplies to the Crown as a gift.[18] The lawmakers did not observe the letter of the law, but Franklin quickly pointed out that they had not violated its spirit. No soldier stationed in New Jersey, he hotly proclaimed, had ever complained about supplies. Indeed, he said, many soldiers "acknowledg'd they were better accomodated here than they had ever been at Barracks in Europe."[19] He begged the ministers to allow him a little leeway in dealing with an assembly that was anxious to do its part to defend the empire. He had no desire to pick an unnecessary quarrel with his legislature, and he hoped the ministry would be persuaded—for its own good—to understand his position. Thus Franklin was dismayed when the Crown disallowed successive New Jersey supply bills. He thought the ministry's legalistic quibbling was counterproductive. "The only difference is about Mode," he protested, "not the Essentials."[20]

In November 1768, the governor received a rude shock. Lord Hillsborough had not only disallowed the previous year's supply bill—which Franklin had fully expected—but he also launched a stinging personal attack on Franklin's own conduct. Always a little insecure, never able to accept criticism gracefully, in this case William was bewildered by a condemnation that struck him as fundamentally unfair. He had done his best to convince the assembly to conform to the Mutiny Act. Failing in his endeavors, he had had two choices. He might have vetoed the bill, winning a few points on principle but leaving the king's troops with no supplies for an entire year. Or he could have signed the bill, thus guaranteeing adequate provisions for another season. As he saw it, common sense dictated that he opt for the latter course.

The issue was finally resolved in 1769 when Parliament modified the Mutiny Act, making it easier for the New Jersey assembly to comply with its terms. Still, the quarrel had been unpleasant, even frightening, and in this instance, as in so many others in the late 1760s, Franklin agreed with his assembly.

The governor faced a more critical threat to his well-being with the passage of the Townshend Acts. Like his father, William expressed no special alarm at first. He knew that most Americans would object to Parliament's latest attempt to obtain revenue from the colonies. The issue was the same as it had been during the Stamp Act crisis. The colonists refused to be taxed by a body in which they had no representation. Moreover, taxation was not the only issue that the Townshend Acts introduced. The money collected by the new, overaggressive customs collectors was intended to be used not only for defense but to pay the salaries of all Crown officers in the colonies, including the royal governors. Their control of the governors' salaries was one of the assemblies' most jealously guarded rights. For if the governors no longer depended on lawmakers for their stipends, they would have no reason to compromise with members of the lower house. Many of them might decide never to convene their assemblies again.

At the beginning of 1768, the Massachusetts legislature sent a circular letter to the other colonies attempting to organize resistance to the Townshend Acts. Unfortunately for William Franklin, the New Jersey assembly was in session when the letter arrived. The lawmakers, with little fanfare, agreed to appoint a committee to consider the Bay Colony's proposal, before turning to more pressing business. The governor was relieved to be told that the assembly did not wish to join any intercolonial resistance effort. Rather, it planned to send a humble, and entirely legal, petition to the king asking for repeal of the Townshend duties. No one bothered to inform Franklin that the legislators planned to write to the Massachusetts assembly as well.

Even as the assembly was preparing its response to the Bay Colony's initiative, Lord Hillsborough was sending instructions to the royal governors telling them to prorogue their respective assemblies if the legislatures tried to acknowledge the Massachusetts letter. Hillsborough's instructions and the New Jersey petition probably passed each other in transit. When Franklin received the secretary's missive in June, he could do nothing but write to the minister, explaining his dilemma and insisting that his assembly had no subversive intentions and no desire to enter into any "unwarrantable Combination" with the other colonies.[21]

Hillsborough was not mollified. In the same letter containing the king's disallowance of the 1767 quartering bill, the secretary berated both governor and assembly for what he saw as a blatant assault on parliamentary supremacy. Indeed, he claimed, the New Jersey response to the Massachusetts letter was an act of "rebellion."[22] Worse, he blamed Franklin for the debacle, and he wondered if William had the proper temperament, or even the proper loyalties, to continue as governor. Angry and frightened, Franklin struck back. In a long, rambling, sometimes incoherent diatribe, he tried to justify both himself and his assembly. The letter touched all the bases, as the governor defended his honor, explained his actions, and even complained about his salary. The letter is particularly interesting because it reveals something of Franklin's political views in 1768 (see Part Two, Document 4).

The governor exhibited an unusual willingness to defend his assembly's position on imperial issues. If he did not admit that he agreed with the colonists, neither, significantly, did he condemn them. Nor did he shrink from offering the ministry a little unsolicited advice. Parliament's attempts to tax the colonies were, he thought, even if technically legal, extremely ill advised. Americans, he pointed out, had never accepted the logic of the Declaratory Act—Parliament's face-saving declaration of its right to legislate for the colonies in all cases—issued along with the repeal of the Stamp Act. Still, they had "quietly acquiesc'd in it," assuming that Parliament would be content to make its point and then let the matter drop. Now England had "rekindled the Flame."[23] Even worse, the government had recently sent troops to Boston to maintain peace in a town that was becoming notorious for its radicalism. The troops, he admitted, would undoubtedly prevent "scandalous Riots and Attacks on the Officers of Government."[24] But this did not solve the underlying problem. Indeed, it exacerbated the situation. The colonists, like English subjects everywhere, believed that standing armies in time of peace were a sign of impending tyranny. The presence of troops in Boston appeared to threaten the basic liberties of the king's subjects, proving to many that their freedom and independence were in danger. "Men's Minds are sour'd," he told the secretary, and "a sullen Discontent prevails." There was "no Force on Earth" that would "make the Assemblies acknowledge by any Act of theirs, that the Parliament has a Right to impose Taxes on America."[25] The government might be able to control the actions of the colonists, he thought, but unless it changed its tactics, it would never be able to capture their hearts and minds.

Franklin's letter virtually invited a reprisal from London, and he later claimed that he expected to be removed from office as soon as his communication reached Lord Hillsborough's desk. But while his treatment of the governor remained cool, at times even hostile, the secretary ignored his diatribe. Had Franklin been deprived of his office in 1768, he might well have joined his father in the move toward independence. But despite his unhappiness with the ministry, he was incapable of taking the initiative and actually quitting his post. Not so many years ago, he had wanted to break his engagement to Betsy Graeme, but he had forced Betsy to do the job for him.

Now, when the stakes were much higher, he waited nervously for Hillsborough to free him from his obligations to the Crown. But the secretary refused to make the first move. Consequently, William Franklin continued to serve the king.

Throughout the late 1760s, whatever differences Benjamin and William Franklin had with Crown policy, they continued their efforts to balance the competing demands of king and country. Despite the physical distance that separated them, their personal and political partnership grew steadily stronger. William's admiration for his father was boundless. He thought that men "of all Parties" wanted to see his father's political star rise to even greater heights.[26] Both he and Joseph Galloway were convinced that if the colonists knew even half of what Benjamin did for them "they would go near to deify" him.[27]

William's personal services to his father were of immeasurable importance. Without his son's willingness to assume responsibility for his extended family, Benjamin would have found it difficult to remain in London. William sent money and provisions to various relatives and used his influence to secure government positions for his less successful relatives. He paid special attention to the interests of Sally and Deborah. When Sally, with her mother's blessing, decided to marry Richard Bache, a relative newcomer to Philadelphia, William investigated his future brother-in-law's prospects. Alarmed by what he saw as a pattern of profligacy and bad judgment, he did his best to prevent the match. Bache was, he thought, a "mere Fortune Hunter" who only wanted a "Family that will support him."[28] Benjamin agreed, and he tried to divert Sally's attentions by suggesting that she visit him in London. This ploy had once worked for William. Perhaps it would do for Sally as well. On this occasion, however, the Franklin women triumphed, and William grudgingly accepted his sister's decision, even serving as godfather to the Baches' first child, Benjamin Franklin Bache. Sometime in the winter of 1769, Deborah suffered a stroke, rendering William's family cares more burdensome than ever. Her appetite dwindled, she grew reclusive, and she suffered lapses of memory, becoming depressed and "verey lonley."[29] William tried to make her comfortable, and she derived inestimable joy from the "King Bird," as she dubbed the Baches' son. But no one was a substitute for Benjamin Franklin.

William also tended to his father's business and political affairs. He looked after Franklin's investments in Nova Scotia. He wrote pamphlets intended to lay to rest any lingering doubts about Benjamin's loyalty to America. He made sure that all of his father's tracts were published in the local press and helped finance a new Philadelphia newspaper that he hoped would be a mouthpiece for the Franklins and their allies.

The relationship was not a one-way street. If William shouldered the responsibility for Sally and Deborah, Benjamin looked after the interests of his grandson. He insisted that William foot the bills for Temple's expenses, but it was Benjamin who cared for the boy on a regular basis. Politically, Franklin was his son's invaluable ally. He offered advice on the best way to deal with the ministry. After William's quarrel with Lord Hillsborough, Benjamin agreed to edit his son's letters to the secretary before forwarding them to their final destination. He lobbied for many of William's pet projects and put in a good word for both the governor and the colony of New Jersey whenever he could. In December 1769, the New Jersey assembly asked Benjamin Franklin to serve as its London agent. No royal governor enjoyed such a close relationship with the person chosen to represent the lower house.

There was yet another interest that bound Benjamin and William Franklin in these years. Like many ambitious Americans, father and son had become deeply involved in a series of interlocking schemes designed to reap a profit from speculation in the land west of the Proclamation Line. Their venture depended upon ministerial whim, for they could not found a colony in the Illinois country so long as the Proclamation Line remained in place. Thus, both men strove to remain in the ministry's good graces. As they continued to confront a wall of intransigence, however, they were forced to admit that English policy was not always compatible with the interests of even the king's most loyal subjects.

This became obvious at the very time when the Franklins thought that their plans for a western colony were about to be realized. On December 23, 1767, the Board of Trade succumbed to intense lobbying efforts, recommending that the Proclamation Line be moved farther west. The way was evidently clear for the Franklins and their speculator friends to begin establishing their western empire. Unfortunately, in June 1768, the speculators' plans were dealt a blow from which they would never recover, when Lord Hillsborough became president of the Board of Trade. Hillsborough had never been sympathetic to western expansion, fearing that it would encourage his own countrymen in Ireland to migrate to America in greater numbers. Moreover, he was not especially fond of either of the Franklins. Within weeks of Hillsborough's accession to the Board of Trade, Benjamin glumly announced that the ministry had put the entire project on hold.

Despite their repeated failures, both Franklins remained hopeful about their plans for western expansion throughout the 1760s. When one project failed, they eagerly devised another. Convinced that their private ambitions and the interests of the British Empire were not in conflict, they blamed individual ministers, not ministerial policy as a whole, for their disappointments. Thus their repeated failures gave them no reason to question their loyalty to king or empire. The cumbersome machinery of the British government always operated more slowly than they liked, but they believed that if they were patient it would ultimately work to their benefit.

There were, if anyone cared to notice, occasional signs of tension in the relationship between father and son in these years. Benjamin was embarrassed when some colonists expressed doubts about his loyalty to American interests because he had a son who served the Crown. William sometimes wondered if Hillsborough's hostility toward him was occasioned by his filial relationship to the often troublesome Benjamin Franklin. Still, neither man cared to blame the other for his disappointments.

The Franklins maintained, even nurtured, their relationship in these years, not only because of their mutual and abiding affection, but because it suited their interests to do so. Just as important, their attitudes toward the British Empire were not markedly divergent in this period. Both were loyal to the king and longed to resolve those issues that divided England and America. Both strove, at least publicly, to pursue a moderate course. William balanced the interests of Crown and assembly, England and America, with dexterity. Benjamin tried to placate the ministry, even as he urged Americans to adopt a firm but prudent course of action in defense of their rights. William always emphasized America's need for England; his father talked of the mother country's dependence on its colonies. But both continued to long for a "consolidating Union," the "only firm Basis" on which the empire's "Grandeur and Stability" could be founded.[30]

NOTES

[1] WF to BF, 3 Sept. 1758, *PBF* 8:132.

[2] BF to John Ross, 14 Feb. 1765, ibid. 12:67.

[3] Joseph Galloway to BF, 18 June [July] 1765, ibid., 218; 27 Feb. 1766, ibid., 13:180.

[4] Richard Jackson to BF, 11 Aug. 1764, ibid. 11:313.

[5] BF to Charles Thomson, 27 Sept. 1766, ibid. 13:428.

[6] BF to Jane Mecom, 2 Mar. 1767, ibid. 14:72.

[7] Lord Shelburne, one of America's best friends in the ministry, replaced Pitt. In 1768 he was followed by the weak and ineffectual Duke of Grafton. Only in 1770, with the selection of Lord North as the king's first minister, did the government even approach a measure of stability.

[8] BF to Pennsylvania Assembly Committee of Correspondence, 10 June 1766, *PBF* 13:298.

[9] Report on a Debate in the House of Lords, [11 April 1767], ibid. 14:108, 109.

[10] BF to Joseph Galloway, 8 Aug. 1767, ibid. 14:230.

[11] BF to James Bowdoin, 13 July 1769, ibid. 16:176.

[12] BF to Joseph Galloway, 9 Jan. 1769, ibid., 11.

[13] BF to James Bowdoin, 13 July 1769, ibid., 176.

[14] WF to BF, 11 May 1769, ibid., 127.

[15] *Votes and Proceedings of the General Assembly of the Province of New Jersey* 71A:32.

[16] WF to BF, 1 Sept. 1769, *PBF* 16:189.

[17]Ironically, BF had a hand in drafting the Mutiny Act and had evidently foreseen no constitutional difficulties with its provisions. He was mainly concerned with securing Parliament's promise that no soldiers would be quartered in private homes.

[18]WF to Earl of Shelburne, 18 Dec. 1766, Shelburne Papers 51:786, William Clements Library, Ann Arbor, Michigan.

[19]Ibid., 790.

[20]WF to Lord Hillsborough, 14 June 1768, F. W. Ricard and William Nelson, eds., *Documents Relating to the Colonial History of the State of New Jersey* (1757–67), 10:33.

[21]WF to Lord Hillsborough, 16 June 1768, ibid., 35.

[22]Lord Hillsborough to WF, 16 Aug. 1768, ibid., 46.

[23]WF to Lord Hillsborough, 23 Nov. 1768, ibid., 69.

[24]Ibid., 70.

[25]Ibid.

[26]WF to BF, 10 May 1768, *PBF* 15:123.

[27]WF to BF, 22 Aug. 1767, ibid. 14:234.

[28]WF to BF, [? May 1767], ibid., 174.

[29]DF to BF, 20[–27] Nov. 1769, ibid. 16:230, 231.

[30]BF to Lord Kames, 25 Feb. 1767, ibid., 14:65.

5

The Making of a Patriot

In 1751, Benjamin Franklin wrote a pamphlet, "Observations concerning the Increase of Mankind," in which he argued that America's population was doubling every generation. If this astounding growth rate continued, he predicted, British Americans would outnumber their counterparts in the mother country within a century. So long as settlers were allowed to move west, Americans would be farmers, not manufacturers. Thus America's population explosion and its vast domain would benefit the mother country, as the colonists would provide an ever-expanding market for English goods. Americans would strengthen the empire, complementing instead of competing with their English cousins. Moreover, the West would act as a safety valve for poor and disaffected English subjects everywhere. And prosperous Americans, grateful to a benevolent monarch, would gladly support the empire's military endeavors.[1]

Franklin's pamphlet reveals some of his earliest thoughts about the nature of the British Empire. He clearly saw America as an important and unique part of the British system and believed that in time England would need the colonies more than the colonies would need England. Still, he saw no reason for America to sever its connection to the mother country. Indeed, he thought their interests were mutual. As America grew in population and power, Franklin hoped that English people everywhere would eventually be equal partners in a "consolidating Union."[2]

Franklin did not easily relinquish his dream of a united empire. Nevertheless, in the years after the passage of the Townshend Acts, events forced him more and more often to reflect on and to modify his views concerning the relationship between England and America. This was especially true after 1771, when the Massachusetts legislature made him its London agent, and he became increasingly familiar with the perspective of American radicals. Throughout the 1770s, he grew ever more disgusted with government policy, more jaded by his experiences in England, and more contemptuous of those who served the king.

Benjamin Franklin's political views changed in fits and starts in the years following the passage of the Townshend Acts. His perspective was shaped by his particular experiences as well as by the political events of the day. It would be futile to assess the relative weight that personal pique and public policy had in impelling him to reevaluate his views. Nevertheless, the colonial reaction to the Townshend Acts, his quarrels with Lord Hillsborough, and his growing contact with leaders in Boston all did their part in determining his political stance. The 1773 Tea Act and its aftermath simply reinforced the views that Franklin had gradually—and reluctantly—developed in the years after 1767.

The quarrel over the Townshend Acts was quieter but more protracted than the crisis occasioned by the Stamp Act had been. Consequently, as the debate continued, Franklin was able to consider his evolving views toward English policy at a leisurely pace. His mood and his views fluctuated. He always urged the colonists to restrain the hotheads in their midst. There was no need to give America's enemies any excuse to enact harsher measures. Still, he insisted that the colonies must keep up their pressure against England, maintaining their boycott of British goods until Parliament repealed the Townshend Acts. Convinced that the mother country could not survive without its colonial markets, he was certain that America's economic strength would ultimately win the day. Significantly, Franklin began to insist that Parliament must concede that it had no right to tax the colonists. In 1766, he had been satisfied when the government backed down on the grounds of expediency, and he had even swallowed the Declaratory Act with relative grace. By 1770, his stance had hardened.

Franklin's attitude toward the ministry also fluctuated. At times he was convinced that most English subjects, even most ministers, were favorably inclined toward America. There was a "general Disposition in the Nation" he told Joseph Galloway, "to be upon good Terms with the Colonies."[3] As late as 1770, when Lord North assumed control of the government, he remained guardedly optimistc that the Townshend Acts would be completely repealed. Still, almost in the same breath, he talked ominously about the "Malice against us in some powerful People," and he feared that men of the ilk of the despised Lord Grenville would assume power, destroying American liberties once and for all.[4]

Neither Franklin's worst fears nor his highest hopes were realized. In March 1770, Parliament repealed most of the Townshend duties, leaving only the levy on tea as a symbol of its right to tax the colonies. Like many colonists, Franklin was not satisfied with this halfway measure. So long as the tea tax remained, the constitutional issues dividing England and America were as troublesome as ever. Thus he urged his compatriots to continue their boycott on English goods until Parliament totally rescinded the Townshend Acts. To do otherwise would prove that the colonies were motivated by pecuniary interest, not unselfish patriotism. In July, however, New York's merchants relaxed their embargo, promising only to refuse to accept any British tea. Merchants elsewhere eagerly followed suit, and by fall the boycott had collapsed.

Franklin was discouraged by the colonial failure to maintain the boycott. Like many Americans, he believed that liberty was best protected when it rested in the hands of a virtuous and independent populace. Virtue in the eighteenth century meant, among other things, patriotism, a willingness to sacrifice private interest for the public good, and the ability to shun luxury in favor of a simple, almost spartan existence. Only individuals who were independent, who owed their livelihood to no other person or special interest, could be virtuous. By definition, male property owners were the most likely possessors of virtue. The collapse of the boycott threatened "republican virtue," as many dubbed it, in a number of ways. It implied that American merchants and consumers were more committed to their own interests than to the public welfare, when they so readily sacrificed their principles for private profit or the opportunity to purchase a few luxuries. Moreover, with the end of the boycott, Americans became more dependent than ever on English goods. Some became mired in debt to British creditors. Many more became psychologically dependent, as they eschewed good American-made products in favor of English finery.

As Franklin watched the controversy over the Townshend Acts develop and worried over its effect on American virtue, he began to reexamine his views of the relationship between America and England (see Part Two, Document 5). He did not abandon his desire for a "consolidating Union of the whole," but he realized that most members of Parliament thought "too highly of themselves to admit Representatives from us."[5] That being the case and likely to remain so, Franklin became more determined than ever to limit Parliament's authority in America.

Franklin was one of many Americans who responded to the colonies' seemingly unending quarrels with the government by questioning Parliament's power. By 1768, he had begun to reexamine his old belief that Parliament could regulate colonial trade but could not tax Americans. Instead, he joined with a growing number of colonial leaders who argued that Parliament either had the right to make laws for the colonies or it did not. There was, he wrote to William, "no middle doctrine." If that was true, he favored the latter position.[6] He obviously found his own argument somewhat troubling. For in the same letter he admitted that he thought Parliament had the right to regulate colonial trade and even to lay duties on English imports. Like most colonists, he was still trying to work out his perspective and was reluctant to accept the ramifications of his own logic.

Nevertheless, by 1768 Franklin's thoughts had begun to crystallize. Beginning with his belief that English people on both sides of the Atlantic were equal and enjoyed identical rights, he argued that Americans were bound to the mother country only through their relationship to the king. While the colonists had always cherished their ties to the monarch, now, he complained, "a new kind of loyalty seems to be required of us, a loyalty to P[arliamen]t."[7] And Parliament, Franklin said, had no authority in the colonies. Its members, like their counterparts in the assemblies, were mere "Subjects of the King." And "*Fellow Subjects* in one Part of [the King's] Dominions are not Sovereign over *Fellow Subjects* in any other Part." Franklin knew that even America's most sympathetic English friends would view his pronouncements as "little less than Treason."[8] In England, parliamentary supremacy was an unquestioned article of faith, and Parliament would never consent to share its power with the colonial assemblies. They want, he sniffed, to be "*omnipotent* without being *omniscient*."[9]

Throughout the 1760s, and well into the 1770s, America's quarrel was with Parliament, not the king. Franklin, like all colonists, continued to proclaim that he could "scarcely conceive a King of better Dispositions, of more exemplary Virtues, or more truly desirous of promoting the Welfare of his Subjects" than George III.[10] He was obviously pleased whenever he heard that the king spoke of him "with regard," and he even continued his efforts to procure a ministerial appointment.[11] Still, if Franklin refused to criticize the king, he developed a profound antipathy for some of the king's ministers, especially his son's nemesis, Lord Hillsborough. In January 1768, when Hillsborough had become in rapid succession secretary of the American Department and president of the Board of Trade, Franklin had been sanguine. He hoped Hillsborough's control over American affairs would result in more stability, and he thought the secretary harbored "favourable" views toward the colonies, at least "so far as he thinks consistent with what he supposes the unquestionable rights of Britain."[12]

In August, Franklin's attitude toward Lord Hillsborough changed dramatically when he had a "long Audience" with the secretary to lobby, once again, for Pennsylvania's petition for a royal government. He came away bitter and discouraged. Hillsborough, it turned out, had a "stronger Partiality for Mr. Penn than any of his Predecessors," and Franklin determined that it would be futile to broach the subject again until the secretary left office.[13] Franklin's hatred of the Penns was visceral, and he could never tolerate anyone who befriended them. Moreover, with his dreams for a royal government—and perhaps for a royal governorship for himself?—dashed, he had less reason than before to curry favor with the ministry.

Franklin's relationship with Lord Hillsborough reached its nadir at the beginning of 1771. In the fall of the previous year, the Massachusetts house had made Benjamin its agent. Franklin was familiar with the duties of colonial agents. He had served as Pennsylvania's representative to England since 1764 and added Georgia and New Jersey to his list of responsibilities in 1768 and 1769 respectively. But these colonies were moderate; their assemblies were followers, not leaders, whenever English-American relationships were at stake. This was not the case with Massachusetts. Moreover, Franklin's appointment had met with considerable opposition from some assembly members. He and his son, after all, both "held Places of Importance under the Crown," and there were some who feared that Franklin would not be sufficiently aggressive in supporting the assembly's agenda.[14] Because he had come to the Massachusetts agency under a cloud of suspicion, he may have felt compelled to prove that his detractors' fears were unfounded.

Massachusetts had long been a troublesome colony. By the mid-eighteenth century, the port city of Boston had begun to experience a steady erosion of its economic fortunes. Its trade had declined; its shipyards and distilleries had suffered reverses. Throughout the century, Massachusetts had participated enthusiastically in England's wars with France. Its men had fought and died in those wars, leaving countless widows and orphans to be cared for at public expense. With unemployment on the rise and taxes soaring, many Bostonians blamed imperial policy—especially tighter trade regulations and Parliament's efforts to tax the colonists—for their plight.

Boston had been the scene of the first, and arguably the most violent, colonial riots against the Stamp Act. The Massachusetts assembly had taken the lead in organizing intercolonial opposition to the Townshend Acts. In 1768, customs commissioners stationed in the capital city had been so intimidated by the threat of mob action that they had requested—and obtained—two regiments of soldiers to patrol the streets of the town and to protect them while they endeavored to enforce the Townshend Acts. The troops had remained in Boston for two years, a concrete reminder of England's unpopular policies toward America. Soldiers and townspeople never got along, as soldiers drove up prices and took jobs that many thought should have gone to native Bostonians. On the night of March 5, 1770, the simmering antagonisms between civilians and the military came to a boil when townspeople took to the streets, advancing on the barracks, shouting obscenities, and throwing rocks and huge chunks of ice at the soldiers. A few soldiers fired at the crowd, killing five rioters and wounding several others in what became known as the Boston Massacre. Almost immediately, the king agreed to remove the troops from Boston. At the same time, Parliament repealed most of the Townshend Acts. Still, the Boston Massacre excacerbated tensions between Massachusetts and America, and it made many local political leaders more determined than ever to protect American liberties from the attacks of what appeared to be a corrupt and tyrannical government in England.

The significance of Benjamin Franklin's decision to accept the Massachusetts agency cannot be underestimated. The first letter of instructions he received from Thomas Cushing, speaker of the house, indicated just how demanding the position would be. Other assemblies merely asked Franklin to help them secure the ministry's favor for various pieces of provincial legislation. The Massachusetts speaker began his correspondence with a long list of the colony's grievances against the British government, as he expressed the assembly's "total alienation" from a ministry that treated its members like "Vassals and Slaves."[15]

The longer Franklin served the Massachusetts assembly, the more critical of ministerial policy he became. This was in large measure because after 1770 he received more news from the pens of political activists in Massachusetts than he did from old cohorts like Joseph Galloway. To be sure, William continued to write to his father. But he was often circumspect, avoiding any topic that might provoke a quarrel. What Franklin heard from Boston, often as not, was that the "Ministry have adopted a settled plan to subjugate America to arbitrary power" and that colonists everywhere were growing more determined to thwart Britain's conspiracy against their liberty.[16]

Franklin's appointment to the Massachusetts agency was significant for another reason. It provided the pretext for his public estrangement from Lord Hillsborough. Hillsborough was an affable man, well liked in his own social circles. But when it came to his perceived duty to defend the king's prerogative, he was, as William Franklin had already discovered, unbending. As part of his attempt to clean up the sloppy practices of previous ministers, as well as his campaign to exert firmer control over the colonies, Hillsborough refused to approve the credentials of any colonial agent who received his appointment solely from the lower house. He insisted that an agent represented the entire colony, not just the people, and thus the governor and council had to have a hand in selecting him. Moreover, because Massachusetts had a reputation as a troublemaker, Hillsborough surely wanted to teach its assembly a lesson or two.

The stage was set for a showdown when Franklin met with Hillsborough on the 16th of January 1771 to present his credentials. Predictably, the minister refused to accept them. Benjamin complained that Hillsborough's conduct throughout their meeting was arrogant and rude. He should be known, Franklin fumed, by his "Conceit, Wrong headedness, Obstinacy and Passion" as well as by his "perverse and senseless Management."[17] As he left the secretary's chamber, the usually affable Franklin muttered that it was really "of no great Importance whether the Appointment is acknowledged or not," for, he added meaningfully, "I have not the least Conception that an Agent can *at present* be of any Use to any of the Colonies."[18] For all practical purposes Franklin had severed his ties with Hillsborough. He had no official contact with the ministry for a year and a half.

Franklin's estrangement from the government came at a time when the Massachusetts assembly sorely needed his services. While relations between England and America were relatively amicable after the partial repeal of the Townshend Acts, they never ran a completely smooth course, especially where the Bay Colony was concerned. One issue that was especially troublesome was the ministry's determination to use the proceeds from colonial customs duties to pay the salaries for royal governors, thus freeing the king's representatives from assembly control. The colonists knew that the king's own salary did not depend on Parliament's approval, but they argued that the American situation was different. The king resided in England, and his interests were tied to the well-being of his subjects. A governor, however, was an interloper. He generally came "from another Country to make Money" and eventually intended to leave the colonies and return home, "where he will not hear the Complaints and Curses of those he has oppress'd and plunder'd."[19]

Franklin had known for some time that Whitehall wanted to use the proceeds from Townshend's tea duty to pay the salaries of colonial governors. That was one reason he urged Americans to refuse to import any British tea. A "true American," he proclaimed, would be "half choak'd at the Thought" of drinking a brew that "contributed to the Salaries, Pensions and Rewards of the Enemies and Persecutors of his Country." And he thought "no Quantity of Sugar sufficient to make the nauseous Draught go down."[20] In the fall of 1770, when the Massachusetts assembly sent its first instructions to Franklin, it had complained of the government's plan to make not only the governor, but judges as well, financially independent. If colonial officeholders, who already owed their appointments to the Crown, also depended on the king's men for their salaries, they would become mere ciphers, ready to do the bidding of anyone who pulled the strings in London. The Massachusetts lawmakers thought that this would subvert the very nature of a "free Constitution" and would "firmly establish a Tyranny upon its Ruin."[21]

At the beginning of 1771, Franklin informed the assembly that Parliament finally intended to act on its plan to make the governors, at least, financially independent. In the spring of 1771, events in Massachusetts came to a head when Governor Thomas Hutchinson announced that he intended to refuse his annual salary from the house. By the following year, everyone knew that the king had granted Hutchinson a salary of fifteen hundred pounds per annum.

Like William Franklin, Hutchinson was an American. Indeed, his roots in Massachusetts stretched back to the founding of the colony. He had devoted his entire life to public service, filling both elective and appointive offices. He was, at one time or another, a member of the assembly, a councilor, and a lieutenant governor, and he had also held various local judgeships. In 1769 he had become acting governor of the colony, and two years later he was governor. His most controversial appointment came in 1760, when he became chief justice of the Massachusetts Superior Court, angering fellow colonial James Otis, Jr., who thought his father deserved the position. Otis, who was allied with Samuel Adams, leader of the colony's nascent patriot faction, swore that he would have his revenge against the man who had usurped his father's rightful place.

In fact, Hutchinson sympathized with America's quarrels with the ministry and deplored Parliament's attempts to tax the colonies. Nevertheless, by the mid-1760s he had alienated a sizable segment of Massachusetts' population. His wealth and power offended many, who saw in his ability to amass numerous political offices a plot to dominate the colony. Moreover, as lieutenant governor, he had tried to enforce the Stamp Act, even while he worked to get it repealed. For his troubles, a Boston mob had ransacked his house. While Hutchinson was an American, his power increasingly emanated from sources outside Massachusetts, notably from the king. Thus he become a perfect symbol for protesters, as he provided solid evidence that the ministry's corrupting tentacles had already reached Boston.

In July 1771, the assembly adopted a petition begging the ministry to reconsider its decision to pay Hutchinson's salary. It argued that the Massachusetts charter of 1692, which formed the basis of the colony's government, was a contract between Crown and colony, and as such it could be altered only by an agreement between both parties. Thus, unless the assembly willingly abrogated its charter right to pay the governor's salary, the king could not change the rules. The assembly's argument was significant, going further than Benjamin Franklin was ready to go. For it sought not simply to deny the authority of Parliament but to limit the power of the king.

Franklin responded cautiously to the issue of the governors' salaries. He tried to keep up with the views of the Massachusetts assembly, but he was by nature a moderate. "Every affront is not worth a Duel," he liked to point out, and "every Injury not worth a War." Most important, "every Mistake in Government, every Incroachment on Rights is not worth a Rebellion."[22] Consequently, his comments were confusing, even contradictory, as he tried to resolve the issues dividing two adversaries who were increasingly unwilling to compromise. He admitted that Parliament's attempts to govern the colonies were a "usurpation" of the assembly's powers, but he also wondered if it might not be "prudent in us to indulge the Mother Country," to obey its laws, "to submit at present in some Instances" to "unjust Authority." A "general open Denial" of Parliamentary sovereignty would, he thought, "bring on prematurely a Contest" that the colonies might not be able to win.[23]

Even when his attitude toward Parliament was firm, Franklin remained reluctant to attack the king's authority. He sometimes agreed that the Crown had no right to alter the Massachusetts charter without the assembly's consent, thus implicitly acknowledging a limitation on the monarch's power. Yet he continued to urge the colonies to maintain a "steady dutiful Attachment to the King and his Family."[24]

While the vast majority of Americans probably agreed with Franklin's reluctance to attack the king's authority, his caution won him no friends in London or in the Massachusetts assembly. The house was horrified at his proposal that it should submit to "unjust Authority."[25] Arthur Lee, Franklin's alternate as agent of the Massachusetts assembly, was especially harsh. Franklin was a ministerial collaborator, he said, "the willing instrument of Lord Hillsborough's treachery."[26] But while Bay Colony leaders accused him of going too slowly, many in London thought Franklin was too radical. Hillsborough refused even to receive him, and there were many who thought his attacks on Parliament had made him unfit to fill his post office position. As is so often the case, moderates like Franklin pleased no one.

Franklin's moderation was based, at least in part, on his belief that undesirable ministerial policy did not have the support of the king or even of most of the ministers. "The Ministry are not," he maintained, "all of a Mind."[27] In the beginning, he blamed America's problems on "the *policy of one man*," George Grenville.[28] By 1770, he thought that Lord Hillsborough was the fly in the ointment even as he insisted that the secretary's "Conduct is far from being approved by the King's other Servants."[29] So long as Franklin convinced himself that the policies he opposed were the responsibility of a few wrong-headed individuals, he remained optimistic that in time America and England could return to the relationship they had enjoyed prior to 1763. The colonies still had many friends in Parliament. The king was surely a benign ruler who wished to preserve the rights of his American subjects. Patience and prudence would, he hoped, carry the day.

Franklin's faith in the British government was tested after the fall of 1772, when Lord Hillsborough resigned from both the Board of Trade and the American Department, and Lord Dartmouth, known for his sympathy toward America, replaced him. Ironically, it was the Franklins' interest in land speculation that provided the excuse, if not the reason, for the secretary's demise. In April 1772, the Board of Trade, at Hillsborough's behest, rejected yet another attempt by the Franklins and their speculator friends to obtain a grant of land in the American West. This time, however, Hillsborough was thwarted when, on July 1, the Privy Council recommended approval of the grant. Hillsborough, furious at being outmaneuvered, offered the king his resignation, and George III accepted it. By August, the Franklins' nemesis was no longer in a position to obstruct their plans.

Franklin was delighted with the selection of Lord Dartmouth as Hillsborough's successor to both his positions, believing that his and America's problems would finally be resolved now that a man of sympathy and understanding was in charge of colonial affairs. Once more, Franklin was welcome in government circles and was even singled out for "particular Respect."[30] Once again he acted, for all practical purposes, as the Massachusetts agent. Most important, he was able to discuss imperial issues with someone who was sincerely interested in finding a way to resolve the differences dividing England and America. Unfortunately, political reality, especially the heated quarrels between Governor Thomas Hutchinson and the Massachusetts assembly, forced him to confront the limits that even the best-intentioned leaders faced when they attempted to find a compromise in an atmosphere tainted by suspicion.

It was the Crown's decision to assume responsibility for the salaries of Massachusetts' government officials that occasioned the beginning of an all-out war between Hutchinson and the lower house. In September 1772, a little over two months after the assembly had sent its strongly worded petition to London asking the King to return control of the governor's salary to the legislature, rumor spread that the colony's judges would soon become similarly independent. A series of town meetings to protest the new policy culminated in November in resolutions that went further than even Boston's leaders had heretofore dared to go. Basing their resolves on the "rights of man" and on natural law—not merely on the rights of Englishmen—the protesters claimed the right to govern and tax themselves, denied Parliament's authority to substitute its judgment for the will of the colonists, and questioned the Crown's authority. The resolutions were, raged Governor Hutchinson, a "declaration of independency" and he determined to answer every claim their authors made.[31]

In January, the governor delivered a speech to the Massachusetts house defending the traditional view of the Crown's authority over its dominions, denying the colonists' right to be represented in Parliament, and asserting that body's right to legislate for them. Each side had staked out its position; retreat for anyone would be difficult. When the assembly's July petition, as well as its November resolutions and Governor Hutchinson's response to those resolutions, reached London, Benjamin Franklin had to deal with their consequences. The quarrel between Thomas Hutchinson and the Massachusetts assembly poisoned the atmosphere between England and America, between Franklin and the ministry. Dartmouth had no desire to argue with the colonies, but he could not tolerate an attack on the king's prerogatives or Parliament's supremacy. Franklin was similarly eager to avoid a fight. But as agent for the Massachusetts assembly, he had no choice but to defend the colony's position. Dartmouth was especially concerned about the assembly's November resolutions, and he predicted that many members of the House of Commons would insist that the assembly retract its claims. Franklin predicted that the Bay Colony would never back down voluntarily, and he was sure that efforts to force it to do so would backfire. He thought Parliament's best course would be simply "to turn a deaf Ear and seem not to know that such Declarations had ever been made." After all, he pointed out, "it is *Words* only. Acts of Parliament are still submitted to there." Why, he wondered, make a mountain out of the proverbial molehill?[32] But both men were helpless. Parliament would not let challenges to its sovereignty go unanswered, and the Massachusetts house would never submit to Parliament's authority.

Meanwhile, leaders in the other colonies watched the quarrel between Governor Hutchinson and the Massachusetts assembly, and many of them were favorably impressed by the assembly's actions. With Virginia leading the way, a number of colonies—including William Franklin's New Jersey—began to develop committees of correspondence to enable the various assemblies to communicate more effectively and more regularly with one another. Without quite realizing the implications of their actions, the colonial governments were creating the instruments that would help them develop a united resistance to English policy.

As the controversy surrounding the salaries of Crown officers continued, two other issues, potentially even more explosive, were gathering force. One was precipitated by Parliament; the other, ironically, was the responsibility of Benjamin Franklin. In December 1772, Franklin sent a packet of letters to the Massachusetts speaker, Thomas Cushing. The letters, penned by Thomas Hutchinson and Lieutenant Governor Andrew Oliver, were all written between 1767 and 1769. At some point they had fallen into the hands of Thomas Whately, a Grenville protégé and a staunch supporter of the Stamp Act. Whately was now dead, but the letters remained attached to his estate. The missives were highly inflammatory. They described a Massachusetts government that was rapidly moving toward independence, and they begged for a firm ministerial hand to stay the forces of violence and anarchy. They even asked for an alteration of the Massachusetts charter, which residents of the colony considered nearly sacred. The letters were not calculated to ingratiate Hutchinson and Oliver, unpopular American beneficiaries of British patronage, with most Massachusetts inhabitants.

Even today, historians do not know how—or from whom—Franklin obtained the incendiary missives. Much more important than solving the riddle of the source of the letters is the question of his motivation in sending them. Franklin instructed Cushing not to publish or copy them. Yet he also told the speaker to show them to "some Men of Worth in the Province for their Satisfaction only."[33] Franklin always claimed that he hoped the letters would "promote a Reconciliation" between Massachusetts and England.[34] His own resentment against the ministry, he explained, had been "considerably abated" when he read the letters. For they proved that the government's view of the colonies had been distorted by "Men of Character" in America who, for private gain, had not been averse to "bartering away the Liberties of their native Country" or "exciting Jealousies in the Crown," thus betraying the colony they were sworn to serve. The letters proved that it was not the king or even his ministers who were to blame for the troubled relationship between England and America. The responsibility lay with misinformation sent to England by a few ambitious colonists.[35]

The letters could not be kept secret for long. When the Massachusetts assembly convened in the spring of 1773, Boston was already buzzing with rumors about their contents. Under the circumstances, it seemed best to read them in a closed session of the house. After that, it was impossible to keep them out of the public eye. Thus Cushing and his cohorts decided to publish the letters in the local newspapers.

With the publication of the letters, Hutchinson's and Oliver's ability to govern Massachusetts was over. On the 16th of June, both the governor's council and the assembly sent petitions to the king asking him to remove the two from office. The petitions were a measure of the evolution of political thought in the Bay Colony. Everyone knew that colonial governors were responsible to the king, not to the people, and it was the king's confidence that determined how long any officer would remain in his post. Although the council and assembly accompanied their petitions with conciliatory letters to Lord Dartmouth, assuring him of their continued loyalty, the petitions were nevertheless bound to confirm the suspicions of many ministers that Massachusetts was spinning out of control. In August, William Bollan, the council's agent, and Benjamin Franklin received the petitions. They immediately forwarded them to Lord Dartmouth, who in turn presented them to the king.

Even as the controversy over the Hutchinson-Oliver letters was heating up, yet another crisis was brewing. This problem had its roots in what appeared to be the imminent financial failure of the British East India Company, which had a monopoly on tea sent to the colonies. After the passage of the Townshend Acts, American purchases of British tea had plunged. In 1771, with the collapse of the colonial boycott on British imports, a few colonists began to buy British tea, ignoring the cries of patriot leaders that they paid an unconstitutional tax whenever they did so. Many others, however, purchased blends smuggled into the colonies by the Dutch or even concocted their own home brews rather than pay the duty on tea. Its market collapsing, by 1773 the East India Company had more than seventeen million pounds of surplus tea rotting in London warehouses. Parliament, many of whose members were East India stockholders, wanted to find an inexpensive means to prop up the ailing company. In March 1773, the company suggested a possible solution. If Parliament quietly dropped the old Townshend duty on tea, which most colonists were not paying anyway, East India tea prices would go down and American scruples over parliamentary taxation would no longer be an issue. Consequently, the colonial demand for British tea would increase.

The House of Commons began to discuss the East India Company's problems in April 1773. At first, Franklin hoped the house would adopt the company's proposal, thus repealing the last significant remnant of the Townshend Acts, but it soon became clear that Parliament was reluctant to abandon the tea tax. Most members of the House of Commons were motivated at least as much by their desire to make some profit from customs duties as they were by any principled commitment to the tax. But Franklin insisted that they were determined to "keep up the Exercise of the Right" to tax the colonies, believing that the promise of cheap tea would be "sufficient to overcome all the Patriotism of an American!"[36]

Whether or not Franklin was right about Parliament's motives, when the Tea Act became law in May, the lawmakers did not repeal Townshend's tea tax. Instead, the government advanced the company a large loan, and it agreed to let the East India Company ship its tea directly from China to American retailers. Before 1773, the company's ships had to pass through England on the way to the provinces, selling their tea at auction to London wholesalers, who in turn sold it to American merchants. This process impelled the company to pay an export duty when its cargo left England. It also added unloading, storage, wharfage, auction, and reloading expenses to the price of the tea. By eliminating the London leg of the journey, Parliament made it possible for the company to lower its prices. The Tea Act would make British tea competitive with its Dutch rival, even with the retention of the three pence per pound Townshend duty.

When he heard about the Tea Act, Franklin hoped that the colonists would resist its implementation firmly but peaceably. He believed that if Americans remained united and avoided rash behavior, they would prevail and the act would "undoubtedly be repealed."[37] To help the colonies organize a united front, Franklin proposed that they convene a "general Congress now in Peace to be assembled," to discuss their grievances and to demand redress. Franklin recommended the congress because he believed that the time had already come when England needed America more than the colonies needed an "infirm" and "aged Parent."[38] Parliament might still have the power to force its will on the colonies, he thought, but it would not retain that power much longer. Partially abandoning the arguments he had made in 1751 in his "Observations concerning the Increase of Mankind," he clung to his hope that Anglo-American union would "long be continued," but he now thought that the growth of the colonies' natural and human resources meant that such a union could be preserved only on American terms.

Throughout the summer of 1773, Franklin alternated between optimism and pessimism, conciliation and a hard-line approach. On the one hand, he told everyone in America that if they would stand firm, refusing to buy British tea until their grievances were resolved, then England would repeal the tea tax. He argued that most of the king's subjects had grown to admire America in general and the inhabitants of Massachusetts in particular. He believed, probably wrongly, that a growing number of English people were disgusted with a ministry whose members were more interested in self-aggrandizement than the public good and with a Parliament that no longer resisted the corrupting influences of a power-hungry ministry. As they saw their own liberties disappearing, he told Samuel Cooper, the English began to believe that freedom and independence were now safe only in America. The "general Sense of the Nation," he insisted, "is for us," as people everywhere begin to realize that Americans had been "ill-us'd, and that a Breach with us would be ruinous to this Country."[39] The next parliamentary election, he predicted, would bring a new government on the scene whose approach was sure to be more conciliatory. Franklin's rosy scenario was designed, at least in part, to stiffen colonial resistance, giving Americans reason to believe that their petitions and resolutions were having some effect. It was, however, not much more honest than the picture of colonial rabble-rousers that colored the letters of Thomas Hutchinson and Andrew Oliver.

If Franklin sometimes convinced himself that American popularity was growing daily throughout England, at other times he was uncharacteristically pessimistic. His pleasure at Dartmouth's appointment as American secretary was soon followed by disillusionment, as he realized that even a sympathetic minister could not bridge the widening gap between the Crown and its colonies. Dartmouth was, Franklin glumly admitted to his son, "a good Man, and wishes sincerely a good Understanding with the Colonies, but does not seem to have Strength equal to his Wishes."[40] More ominously, for the first time he began to question the king's right to govern the colonies and to suspect that the king, not just the ministry and its parliamentary minions, was responsible for the government's attacks on colonial liberty. Most of the time, Franklin kept these ideas to himself, sharing them with only a few close friends and his son. Still, if he ever followed them to their logical conclusion, he would have to admit that there was no good reason to preserve the ties that bound the empire and its colonies.

In fact, Benjamin Franklin's own ties to the empire began to unravel in the late winter of 1773. On Christmas day, a brief announcement appeared in the pages of the *London Chronicle*. Benjamin Franklin admitted publicly that he was the source of the now infamous Hutchinson-Oliver letters. He was virtually forced to acknowledge his role when William Whately, Thomas Whately's brother, accused Franklin's old friend John Temple of procuring the documents and sending them to Boston. Temple denied the charge; the two men fought a duel in which Whately incurred minor injuries. Rather than risk further sword play between the two antagonists, Franklin stepped forward. He claimed he had done nothing wrong in releasing public letters written by public persons discussing public issues. There were many in London who disagreed.

Although Franklin did not know it, just nine days earlier the inhabitants of Boston had raised their conflict with both England and Governor Hutchinson to a new level. On the night of December 16, approximately fifty men disguised with Indian blankets and warpaint boarded three ships resting in Boston's harbor, dumping their cargo, 342 crates of East India tea, into the harbor. When British tea had reached most colonial ports, the ships' captains either had been "persuaded" to leave immediately or had agreed to stow their unpopular cargo in warehouses. But in Massachusetts, Thomas Hutchinson was determined to force the colonists to purchase the tea, and he would not allow the ships to leave the harbor or simply to store their cargo. The Bostonians responded to the governor's challenge with the Boston Tea Party. As the little drama unfolded and the bulging crates of tea sank to the ocean floor, any hopes Franklin had for an amicable solution to the issues dividing England from the colonies sank with them.

The stage was set for Franklin's public confrontation with the ministry. Throughout the fall, he had continued to insist that he was doing everything in his power to restore harmony between the "two Countries." Still, even Franklin had to admit that his propaganda pieces defending the colonies had become increasingly "saucy." He knew that he had angered a number of influential men, and he feared that they would make him "feel their Resentment."[41] Still, he clearly had no conception of the fury that was about to be unleashed upon him.

By early December 1773, the ministry had finally begun to consider the Massachusetts petitions for the removal from office of Thomas Hutchinson and Andrew Oliver. On January 8, Franklin received a summons to appear at the Privy Council's hearing on the petition, which was scheduled for January 11. Not until the 10th did Franklin learn that Hutchinson had retained a lawyer to represent him at the session. Caught by surprise, Franklin consulted William Bollan, the council's agent. They agreed to seek a postponement of the hearing, which they received with little difficulty. The hearing would be held on January 29.

Unfortunately for Franklin, word of the Boston Tea Party reached London on January 20. The news struck a chord. Angry, frustrated, feeling increasingly ill used and bewildered, the members of the administration lashed out at their most convenient scapegoat. Already smarting from the repercussions of the release of the Hutchinson-Oliver letters, embarrassed by Franklin's increasingly pointed barbs in the press, and furious at the latest example of colonial disloyalty, the ministry was determined to seek revenge.

The moment Franklin entered the section of Whitehall aptly named the Cockpit, he knew that this would not be the ordinary, dry Privy Council hearing. The room was jammed with spectators. Thirty-four Privy Councilors showed up, including Lord North himself. Hillsborough was also there, smiling in anticipation of the humiliation awaiting the man he still blamed for costing him his job. Dartmouth, too, took time from his busy schedule to observe the "entertainment."[42] Even a few members of the public managed to shove their way into the crowded little room, lending a circus atmosphere to the proceedings.

The man Hutchinson chose to represent him was Alexander Wedderburn, a formidable and unprincipled Scottish lawyer who clearly relished his day in the sun. He spoke for nearly an hour, delighting his audience, who frequently laughed aloud at the "torrent of virulent abuse" the attorney heaped on his victim. Benjamin Franklin stood silently throughout the proceedings, a faint smile frozen on his face. He was, said William Bollan, a perfect picture of "philosophic Tranquility and sovereign Contempt."[43] Wedderburn accused Franklin of engineering a grand conspiracy to dupe the people of Boston into near treasonous activity. He was, said the attorney, the "actor and secret spring by which all the Assembly's motives were directed." Due to his "treachery," he shouted, England faced a "whole province set in flame." Franklin, said Wedderburn, wanted nothing short of independence. He was a "true incendiary," whose underhanded lies and machinations had alone nearly destroyed a relationship that had once been the pride of the British Empire.[44]

Although Benjamin Franklin stood silently throughout his ordeal, he never forgot the public, almost ritual humiliation he suffered at the hands of the ministry. The king's men won a Pyrrhic victory that day, for their momentary satisfaction came at a high price. They succeeded in alienating one of England's most influential American friends. Until 1774, Benjamin Franklin was a conciliator, a man who reacted cautiously to events, who liked to take the line of least resistance whenever possible. He was surely no "incendiary." But the longer he remained in England, the more disgusted Franklin became with English society, as he railed against the "Party Contentions about Power and Profit," the "Court Intrigues and Cabals" that were the hallmark of British politics.[45] Parliamentary elections, he said, were characterized by "Confusion and Disorder . . . and such Profusion of Money as never was known before."[46] Still, if elections "debauched" the people, turning them into "drunken mad mobs," it was no more than they deserved.[47] For the English people were "full as corrupted and venal" as the men they chose to represent them.[48] They were all "ungratefully abusing the best Constitution and the best King any Nation was ever blest with, intent on nothing but Luxury, Licentiousness, Power, Places, Pension and Plunder."[49]

As Franklin's disenchantment with English corruption grew, his idealization of America proceeded apace, and he became, more than ever, the self-appointed promoter of republican virtue. Colonial governments, he proclaimed, were "uncorrupted."[50] American merchants were actuated by a *"noble disinterestedness* and *love to their country,* unexampled among Traders in any other age or nation."[51] While England represented all that was venal in the modern world, America had become, for Franklin, the world's last hope for republican simplicity and the preservation of liberty.

Until 1774, despite his quarrels with the government and his disillusionment with the king's men, even with the king himself, Franklin continued to believe that the British government was the best on earth. It needed reforming, to be sure, but despite all the mother country's problems, he remained proud of being an Englishman, and he thought the colonial tie with the mother country was, at the very least, "worth preserving."[52] Now he was not so sure. The Privy Council had rejected the Massachusetts assembly's petition to remove Hutchinson and Oliver. Worse, it had implied that the leaders of the colony, simply by submitting the petitions, were seditious. Benjamin Franklin, "the mere pipe" who conveyed those petitions to the ministry, had become "obnoxious" to the authorities.[53]

Two days after the hearing at the Cockpit, Franklin was stunned to learn that he had been removed from his position as the post master general of North America. Publicly he pretended that even this last indignity did not faze him. "Intending to disgrace me," he wrote his beloved sister Jane, "they have rather done me Honour." It was a "Testimony of my being uncorrupted."[54] But while he remained outwardly cool, he seethed in private. He had been personally humiliated. Moreover, the experience proved, at least to him, that in the eyes of the ministry Americans were second-class subjects. If Americans could not petition for redress, he pointed out, if their most humble complaints were "deemed affronts," then they could not redress their wrongs: "Where complaining is a crime, hope becomes despair."[55] Perhaps American radicals were right when they argued for the existence of a ministerial conspiracy against liberty.

NOTES

[1]See BF, "Observations concerning the Increase of Mankind," *PBF* 4:225, 234.

[2]BF to Lord Kames, 25 Feb. 1767, ibid. 14:65.

[3]BF to Joseph Galloway, 11 June 1770, ibid. 17:170.

[4]Ibid.

[5]BF to Joseph Galloway, 14 April 1767, ibid. 14:125; BF to Cadwallader Evans, 9 May 1766, ibid. 13:269.

[6]BF to WF, 13 Mar. 1768, ibid. 15:75, 76.

[7]BF, "Causes of the American Discontents before 1768," ibid. 12.

[8]BF to WS, 29 Nov. 1769, ibid. 16:246.

[9]BF to Lord Kames, 25 Feb. 1767, ibid. 14:65.
[10]BF to Samuel Cooper, 27 Apr. 1769, ibid. 16:118.
[11]BF to WF, 19[–22] 1772, ibid. 19:259.
[12]BF to Joseph Galloway, 2 July 1768, ibid. 15:164.
[13]BF to Joseph Galloway, 20 Aug. 1768, ibid., 189.
[14]Samuel Cooper to BF, 6 Nov. 1770, ibid. 17:274.
[15]Massachusetts House of Representatives, Instructions to Benjamin Franklin as Agent, 6 Nov. 1770, ibid., 275–83.
[16]Charles Thomson to BF, 26 Nov. 1769, ibid. 16:237.
[17]BF to Samuel Cooper, 5 Feb. 1771, ibid. 18:24.
[18]BF's Account of His Audience with Hillsborough, 16 Jan. 1771, ibid., 15, 16.
[19]BF to Samuel Cooper, 30 Dec. 1770, ibid. 17:312.
[20]Ibid., 313.
[21]Massachusetts House of Representatives to BF, 29 June 1771, ibid., 18:149.
[22]BF to John Winthrop, 27 July 1773, ibid. 20:330.
[23]BF to Samuel Cushing, 10 June 1771, ibid. 18:122, 123.
[24]BF to Thomas Cushing, 10 June 1771, ibid., 123.
[25]Massachusetts House of Representatives to BF, 29 June 1771, ibid., 150.
[26]Arthur Lee to Samuel Adams, 10 June 1771, ibid., 128.
[27]BF to Jonathon Williams, Sr., 6 June 1770, ibid. 17:157.
[28]BF, "Subjects of Subjects," *Gentleman's Magazine* [Jan. 1768], ibid. 15:38.
[29]BF to Thomas Cushing, 10 June 1771, ibid. 18:122.
[30]BF to WF, 3[–4] Nov. 1772, ibid. 19:361.
[31]See ibid. 20:82–84.
[32]BF to Thomas Cushing, 6 May 1773, ibid., 20:201.
[33]BF to Thomas Cushing, 2 Dec. 1772, ibid. 19:411.
[34]BF to Joseph Galloway, 18 Feb. 1774, ibid. 21:109.
[35]BF to Thomas Cushing, 2 Dec. 1772, ibid. 19:412.
[36]BF to Thomas Cushing, 4 June 1773, ibid. 20:228.
[37]BF to Joseph Galloway, 1 Nov. 1773, ibid., 462.
[38]BF to Massachusetts House of Representatives, 7 July 1773, ibid., 282, 283.
[39]BF to Thomas Cushing, 1 Nov. 1773, ibid., 456.
[40]BF to WF, 14 July 1773, ibid., 308.
[41]BF to Jane Mecom, 1 Nov. 1773, ibid., 457, 458.
[42]BF to Thomas Cushing, 15[–19] Feb. 1774, ibid. 21:92.
[43]William Bollan to the Massachusetts Council, n.d., quoted in ibid., 40n.
[44]Wedderburn's Speech before the Privy Council, 29 Jan. 1774, ibid., 58, 60.
[45]BF to Joseph Galloway, 8 Aug. 1767, ibid. 14:228.
[46]BF to Joseph Galloway, 13 March 1768, ibid. 15:79.
[47]BF to WF, 16 Apr. 1768, ibid., 98.
[48]BF to Joseph Galloway, 20 Apr. 1771, ibid. 18:78.
[49]BF to John Ross, 14 May 1768, ibid. 15:129.
[50]BF to [WF, 12 Oct. 1774], ibid. 21:333.
[51]BF to Thomas Folger, 29 Sept. 1769, ibid. 16:209.
[52]BF to John Winthrop, 29 July 1773, ibid. 20:331.
[53]BF to Thomas Cushing, 15[–19?] Feb. 1774, ibid. 21:93.
[54]BF to Jane Mecom, 17 Feb. 1774, ibid., 103.
[55]BF to Thomas Cushing, 15[–19?] Feb. 1774, ibid., 94.

6

The Making of a Loyalist

William Franklin had learned his first and most enduring political lessons at his father's knee, and nothing that happened after he began to lead an independent life made him question the usefulness of those lessons. To the contrary, his experiences as royal governor of New Jersey merely reinforced what seemed to him to be eternal verities. As his father once had done, he grounded his political philosophy on a faith in the identity of English and American interests. He saw Britain as an organic whole whose integrity could not be violated without certain disaster for English subjects everywhere. And he was firmly convinced that the colonies' "Prosperity and Happiness" could be assured only by their "truly dutiful Behaviour" to a sovereign "from whom they derive Protection in the Enjoyment of their Liberties, Properties, Religion and every thing that is valuable."[1] While he was always willing to criticize government policy, he was determined to uphold the authority of king and Parliament in America. "I think," he told his father, "that all Laws until they are repealed ought to be obeyed and that it is the Duty of those who are entrusted with the executive Part of Government to see that they are so."[2]

The longer he served as royal governor, the more determined Franklin became to uphold the Crown's prerogative. While he did not question the right of the assemblies to exist and thought the people's representatives served a valuable function, he grew increasingly fearful that the "democratical" part of colonial government was overstepping its bounds, destroying the fragile balance that alone could guarantee stability in the colonies. Any student of history knew that if the balance tipped too far toward the legislature, anarchy would result, and as early as 1767 he was complaining that the assemblies "already Claim and exercise more Power . . . than a British H: of C would presume to do."[3]

Much of Franklin's dogged determination to uphold his—and hence the Crown's—prerogatives was practical. He owed his position to the king. One false move and a promising career would be destroyed. As an American, if he ruined this opportunity, his chances of securing another sinecure were slim, and unlike his father he had no other irons in the fire. The elder Franklin clung to his post office position as long as he could, but when he lost it, he continued serving the colonial assemblies. Because he never owed his livelihood to a single source, he had the luxury of being his own person. William was not so fortunate, and he would have a difficult time of it if he lost royal favor.

The younger Franklin's growing attachment to the king's prerogative was not merely the product of an instinct for survival. His experiences in Pennsylvania, as well as his work with New Jersey lawmakers convinced him that Americans were not fit to rule themselves. Increasingly, he viewed the assemblies' refusal to contribute to the empire's defense as unadulterated miserliness, their insistence on constitutional rights as mere window dressing. Moreover, he knew from experience that the colonies were weak and disunified. The lack of unity was especially dangerous in times of military crisis. Then each province seemed more intent on keeping its own contributions to the common defense as low as possible than it was on fighting a common enemy. As a young man, Franklin had helped fight a war under the old requisition system, and he had seen how disastrous local jealousies could be for the men who had to cope with inadequate supplies while the colonies wrangled over the portion each would pay for the soldiers' upkeep. He had also seen the Albany Plan, his father's project for uniting the colonies, ignored by assemblies that cared more for their own rights than for the common good. Left to themselves, the American provinces would tear one another apart. The elder Franklin was convinced that the time was soon coming when the colonies would be an equal, even a dominant, partner in a unified British Empire. His son believed just as firmly that the colonies would disintegrate without a firm hand at the helm. Both men loved England and America. But their visions of the future were beginning to diverge.

If Benjamin Franklin was confident of his ability to maintain a working relationship with the English government in the years immediately following the partial repeal of the Townshend duties, his son was optimistic about his own chances for remaining on cordial terms with the New Jersey assembly. Indeed, even into the 1770s, his quarrels were more often with London than with America. No matter how careful he tried to be, he ended up displeasing someone in the ministry. Before 1772, that someone was generally Lord Hillsborough. Clearly, the secretary did not trust him, perhaps because of his father, perhaps not. Franklin never knew. But he did know that he was constantly receiving "dark hints" that he was "at present out of Favour" in London.[4] Hillsborough never gave the governor any credit when he accepted William's recommendations of New Jersey inhabitants for lucrative posts. The secretary refused to sign his letters with the pro forma expression of "regard" for the chief executive, and Franklin was even convinced that Hillsborough intercepted his personal mail. "There is a Meanness in this kind of Conduct," Franklin complained, that is "extremely unbecoming one in his Station."[5] He could not help hoping that his loyal service to the king would one day be rewarded—perhaps with a promotion to the governorship of Barbados, where Elizabeth could be reunited with her family. Unfortunately, he told his father, "I stand no Chance for any Promotion . . . while Lord H. is at the Head of the American Department, and is so much displeased with your Conduct."[6]

Franklin may have been unhappy with an administration that was too intrusive, that did not allow him any discretion, any opportunity to make the little compromises so necessary to the success of all political leaders. He was, however, generally pleased with his relationship with both his assembly and his council. He developed solid friendships with influential councilors like William Alexander, and he learned how to work effectively with the colony's representatives, mostly amiable types who, while a bit tight-fisted, were not prone to pick unnecessary quarrels with the governor. The colony's moderation, coupled with Franklin's natural charm and astute political sense, augured well. He always "endeavored," he said, "to steer my little bark quietly through all the storms of political contest with which I was everywhere surrounded."[7] While it was often difficult to steer a middle course, to avoid the rocks and undercurrents that threatened to capsize him, he managed for longer than most royal governors to please the colonists without destroying his credibility in London.

When Parliament passed the Townshend Acts, Franklin had carefully avoided antagonizing the New Jersey assembly. While he could hardly be expected to question Parliament's authority, there is some evidence that he understood the colonists' position. For practical reasons alone, he wished Parliament would quit trying to tax its provinces, for he knew that every such attempt was bound to embroil him in a quarrel with the New Jersey assembly. At the very least, he was willing to argue against the "Impropriety" of imposing taxes in America, and he assiduously avoided any public condemnation of the colonial boycott of British imports.[8] Agreeing that discretion was surely the better part of common sense, if not of valor, he refused to convene the assembly for a year and a half rather than risk being drawn into a fruitless quarrel over the Townshend Acts with New Jersey's representatives. Only in October 1769, when he was able to announce that the detested legislation would soon be repealed, did he call the lower house to Burlington.

The session, which was devoted to the disposal of a backlog of routine matters, proved to be amicable, justifying the governor's decision to avoid any risk of a confrontation with the colony's lawmakers. No one muttered a complaint when he begged in his opening speech to the assembly for a return to "that mutual Confidence and Affection" that was "essential to the Glory and Safety of the whole British Empire."[9] Americans may have been embittered by the Townshend duties, but at least in New Jersey most people were ready to get on with their lives.

In 1770, Franklin had an opportunity to work in concert with the New Jersey assembly as they struggled together to quell popular uprisings in the East Jersey counties of Monmouth and Essex. In Monmouth, a weak economy and an almost instinctive distaste for rapacious lawyers who charged what many thought were exorbitant fees were at the root of the problem. In Essex, the issue was not court reform but conflicting claims to land titles. In both cases, the assembly had failed to respond to their constituents' pleas for reform. Consequently, disenchanted protesters took to the streets, shutting down the courts in Monmouth and nearly doing the same in Essex. One small group of protesters in Essex even visited the farm of Judge David Ogden in the dead of night, where they burned two barns to the ground. Public protests had worked against England during the Stamp Act crisis. Perhaps, reasoned the rioters, they would do the trick at the local level, as well.

William Franklin's desire to uphold the law, defend the rights of property, and maintain order knew no bounds. He quickly swung into action, with the support of most New Jersey leaders. Future loyalists and future patriots alike were panic-stricken by the events in East Jersey, as they wondered if the conflagration that had destroyed David Ogden's barns would spread to their own homes. Many imagined that all the talk of "liberty" and "rights," so popular when it had been directed against the English government, had gotten out of hand. Few pointed out that there was no causal link between the Monmouth and Essex riots or between the Stamp Act protests and the uproar in East Jersey. To many, including William Franklin, it all seemed part of a general pattern of assault on authority, and as such it had to be nipped in the bud.

Thus Franklin called an early session of the assembly in March 1770 and devoted his entire opening speech to the court riots. The protesters, he cried, were "factious designing Persons" who were using the "Licentiousness of the Times" to stir a "deluded populace" into action.[10] Instead of appealing to their representative assemblies, the proud birthright of all Englishmen, a few "artful and designing" troublemakers were preying on the emotions of the majority, destroying the law, "the best Cement of Societies," for their personal gain.[11] If they were not stopped, he predicted, they would lead America inexorably toward anarchy.

As late as the winter of 1771 Franklin could congratulate himself on his relationship with his assembly. Unlike Thomas Hutchinson, he faced no hostile group of legislators who questioned his every move. Nor did he do anything to incur the distrust of the members of the lower house. Perhaps nothing better illustrates his ability to work with New Jersey lawmakers than the way he managed to avoid a quarrel with them over the method of appointing the colony's London agent. For Benjamin and William Franklin, the incident also reveals how far apart father and son had drifted over the years.

In June 1771, the Board of Trade ordered the governor to persuade his assembly to share its power of appointing the colony agent with the governor and his council. Benjamin Franklin had served as the New Jersey assembly's agent since 1769. Now, however, the Board of Trade wanted him to represent all three branches of the government. Franklin had already argued with Lord Hillsborough over this very issue in January, and the result, for all practical purposes, had been the nullification of his power as the Massachusetts agent. He had written in anger to his son berating the secretary, proclaiming that any colonial agent selected jointly by governor, council, and assembly would be a mere cipher and insisting that henceforth he intended to "decline serving under every such Appointment."[12] The secretary's rigorous attention to detail had put father and son, governor and assembly, on a collision course.

William was reluctant to confront his assembly with the board's instructions. They were calculated, he complained, "to lead me into another Squabble with the Assembly for it is a Point they will never give up."[13] Still, an order was an order. And so he set to work. Using "a good deal of Persuasion, and many Arguments" he talked to key legislators in "a private way" before he even broached the matter to the assembly as a whole.[14] At first they told him that it would be "impossible" for them to acquiesce to the board's orders.[15] But little by little, using his charm, his persuasive talents, and his political acumen, he brought the representatives around. The fact that his own father currently served as the assembly's agent surely helped his cause. In all likelihood, he told the legislators that he would accept any reasonable nominee they proposed. Thus the assembly would select Benjamin Franklin as its agent, and both the governor and the council would submit separate letters supporting the assembly's choice. Hillsborough would be satisfied that his instructions had been obeyed, and the assembly would retain the real power of selecting the agent.

Franklin was pleasantly surprised when the legislators acquiesced to his request, but he suspected that his father would view his victory with disfavor. Thus he introduced the subject to Benjamin with some trepidation. He could not help but boast of his success, for he had achieved it "contrary to the Expectation of every Body." Still, he knew that Benjamin would "not be altogether pleas'd" with his triumph. "However," he insisted, "it really (*inter nos*) makes no kind of Difference." It simply gave the board the feeling of a "Point gained" without altering the balance of power. It was a matter of form over substance. Surely his father, a man known for his willingness to split the difference with his foes, would understand.[16]

Benjamin never responded to William's letter. Still, despite his earlier fulminations, he continued to serve as New Jersey's agent until the eve of the Revolution. If he was disappointed with his son for compromising on such an important issue, he did not say so, and William could be excused for assuming that his father tacitly approved of his conduct.

William Franklin's ability to perform his delicate balancing act began to decline in the spring of 1771. No one, not even the most astute governors in the most moderate colonies, could have completely escaped the consequences of the growing tension between England and America, king and assembly. While he strove mightily to serve two masters, Franklin had sworn an oath to uphold the Crown's prerogative. He often sympathized with the assembly and certainly understood its role in the imperial scheme of things, but he took his oath seriously. Moreover, after 1771 it was the assembly, not the ministry, that grew more rigid, refusing to give him the breathing room he needed.

It was New Jersey's suffering economy, not arguments over the "rights of Englishmen," that was the immediate cause of Franklin's troubles. New Jersey was still suffering from the effects of the depression that followed the French and Indian War that plagued all the mainland colonies. Moreover, hard money was scarce in the seaboard provinces, and the Board of Trade did not allow its colonial possessions to issue their own paper bills of credit. Under the circumstances, imperial demands for military assistance were bound to be unpopular. The issue was joined in the spring of 1771 when the legislators met for what turned out to be a lengthy session. In his opening remarks to the assembly, the governor asked for additional funds to supply the king's troops for another season. He dusted off his usual arguments to persuade the lawmakers to accede to the king's request: New Jersey's support of the empire would benefit the colonies at least as much as it would the mother country. The king's army allowed Americans to live in peace, for only royal troops possessed the experience and training necessary to defend the colonies effectively. He airily dismissed the abilities of the local militia. The militia meant well, he admitted, but it was too scattered, too undisciplined to do the job. Thus sheer "Loyalty and Gratitude" to the king, as well as the colonial need for "Security and Defence," mandated a favorable response to the governor's request.[17]

Assemblies everywhere were becoming restive by 1771. Their members were aware of the quarrels over rights and prerogatives that dominated relations between Massachusetts and London. Moreover, their own experiences had made them increasingly suspicious of the home government. They had endured the consequences of a reorganized and reinvigorated customs administration. Three times in less than ten years, Parliament had attempted to tax them. Even now, a tea tax remained on the books, a constant reminder that Parliament did not intend to abandon its claim to the right to tax the colonies. The Boston Massacre in March 1770 had reinforced colonial beliefs that standing armies in time of peace were a sign of tyranny. The colonists still blamed the ministry, not the king, for their unhappiness. Still, no one, even in moderate New Jersey, was ready to comply without hesitation to government directives.

Its suspicions of ministerial motives as well as its worries about the colony's economic condition made the New Jersey assembly balk at Franklin's request for military aid. The legislators waited only one day to respond, resolving, with only three dissenting votes, that the assembly could not afford any additional military expenses unless it raised taxes in the colony. Land values were declining, the treasury was in a sorry state, and while they meant no disrespect to the governor, they insisted that it was impossible even to consider increasing taxes under the present circumstances.

Franklin was furious—and a little frightened as well. Not since the Stamp Act crisis had the assembly so bluntly defied his wishes. What would Hillsborough say when he heard that the New Jersey legislature had turned a deaf ear to a direct and altogether reasonable request from the king? Franklin had been working hard in recent months to return to the secretary's good graces. Now all his efforts seemed to have been wasted, and he was in danger of having to relive the experience he had endured in 1768 when Hillsborough had attacked him so viciously. Once again he would have to prove his loyalty to the Crown, and once again he would have to show that he could control his own legislature. Moreover, and perhaps most important, Franklin's sympathies lay with the ministry, for he thought that in this instance colonial rights were clearly not an issue. He believed that the assembly had refused to supply the king's military needs for only one reason: stinginess, not principle. This time Franklin, not the assembly, held the high moral ground.

Like all royal governors after 1770, William Franklin was beginning to realize just how difficult it had become to serve the interests of both king and colony. As the assemblies grew more suspicious of ministerial motives and more confident of their ability to resist unpopular policy, they were less willing to compromise. Assembly intransigence, of course, only provoked the ministry, making it determined to keep the colonies from sliding into independence. Royal governors were caught in the middle. On the one hand, they had to enforce policies that they had no hand in making. Their failure to do so would cost them their jobs. On the other hand, the growing self-confidence of the colonial assemblies made it nearly impossible for the governors to secure compliance with unpopular directives. As a low-born American, William Franklin had always been a little more insecure than many other royal governors. By now, however, there was scarcely a governor in America who did not occasionally sense that he was losing control of his own colony.

When Franklin was insecure, he struck back with every weapon at his disposal. Unfortunately, his reaction made compromise virtually impossible. Although he surely knew better, he insisted that New Jersey's economy was enjoying a "gradual Course of Improvement."[18] He argued that the colony was not overtaxed. Moreover, he claimed that there was plenty of money in the treasury to supply the king's troops without resorting to further taxation. As Franklin saw it, New Jersey's legislators were using the supply bill as an excuse to set themselves up "in Opposition to the King and Parliament."[19]

By questioning the assembly's integrity, Franklin had made it impossible for him and the legislators to arrive at a middle ground. Thus the argument degenerated into a series of mutual recriminations and outraged denials until, at the end of April, Franklin reluctantly prorogued the assembly. When the assembly reconvened at the end of May, however, no one's position had changed. Again, the governor prorogued the house, at the same time turning to London for advice. His characterization of the assembly was more critical than it had ever been. Always before when he had reported popular opposition to ministerial policy, he had put New Jersey in the best light possible. Now he was not so charitable. The assembly's behavior, he told Hillsborough, was "entirely inexcusable," for the colony had never been more "flourishing." The legislators, who were momentarily expecting new elections, were merely posturing in an effort to gain support from the voters.[20]

Whether he realized it or not, Franklin was reinforcing Hillsborough's prejudices against the colony. Moreover, by siding with the ministry against his own assembly, he was inching away from his self-described role as disinterested moderator and toward a position that would one day put him firmly in the king's camp. In the days and months following his quarrel with the legislature, he did not regret his course of action, especially after Lord Hillsborough grudgingly expressed his approval of the way Franklin had handled the affair. Obviously, London's favor could be most easily won by a firm stand against colonial obstinacy.

Ironically, it was the usually obdurate Lord Hillsborough who found an honorable way to resolve the impasse. In October, he removed the troops remaining in New Jersey to St. Augustine, Florida. It was London that gave Franklin a graceful way out of an impossible situation, London that was willing to accept a reasonable compromise. It was the colonial assembly whose members refused to alter its course.

Franklin was relieved but disquieted by Hillsborough's decision. In the short run, it made his own life easier. With the quarrel over the supply bill at an end once and for all, he could begin to mend fences with the assembly. At the same time, he thought his standing with the ministry had never been better. Still, he was vaguely troubled by the home government's inability to secure compliance with reasonable requests. If American assemblies could defy king and Parliament at will, what did this mean for the future of a united empire?

For a time, Franklin managed to shrug off his uneasiness. Admittedly, he had been angered and a little unnerved by the ferocity of the debate over the supply bill. Still, he could claim, with considerable justification, that most inhabitants of New Jersey bore him no personal animosity. At the same time, he could argue that he had served the Crown with honor. Perhaps, he thought, it was still possible for a prudent leader to "steer his little bark" between his various interests and loyalties with grace. But even as Benjamin Franklin was confronting the limits of his ability to influence ministerial policy, his son had begun to discover how weak his own position in New Jersey had become. If the elder Franklin abandoned hope for compromise with London in 1774 after his humiliation before the Privy Council, the governor began to doubt his ability to work with the legislature several years earlier, in the days after the East Jersey treasury robbery.

There was nothing about the robbery that should have embroiled Franklin and the assembly in a controversy that nearly tore New Jersey apart. The governor himself later asserted that "there never existed a more unnecessary Dispute between a Governor and an Assembly."[21] Had it occurred even five years earlier, the robbery would have merited a mere footnote in the colony's history. But at a time when the relationship between England and America was rapidly deteriorating, when leaders from South Carolina and Virginia to Massachusetts and Rhode Island professed to see tyranny everywhere, when diatribes against the despotic attempts of royal governors to destroy colonial liberties were becoming routine, it is not surprising that New Jersey lawmakers seized upon the robbery of the East Jersey treasury to flex their muscles. Earlier in his career, Franklin might have defused the crisis instead of aggravating it. But this was not a time for reasoned discourse. Governors throughout the colonies were on the defensive. Assemblies everywhere were suspicious, hostile, demanding. Under those circumstances, it was easy for a local issue to assume the proportions of a constitutional crisis.

The details surrounding the robbery of the East Jersey treasury remain somewhat mysterious, but the basic train of events is reasonably clear. On the morning of July 22, 1768, Stephen Skinner, the East Jersey treasurer, was roused from his slumbers by the shouts of his carpenter and a young black servant. Someone had broken into the house and absconded with more than six thousand pounds of New Jersey money.

Reaction to the robbery began routinely enough. Skinner organized a party to search for the thieves, and both he and the governor offered a reward to anyone assisting in the capture of the robbers or the recovery of the treasury funds. The assembly investigated the robbery and concluded that there was no reason to blame Skinner for the unfortunate incident. In the fall of 1770, however, the assembly reopened its investigation. After hearing from a parade of witnesses, the legislators came to a conclusion that differed markedly from the one it had reached earlier. The money was stolen, they now asserted, "for want of that Security and Care that was necessary to keep it in Safety."[22] The assembly concluded that if Stephen Skinner's negligence was responsible for the robbery, then he was obligated to reimburse the colony for the loss it had suffered.

The controversy simmered for two years. Skinner refused to reiumburse the treasury, and the thieves remained at large. At first Franklin ignored the entire matter, but by 1772 his position had weakened perceptibly. He had not entirely recovered from the controversy over the supply bill. In addition, more than half the legislators who gathered in Perth Amboy in the fall of 1772 were first-time members of the assembly. In the last election, the voters had turned many of Franklin's allies out of office. At the same time, the number of West Jersey representatives had increased. It was from the West that the leaders of the anti-Skinner faction came.

The issue was joined in earnest when the New Jersey assembly, led by James Kinsey, a freshman legislator from Burlington, ordered Governor Franklin to force Skinner to reimburse the treasury for its losses. After Franklin refused to comply with the house directive, the controversy escalated, as the assembly also began to demand the power to remove, and eventually even the power to nominate, the colony's treasurers. Franklin saw the legislature's demands as a thinly disguised attack on the Crown's prerogative. Moreover, having publicly declared his confidence in Skinner, he refused to back down.

After that, relations between governor and assembly degenerated. Chief Justice Frederick Smyth, who returned from England in the fall of 1772, was appalled at the "violent contest." And he singled out William Franklin for special blame. While the controversy had left all government "much degraded," he thought Franklin's "extraordinary attachment" to Stephen Skinner was keeping the quarrel alive.[23] Franklin and his supporters, many of whom were East Jersey leaders, disagreed with Smyth's assessment. They were firmly convinced that the legislators were using the treasury robbery as a pretext to expand their own power at the governor's expense. "I believe," said Cortlandt Skinner, Stephen's brother, "that some would rather that the robbery was never discovered than the favorite scheme disappointed." For, he continued, "the nomination of the Treasurer by the House and removal only by them is the darling object to which every other Consideration would be sacrificed."[24] Indeed, James Kinsey had been heard to remark that even if lightning had destroyed the East Jersey money, he would still hold Skinner responsible for the loss.

The controversy dragged on until February 1774, when the legislators lost patience. Using their control of the purse as a weapon, they informed Franklin that approval of the annual support bill hinged on the removal of the treasurer. If Skinner did not resign, no one in the government, including the governor himself, would be paid. When Franklin still refused to budge, launching an intemperate diatribe against the lawmakers, the assembly voted overwhelmingly to deny Skinner control over the colony funds. It also made an end run around the governor, drafting a petition to the king asking for Skinner's removal from office. Franklin shuddered at the thought of involving London in his controversy with the lower house. What if the ministry disapproved of his conduct? It was hard enough to endure the assembly's carping criticisms. To be rebuked by the king would be intolerable.

Something clearly had to be done. Government had ground to a halt, and Franklin's relationship with the assembly had reached its nadir. It was Skinner, not the assembly or the governor, who resolved the conflict. On February 24, the embattled treasurer submitted his resignation. The council urged Franklin to accept it, and William reluctantly bowed to the inevitable.

William Franklin's protracted quarrel with the assembly in the wake of the East Jersey treasury robbery is significant for many reasons. The quarrel over the East Jersey treasurer, like Thomas Hutchinson's dispute with his legislators over his salary, reflected the tensions that plagued all royal governors and their assemblies by 1774. Minor disagreements, which at one time might have been resolved or simply ignored, were now providing the fodder for major confrontations. Even in New Jersey, where the assembly was noted for its moderation, tempers were growing shorter and small slights were viewed with suspicion. Even a governor like William Franklin, an American who prided himself on his ability to work with his assembly, could not always bridge the gap between himself and the lawmakers.

The crisis is also significant because of what it reveals about Franklin's personal and political character in the early 1770s. While he did not like conflict, always preferring to search for a middle ground with his opponents, he was never able to accept a personal attack with equanimity. Thin-skinned, proud, and a little insecure, he tended to lash out at those who questioned his character or motivations. Once he was convinced that his own judgment was correct, he would not alter his course. "Controversy," he said, "is really disagreeable to me; and Tho' I never seek it, yet I never avoid it where it is necessary to my Character, let the Consequences be what they may."[25] He had been particularly stung by Chief Justice Smyth's accusation that he was defending Skinner because the two men were friends. While he insisted that he never pretended to "Infallibility," he did claim to act out of an honest concern for "Principle." His motives were pure, his "Attachments" irrelevant.[26] Because he always claimed the moral high ground for himself, he found it difficult to believe that his opponents might honestly differ with him. Like many loyalist leaders, he attributed ulterior motives to his opponents, seeing his detractors as avaricious demagogues who were using public controversy for their own insidious purposes. Once he had convinced himself that his own motives were noble, while his opponents' were corrupt, he was unable to retreat from his position.

Franklin's response to the controversy surrounding the East Jersey treasury robbery widened the breach between the governor and the lower house. At the same time, it made him more determined to uphold the king's prerogative. He had always tried to find a compromise between the conflicting interests of the New Jersey assembly and the ministry. Now he distanced himself from the lower house, as he tried desperately to defend the rights of a king whose position appeared to be under siege. He had barely survived the controversy engendered by the colony's refusal to supply the king's troops. He had become nervous as he witnessed the heightening political tensions in other colonies. He was beginning to fear that a few colonial malcontents were plotting to destroy the precarious balance between executive tyranny and leveling democracy.

More than any other single incident, the controversy over the East Jersey treasury robbery poisoned William Franklin's relationship with his legislators. Thereafter, the governor never again assumed that New Jersey's lawmakers acted with honorable intentions, and he became more likely to view his adversaries as part of a grand conspiracy whose members aimed at nothing less than the destruction of Crown influence in America. For really the first time, the threat to his own position clearly came not from some officious bureaucrat in London but from his own assembly.

Franklin's tendency to view American affairs through a conspiratorial lens was not unusual. Many colonists had long believed that the ministry was engaged in a conscious plot to destroy liberty in England and America. Indeed, anyone who had read Trenchard and Gordon's *Cato's Letters* knew that the holders of "power" would inevitably destroy the protectors of "liberty," if given half the chance. It did not take much imagination for the men who represented the king's interests in the colonies to turn Trenchard and Gordon's notions on their head and to assume that a few devious American leaders were part of a scheme to destroy the king's prerogatives, tipping the balance of the colonial governments toward the assemblies and leading America toward anarchy.

One immediate consequence of Franklin's struggle with his assembly was his decision, at the end of 1773, to leave his West Jersey home for the more congenial environment of Perth Amboy. He told his father that he planned to move because Elizabeth thought Perth Amboy's climate was better for her health, but in fact it was the political climate of the eastern capital that appealed to him. Over the years, he had become personally and politically comfortable with many East Jersey leaders. The quarrel over the treasury robbery moved him still closer to this group. Once he had resisted the lure of Perth Amboy's sumptuous governor's mansion, but he no longer saw any reason to do so.

The decision to move to the East Jersey capital had both real and symbolic importance. Once the Franklins settled in Perth Amboy, the governor would no longer have easy access to Philadelphia, making it more difficult for him to tend to his father's affairs there. The decision was a public acknowledgment of the distance Franklin was willing to put between himself and his past. It was an indication, as well, that he was not as determined as he once had been to govern New Jersey with an even hand. He seemed to be looking for a comfortable haven from the storm of controversy that threatened to overwhelm him. To be sure, he was not fleeing Burlington in a desperate search for safety. He did not actually move to Perth Amboy for another year, as he took the time to sell his Burlington residence and prepare his new house for occupation. Still, the move was significant, as it helped to insulate him from those forces that might have convinced him to bend his principles, to acknowledge the position of those legislators who distrusted London's motives and who feared that the ministry was trying to destroy colonial liberty.

It would be wrong to imply that Franklin abandoned his efforts to work with his assembly as a result of the protracted quarrel over the treasury robbery. Benjamin Franklin's decision to turn against king and ministry after his humiliation before the Privy Council was abrupt and virtually irrevocable. His son arrived at his own decision to choose between king and country more slowly and by a more circuitous route. In the years immediately preceding the Boston Tea Party, William still had reason to hope that he and New Jersey's lawmakers would be able to smooth away the irritations that troubled their relations. His reluctance to part company with his assembly was to some extent the result of his continued quarrels with the ministry, even after Lord Dartmouth became president of the Board of Trade. While Dartmouth praised William, telling Benjamin that he was an excellent governor who "kept his Province in good Order during Times of Difficulty," his position did not improve materially after the secretary took over American affairs.[27] His salary was lower and his expenses higher than those of most colonial governors, and he thought that his long and loyal service to the colony merited some material reward. Yet in 1773, when he asked for a salary independent of assembly approval, Dartmouth responded with a terse negative. In the years before the Boston Tea Party, Franklin confronted no issue that would irrevocably cut him off from the New Jersey assembly. Neither did he find any reason to embrace the ministry with open arms.

Still, tensions were rising. In the spring of 1773, when William first heard about the Hutchinson-Oliver letters, he was appalled. He himself had experienced the sense of violation that Massachusetts officials now felt when he had suspected that Lord Hillsborough's minions had riffled through his own letters. Moreover, while William had criticized Hutchinson from time to time, arguing that he almost invited confrontations with his assembly, he could not help but sympathize with the plight of a fellow governor. Hutchinson, he told his father, was "gloomy and low spirited" and was preparing to flee the colony before he was subjected to further humiliation.[28] William knew what it was like to be reviled and misinterpreted by self-interested and ambitious colonists. He also believed that Americans had overreacted to the letters' contents. In some ways he agreed with the Massachusetts governor, and he envied Hutchinson's independent salary, even though he knew that it had occasioned hostility between governor and assembly. Like Hutchinson, he deplored the excesses that invariably accompanied mob action, and he worried that democracy in America was getting out of hand.

Franklin assumed that his father would share his sentiments. Benjamin was no friend of democracy gone mad, and, like his son, he had often complained vigorously when political enemies had intercepted his own letters. William surely did not suspect that his father had anything to do with sending the Hutchinson-Oliver letters to the Massachusetts assembly. When rumors began floating through the colonies that the elder Franklin had been the instrument of Hutchinson's destruction, William naturally assumed that the allegations were nothing more than the usual false stories that Benjamin's detractors had invented over the years.

William must have been stunned when he read his father's letter, written on the first of September, telling him what he had carefully hidden from interested parties on both sides of the Atlantic. He was, Benjamin admitted, the source of the "famous Boston letters."[29] Even his claims that he hoped that airing the letters might bring England and the colonies closer together could scarcely have softened the blow. William could take some comfort in the fact that his father trusted him with information that he shared with few others. Still, the letter revealed how far Benjamin had drifted toward the position of Massachusetts radicals, as he wondered how his own son could have failed to appreciate the "heinous" nature of the governor's statements. His cavalier response to Hutchinson's predicament made matters worse. "I don't wonder that he should be dejected," Benjamin said. "It must be an uncomfortable thing to live among people who he is conscious universally detest him."[30]

William told no one about his father's part in an affair that he viewed with horror. He tried to convince himself that Benjamin's motives had been laudable, even if their consequences had been disastrous. For his part, the elder Franklin interpreted his son's comments as charitably as he could. If William did not understand why the letters were so damnable, perhaps, he suggested, his son had not actually read them, but had only heard about their contents secondhand. As late as October 1773, Benjamin excused his son for views that he would have deplored in any other governor. "I know," he said with a tincture of melancholy, "your sentiments differ from mine. . . . You are a thorough government man, which I do not wonder at, nor do I aim at converting you." He only hoped William would perform his job with dignity. "If you can promote the prosperity of your people," he said, "and leave them happier than you found them, whatever your political principles are, your memory will be honored."[31]

Yet another, and in the end more decisive, imperial controversy was developing throughout the summer of 1773. Like his father, William did not immediately appreciate the significance of the Tea Act. He was reasonably confident that in New Jersey, protests against the legislation would be muted at worst. No East India ships would sail into any of New Jersey's harbors. No mobs would be waiting to turn any ships away. Besides, New Jersey was still embroiled in the controversy over the treasury robbery, and until that issue was resolved, colony leaders had interest in little else.

At first, even news of the Boston Tea Party did not disturb William Franklin's sense of well-being. The colony experienced a few isolated protests here and there, but New Jersey's reaction to Boston's intitiative was generally low-key. The members of the lower house were in no apparent hurry to broach the subject, and the governor predicted that the assembly would probably not even form a committee of correspondence. He "took some Pains with several of the principle [sic] Members for the purpose" and thought, despite his recent differences with the legislators, that he still had enough influence to keep matters under control.[32] Indeed, New Jersey was the last mainland colony to form a committee of correspondence, and it did so only after the lawmakers learned that the neighboring colony of New York had formed one. Even then, Franklin assured Dartmouth, they acted only because they did not "choose to appear singular."[33]

All things considered, Franklin remained confident that he—and the empire—would weather the storm that followed the Boston Tea Party. England and America had always survived their differences. There was no reason to believe that they would not continue to do so. Despite his unhappiness with his own assembly, the governor hoped that he would be instrumental in bringing both parties to an amicable resolution of the issues that divided them. He could not imagine that the colonies could survive without the mother country. Nor did he believe that England was engaged in a conspiracy to destroy the liberties of its own colonists. Singing the refrain that was familiar to loyalists everywhere, he insisted that the men who were stirring the colonies to action were a small minority, acting for transparently selfish purposes. He was convinced that in time the vast majority of Americans would come to their senses, reject the overtures of the handful of hotheads among them, and decide to remain loyal subjects of a benevolent empire. He refused even to contemplate the possibility that he would ever be forced to choose between America and England, father and king.

NOTES

[1] *Votes and Proceedings of the General Assembly of the Province of New Jersey* 63A:4, 5.
[2] WF to BF, [3? Sept. 1771], *PBF* 18:218.
[3] WF to BF, 22 Aug. 1767, ibid. 14:236.
[4] WF to BF, 23 Oct. 1767, ibid., 293; WF to BF [3? Jan. 1769], ibid. 16:37.
[5] WF to BF, [3? Jan. 1769], ibid., 37.
[6] WF to BF, 13 Oct. 1772, ibid. 19:336.
[7] WF to William Strahan, 18 June 1771, C. H. Hart, "Letters from William Franklin to William Stroban," *Pennsylvania Magazine of History and Biography* 35 (1911): 448, 449.
[8] WF to BF, 22 Aug. 1767, *PBF* 14:230.
[9] *Votes and Proceedings* 69:5.
[10] Ibid. 70A:5, 7.
[11] Ibid., 8.
[12] BF to WF, 30 June 1772, *PBF* 19:51.
[13] WF to BF, [3? Sept. 1771], ibid. 18:218.
[14] BF to Lords of Trade, 26 Dec. 1771, F. W. Ricard and William Nelson, eds., *Documents Relating to the Colonial History of the State of New Jersey* (1757–67), 10:320.
[15] WF to Lord Hillsborough, 27 Dec. 1771, ibid., 323.
[16] WF to BF, 6 Jan. 1772, *PBF* 19:3.
[17] *Votes and Proceedings* 71A:5.
[18] Ibid., 12.
[19] Ibid., 16.
[20] WF to Lord Hillsborough, 1 June 1771, Ricard and Nelson, *Documents* 10:299.
[21] *Votes and Proceedings* 74:51.
[22] Ibid. 70B:30.
[23] Chief Justice Smyth to Lord Hillsborough, 5 Oct. 1772, Ricard and Nelson, *Documents* 10:380.
[24] Cortlandt Skinner to Philip Kearney, [18 Nov. 1773], ibid. 10:413.
[25] *Votes and Proceedings* 72:92.
[26] Ibid. 74:139.
[27] BF to WF, 3[–4] Nov. 1772, *PBF* 19:360.
[28] WF to BF, 29 July 1773, ibid. 20:332.
[29] BF to WF, 1 Sept. 1773, ibid., 387.
[30] Ibid.; BF to WF, 9 Oct. 1773, ibid., 439.
[31] BF to WF, 6 Oct. 1773, ibid., 437.
[32] WF to Lord Dartmouth, 31 May 1774, Ricard and Nelson, *Documents* 10:458.
[33] Ibid.

7

Toward Independence

The Boston Tea Party set the stage for a series of events that ultimately separated America from England. Those same events led Benjamin and William Franklin to choose opposite sides in a war that both men would have preferred to avoid. By the middle of 1774 the two men simply quit discussing political issues, and by the end of 1775 they no longer communicated at all.

After Parliament passed the legislation that became known as the Coercive Acts in 1774, both Franklins attempted to find some way to resolve the issues that were tearing the empire apart. This time they operated from very different perspectives. Benjamin urged the colonists to cut off all commercial intercourse with England, arguing that if the mother country had backed down before in the face of colonial unity, it would surely do so again. William was convinced that England would not retreat. He insisted that the colonists had to exhibit a willingness to compromise if they seriously wanted a rapprochement. Ironically, he relied on his own father to work out the details of such a compromise.

While the two men surely realized that their political views were diverging in the early 1770s, they continued to try to nurture the personal side of their relationship. Benjamin purchased English goods for the governor and his wife, taking care that every tea urn, every mahogany chair that he sent to America met his son's exacting standards. Whenever he could, he called William's achievements to the attention of the ministry. More revealingly, he shared confidential gossip with his son, regaling him with irreverent stories about government insiders. He also divulged his most subversive thoughts about government policy and imperial affairs to a son he trusted completely. His letters were dotted with reminders that they were meant for William's eyes only—and William never betrayed his father's confidences.

For his part, William continued to support his father, even as he grew uneasy about his politics. He worried about Benjamin's health, urging him to come home before old age caught up with him. He refused to criticize his father, no matter how great the temptation might have been. When William Strahan to warn him that Benjamin was out of touch "with the *Ministry in general*," telling him that some people assumed he held "the same political Opinions with [his] Father," William's reply was circumspect, although he did put some distance between himself and the elder Franklin.[1] There was, he insisted, "no reason (other than the natural connexion between us) to imagine that I entertain the same political opinions with my father.... My sentiments are really in many respects different from those which have yet been published on either side of the question." He knew that he often suffered from his "natural connexion" with Benjamin, but he refused to repudiate a man whose affection he cherished.[2]

Yet despite their best intentions, an aura of animosity increasingly pervaded the letters between father and son in the years before the Revolution. That this should have been the case is hardly surprising. Both men were deeply embroiled in the controversies of the day, and while they both tried to avoid an argument, neither could resist the temptation to lash out at the other from time to time.

As Benjamin grew disenchanted with the ministry, he tried to convey his mood to his son. Generally, he engaged in reasoned discourse, but on occasion he abandoned his pose of disinterested equanimity altogether. He sneered at the views of "great Common Lawyers," noting with false humility that, unlike his son, he himself was "somewhat of a Civilian."[3] And he attacked those sycophants who embarked "on the precarious and degrading business of seeking government dependencies."[4] Apparently forgetting that he had once helped launch William's career as a Crown servant and that he had also sought royal preferment for himself, he now insisted that he "rather wish[ed] to see all I am connected with in an Independent Station, supported by their own Industry."[5] Whenever Benjamin discussed Temple's prospects with William, he implied that he hoped the boy would not follow in his father's footsteps. Independence, not royal patronage, should be the key to Temple's success. Above all, he thundered, "I would have him a Free Man."[6]

Such comments must have made William wince, for their message was unmistakable. Still, he generally refrained from striking back or even acknowledging his father's pointed barbs. And he remained stubbornly convinced that Benjamin had both the will and the ability to find the magic solution that would reconcile the differences between England and America. He thought his father was the one colonial agent whose opinion Whitehall respected. Even Hillsborough, William insisted, saw Franklin as a "Man of great Abilities, and of uncommon Knowledge in American Matters."[7]

William's faith in his father was not as naive as it appears in hindsight. He knew that Benjamin had always harbored a deep and abiding love for the empire. True, the elder Franklin's criticisms of Parliament and the ministry had grown harsh over the years. But William had endured enough of his own quarrels with Whitehall to know that the ministry was capable of making serious errors. Moreover, he had sworn obedience to the king, not to Parliament. So long as his father remained loyal to the Crown, William did not foresee the possibility that he and Benjamin would go their separate ways.

Unfortunately for William, Benjamin Franklin's views of the king's role in imperial affairs were beginning to change. In this instance, he was ahead of most of his American compatriots. The colonists had always insisted that their quarrel was with a Parliament that had been corrupted by a venal ministry. At least in public, they refused to blame the king for their differences with the mother country. By the summer of 1773, however, Benjamin Franklin was finding it increasingly difficult to maintain a belief in the king's innocence. He was also beginning to argue that the colonists owed no absolute obedience to the monarch. When the first settlers came to America, he said, they voluntarily agreed to obey the English sovereign. It went without saying that their descendants had the right to reverse that voluntary decision to obey the king should circumstances warrant it. Even worse from William's perspective, Franklin blamed the king himself for the colonists' continued differences with England. "Between you and I," he confided to his son, speaking especially of the Tea Act, "the late Measures have been, I suspect, very much the King's own. . . . This entirely to yourself."[8]

It is easy to imagine William Franklin groaning aloud when he read these comments, but it would be a mistake to assume that he comprehended their full import. Indeed, for a long time Benjamin himself was not prepared to follow his own arguments to their logical conclusion. Moreover, so long as the vast majority of Americans retained their loyalty to the king, and so long as the elder Franklin kept his darkest thoughts to himself, William did not think he needed to worry unduly about their consequences.

In 1774, however, after his ordeal before the Privy Council, Benjamin's mood changed dramatically. While he pretended to be indifferent to his treatment by the ministry, he was clearly stung by his personal humiliation. He was angered even more when the government stripped him of his post office position. To most people, even to his sister Jane, he hid his anger behind a mask of bland indifference. But when he wrote to William, just two days after he had been fired, Benjamin revealed his pain. It was a terse message, for he was too distraught to discuss his experience in any detail. Nevertheless, his expectation was clear. He assumed that William would resign his position as governor to protest his father's treatment. William now had no chance of being promoted, he pointed out, and his present position was poorly funded and likely to remain so. "I wish," he said, "you were well settled on your Farm. 'Tis an honester and a more honourable because a more independent Employment."[9]

While William sympathized with his father, he had no intention of leaving a position that was his sole source of income, identity, and purpose. Moreover, he was not a man who abandoned his obligations lightly. He had once refused to break his engagement to Elizabeth Graeme, in effect forcing her to do the job for him. In 1768 he had virtually invited Lord Hillsborough to dismiss him, but he had not resigned his post. Most recently, he had stubbornly—some would say foolishly—supported Stephen Skinner in his long battle with the assembly. Once William declared his loyalty to any person or idea, he refused even to contemplate withdrawing his support.

Benjamin's letter came as a shock. It revealed how far his father had moved from England's corridors of power. Not only had the elder Franklin's usefulness to the governor come to an end, but he could now prove to be a detriment. Still, William had no more desire to turn his back on his father than he did to abandon the king. Thus, he simply did nothing.

Benjamin himself temporarily saved his son from an impossible dilemma. A little more than two weeks after his first blunt letter, he wrote again, more calmly this time, instructing William to sit tight. Rumor had it that he would soon be fired anyway. Why not force the ministry to do the dirty work? Do not, Benjamin told his son, "save them the shame of depriving you whom they ought to promote." For "one may make something of an Injury, nothing of a Resignation."[10] William was temporarily off the hook. Still, it was obvious that his father assumed that, one way or another, he would soon vacate his post. Indeed, at the beginning of May 1774 Benjamin wrote a third letter, suggesting that William would be more "comfortable" if he "disengaged" himself from the governorship. He knew that so long as his son retained his position, he would perform his duties honorably. Still, he thought "Independence more honourable than any Service."[11]

In his assumption that William's governorship would soon end, Benjamin Franklin was mistaken. Ignoring his father's mixed signals, William did not resign. Nor was he fired. He continued in his post, wearing a studious "Air of Indifference" while his detractors gleefully speculated about his ability to hold on to his job and about the effect that imperial discord might have on his relationship with Benjamin.[12] He also proceeded with his plans to move to Perth Amboy, seemingly unperturbed by the whispers of gossipmongers throughout the colonies. He kept the lines of communication open both to the ministry and to his own council and assembly. He also made some overtures to his father.

In May, he sent a short but carefully crafted letter to Benjamin indicating his intention to remain in his post. He had just heard from a London friend who had apprised him of Lord Dartmouth's "Sentiments respecting my Conduct." Whatever the secretary said had made him "easy as to my Office."[13] Moreover, he refused to be upset over Benjamin's loss of his post office position. Word had it that his father's own friends in Boston were behind a scheme to do away with the royal postal system. Thus, he said, Benjamin would have lost his salary as postmaster general under any circumstances. Far from being furious at his father's humiliation, William dismissed it as a minor incident.

In the same letter, William stepped up his efforts to convince his father to leave England. Obviously, he said, Franklin had no influence in London. He had friends and family at home who were anxious to see him. Indeed, his "Popularity in this Country," was "greatly beyond whatever it was."[14] Above all, William wanted his father to return home so that he could see for himself what had happened to his beloved colonies during his decade-long absence from America. The elder Franklin, he insisted, saw the colonies through rose-colored glasses. He had not experienced the turmoil and upheaval, the violence and treachery that had come to characterize colonial politics. He was so blinded by the corruption that he saw in London, so angered by his humiliation at the Cockpit, that he had lost his ability to view imperial relations from a balanced perspective. If he returned to America, William was convinced that Benjamin would see affairs there as he himself did. Then his father could use his diplomatic skills to calm colonial hotheads, assuring Americans everywhere that England was involved in no dastardly conspiracy to destroy American liberty.

Events in England and America gave William another opportunity to convince his father to return home. When news of the Boston Tea Party reached London, the government reacted harshly, displaying its determination to flex its muscles and reassert its authority in Massachusetts. At the end of March 1774, Parliament passed the Boston Port Act, closing Boston Harbor to all shipping until the East India Company had been reimbursed for its losses. News of the Port Act reached America in May, and the Massachusetts committee of correspondence responded immediately, asking the other colonies to suspend all trade with England. Merchants in New York and Philadelphia, however, did not view the proposed boycott with enthusiasm. They favored an intercolonial meeting where delegates from all the colonies could discuss their differences with England. While Boston's political leaders were unhappy with what they saw as a delaying tactic, they reluctantly agreed to support the proposal for a continental congress. William tried to use the prospect of the congress to lure his father home. Everyone, he said, valued Franklin's experience and wanted him to attend. Unfortunately, in the same letter, William discussed his views of the Boston Tea Party, suggesting that the Bay Colony would be wise to pay the East India Company for the damages it had sustained. Not only would such compensation accord with the principles of "strict Justice," but it was smart politics as well. It made sense for Massachusetts inhabitants to "do Justice before they ask it of others. . . . Their making Reparation to those whom they have injured would besides give greater Weight to their Representations and do Credit to their Cause."[15]

In September, when Benjamin replied to William's letters, he exploded. In a less contentious time, he had called his son a "thorough government man." But then, he had promised to make no attempt to "convert" him.[16] He was no longer able to maintain a philosophical attitude toward his son's politics. He was deeply hurt by William's apparent indifference to his own public humiliation and pained by the implication that he had outlived his usefulness in London. The fact that the governor seemed more disturbed by Boston's rioters than he was by England's attack on colonial rights also disturbed the elder Franklin.

Thus, he lashed out. "I do not," he wrote with obvious sarcasm, "so much as you do, wonder that the Massachusetts have not offered Payment for the Tea." Although he himself had once proposed that Boston reimburse the East India Company for its losses, he now claimed that America owed England nothing. Rather, Parliament owed the colonies money for the "many Thousand Pounds" it had "extorted" from America over the years. But "you," he said in a tone that revealed the width of the chasm separating him from his son, "who are a thorough Courtier, see every thing with Government Eyes."[17]

Clearly, Franklin had no immediate plans to return to America. To the contrary, despite his occasional fulminations and bitter outbursts, he still entertained some hope that he might be of use in persuading Parliament to soften its stance toward the colonists. Until Parliament passed the Boston Port Act, Franklin had remained surprisingly optimistic about the prospects for reconciliation. He had initially been disturbed by news of the Boston Tea Party, calling it "an Act of violent Injustice on our part" and lamenting the destruction of private property "in a Dispute about Publick Rights."[18] But when the government began to take measures to punish the Bay Colony, Franklin's position hardened. The Port Act had been bad enough. Even worse were the three reform bills that Parliament passed in late May and early June. Known collectively, with the Port Act, as the Coercive Acts, the legislation envisioned a total restructuring of Massachusetts government. Parliament directed local authorities to find convenient quarters for royal troops and allowed the governor to transfer trials to England or to another colony if he thought local juries would be prejudiced against the government's case. It also gave the governor the right to appoint his council and to appoint or remove sheriffs and judges at his own discretion. Finally, it allowed the governor to forbid all town meetings except the annual one to elect officers. To ensure that the Coercive Acts would be administered with a firm hand, the ministry replaced Governor Thomas Hutchinson with General Thomas Gage, who would retain his position as commander-in-chief of His Majesty's forces after he assumed the governorship. In effect, Massachusetts existed under martial law.

England was clearly in no mood to compromise with its colonial possessions. Still, while Franklin admitted that the Tea Party had temporarily "united all Parties here against our Province," he continued to plead America's case.[19] He signed petitions protesting the Coercive Acts. In August, he met with William Pitt, trying to help one of the colonists' staunchest allies use his position in the House of Lords to forge a coalition composed of those members of Parliament who were seeking ways to bridge the gap between the divergent claims of England and America.

Significantly, Franklin assumed that reconciliation would be achieved in terms favorable to the colonies. To put it bluntly, he expected England to cave in. Always before when the colonies had presented a united front to Parliament, the ministry had backed down. Why, he wondered, would the same strategy not work again? Franklin supported the Massachusetts request for a colonial boycott and applauded American efforts to organize a continental congress. Repeatedly he wrote home trying to bolster the American resistance movement with his upbeat assessment of English affairs. The strength and unanimity of the colonies, he said, "surprized and disappointed our Enemies, and the Tone of publick Conversation, which has been violently against us, begins evidently to turn."[20]

By the fall of 1774, it seemed clear that America would maintain the united stance that Franklin advocated. Every colony but Georgia agreed to send representatives to Philadelphia for what became known as the First Continental Congress, and toward the end of August the delegates began to arrive in Pennsylvania. They were a determined, but not a radical, group. Everyone there, including Franklin's friend Joseph Galloway, deplored the Coercive Acts, just as they had opposed Parliament's various attempts to tax the colonies over the years. No one, not even the delegates from Massachusetts, so much as broached the subject of independence. They were all simply searching for the most effective means of persuading England to repeal the Coercive Acts. Resistance, not rebellion, was the aim of the First Continental Congress. Some members, especially the representatives from Massachusetts, thought that a colonial boycott would force England to back down. Others preferred petitions and judicious proposals for a thorough reform of the imperial machinery. No one disagreed about the goals of the congress. Only the best way to achieve those goals was at issue.

In the end, the Massachusetts delegates won the day. In October, the congress devised a Declaration of Rights and Resolves, a spirited statement of the colonists' rights as English subjects. It also adopted the Suffolk

Resolves, advising Massachusetts inhabitants to disobey the Coercive Acts and to prepare to defend themselves from possible British attack. Finally, over the objections of many supporters of the merchants' interests, it voted to cut off all trade with England and it advised each colony to devise a system of committees to enforce the boycott.

Benjamin Franklin confidently predicted that a successful boycott would bring the North ministry to its knees, as the English everywhere began to sympathize with the beleaguered colonists. If the colonists refused to back down, he wrote, "you will undoubtedly carry all your Points: by giving way you will lose every thing."[21] Franklin continued to see colonial unity as the best means of effecting a reconciliation between England and America. Like his compatriots at the Continental Congress, he had not yet begun to think seriously about independence.

Throughout 1774, Franklin continued to insist that "the American Cause begins to be more popular here," but he was clearly misreading the English situation. In fact, America's defenders were few and far between.[22] By the mid-1770s, only a few English merchants depended on American trade for their livelihood, and most of them had grown disenchanted with the colonies. Even Franklin had to admit that his remaining friends in Parliament could find no sympathetic ear in the ministry. And it was the ministry's position that generally prevailed. Colonial influence in England had seriously diminished since the days when Parliament had repealed the Stamp Act.

By the end of November, Franklin was almost ready to abandon all hope. Preparations were begun to send reinforcements to augment the three thousand troops already under General Gage's command in Boston, and time was running out. Benjamin made one last desperate stab at reconciliation before abandoning the process altogether. A number of influential government men—just who they were remains unclear—began to use intermediaries to initiate tentative, secret negotiations with Franklin in an effort to find some middle ground between England and America. While he readily agreed to meet with Whitehall's surrogates, Franklin seemed to realize from the start that the negotiations would bear no fruit. He reminded the men who approached him that he had no authority to speak for the colonies. Only the Continental Congress—a body that the government steadfastly refused to recognize—had the right to negotiate a settlement.

Moreover, Franklin himself was taking an increasingly hard-line stance. His "Hints for a Desirable Union," which he presented to Quaker intermediaries David Barclay and Dr. John Fothergill in December, were more in the nature of demands than an effort to initiate serious negotiations. For a start, he wanted Parliament to repeal the Tea and Coercive Acts, reconsider its policy of regulating colonial trade, abandon any attempt to secure requisitions during peacetime, relinquish its claim to the right to tax the colonies, and guarantee the right of the assemblies to govern themselves and to control the salaries of their respective governors. His demands, if he meant them to be taken seriously, could never be met.

Franklin's on-again, off-again contacts with various government emissaries lasted through the first part of March 1775. But at least by the middle of February, it was clear that Whitehall would not consider any limitations on Parliament's right to legislate for or to tax the colonies, nor would the ministry abdicate its power to alter colonial governments at will. That being the case, there really was nothing more to say. Franklin lost his normally cheery perspective. He was having a hard time sleeping. And he began to worry that nothing, not even the colonial boycott, would force the ministry to back down.

Franklin's only remaining hope—and he knew that it was a long shot—were William Pitt's last-ditch efforts on America's behalf. Franklin began a series of personal discussions with Pitt in December, and on January 19, the "great man" invited the American agent to be his guest at the House of Lords the next day to hear him introduce a bill calling for the removal of General Gage's troops from Boston.[23] Franklin's appearance at court with Pitt "caus'd a kind of Bustle" among the Lords, a reaction that Benjamin obviously relished, but while a few Lords supported Pitt's proposal, "all avail'd no more than the whistling of the Winds."[24] Pitt returned to the upper house on February 1 with a full-fledged plan to resolve the crisis, but once again, ministerial influence prevailed and his bill was soundly defeated.

As he watched the Lords debate, Benjamin realized that any hope for a settlement was futile. Lord Sandwich attacked Pitt's bill with special venom, implying that Franklin was its author. At first, Lord Dartmouth gave the proposal his cautious support, but when he saw which way the winds were blowing he abruptly changed his mind. This from the man Franklin had once valued as a friend to America. Dartmouth was, he sniffed contemptuously, a man who had "in reality no Will or Judgment of his own."[25] The debate only confirmed Franklin in the opinion he had been moving toward for the past year. It made the Lords' "Claim of Sovereignty over three Millions of virtuous sensible People in America, seem the greatest of Absurdities, since they appear'd to have scarce Discretion enough to govern a Herd of Swine."[26] The House of Commons was no better. So long as its members were content to be bribed, bullied, and manipulated by the ministry, there was no hope for virtuous government in England.

After the debate in the House of Lords, Franklin continued his desultory discussions with various ministerial emissaries. But his heart was not in the effort. On February 20, Lord North made what would be his last attempt to settle England's differences with America, offering to refrain from taxing any colony that made a reasonable contribution to imperial expenses. Franklin viewed the proposal with disdain. It meant, he said, that the colonists would have to grant an unspecified amount of money for any purpose the government deemed necessary. Parliament was, he said, like a highway robber "who presents his Pistol and Hat at a Coach-Window, demanding no specific Sum, but if you will give all your Money or what he is pleas'd to think sufficient, he will civilly omit putting his own Hand into your Pockets. If not, there is his Pistol."[27]

By the beginning of March 1775, Franklin was ready to head for home. Thomas Whately's brother William was threatening to sue Franklin in Chancery Court for his part in airing the Hutchinson-Oliver letters. He had received word that Deborah had died, and he needed to return to Philadelphia to wrap up some business affairs there. Temple was old enough to begin preparing seriously for a career, and Benjamin did not want him educated in a corrupt English school. Franklin also thought that he might be able to persuade his son to join him in his own move toward independence. He hoped that a face-to-face meeting with William would somehow effect a change in William's perspective. If William knew what he did about the uncompromising position of king, ministry, and Parliament, he might see old issues in a new light. If he could be made to feel the extent of the decay that permeated London, he would not find it so easy to maintain his loyalty to a government that had done so little to support him over the years. It was surely worth a try.

Benjamin Franklin did not realize the extent of his son's commitment to the king. After 1773, William's activities in New Jersey were in many ways a mirror image of Benjamin's efforts in London. While Benjamin pressured Whitehall for concessions, William directed most of his attention to persuading the New Jersey assembly to soften its stance. While the elder Franklin grew disgusted by what he perceived as the corruption and sheer bullheadedness of England's leaders, his son was alarmed by what he saw as the virtual anarchy in America. Benjamin had been humiliated by his treatment at the hands of the ministry. William was dismayed by his treatment at the hands of lawmakers whom he had once counted as his friends.

As word of the Coercive Acts trickled into the colonies, political tensions everywhere heightened. In Massachusetts, the change was especially noticeable. General Gage controlled Boston, but even there he was hard put to find men to serve on his council. Throughout the rest of the province, extralegal government held sway. Courts ceased functioning, and self-constituted committees assumed the place of outlawed town meetings.

William Franklin was dismayed, but throughout 1774 he remained hopeful. With the controversy over the East Jersey treasury robbery at an end, he had temporarily returned to the good graces of the assembly. Unlike his father, he was convinced that after the Tea Party England would not back down in the face of colonial intransigence. But like Benjamin, he thought that the issues that divided England and America could still be resolved. Neither man was willing to admit that the Boston Tea Party and the Coercive Acts had ushered in a new age, that positions on both sides of the Atlantic were hardening daily, that virtually no one was willing to make the concessions that were necessary to effect a reconciliation. Where the elder Franklin had been confident that Parliament could be persuaded to repeal the Coercive Acts, his son thought that the colonists would eventually see the error of their ways.

When he wrote to Lord Dartmouth in May 1774, William revealed a strangely myopic perception of the colonial situation. After assuring the secretary that "no Attachments or Connexions" would ever impel him to "swerve from [his] duty," Franklin offered an upbeat appraisal of current conditions.[28] Yes, he admitted, a few merchants in Philadelphia and New York were talking of coming to Boston's aid, but they seemed determined to avoid another boycott at all costs. Some were also proposing a continental congress, but the governor doubted that the notion would go much beyond the talking stage. He cavalierly—and unrealistically—dismissed the machinations of the various local committees of correspondance as "absurd" and "unconstitutional." They cannot, he sneered, "even answer their Purpose." For every assembly existed at the pleasure of its governor, and no governor would allow his assembly to do anything "improper." Thus, he triumphantly proclaimed, "whenever an Assembly is dissolved, the power of its Committee is of course annihilated."[29] From a legal perspective, Franklin was on firm ground, but he failed to realize that legal niceties were becoming irrelevant to America's opposition leaders.

In June, William was forced to recognize this very fact, when a group of Essex county protesters gathered in Newark to condemn the Coercive Acts and to express their support for an intercolonial congress. "Meetings of this Nature," he observed, "there are no Means of preventing, where the chief Part of the Inhabitants incline to attend them."[30] Moreover, that same month, colonial leaders defied Franklin's earlier predictions, scheduling an intercolonial meeting in Philadelphia for the fall. At the end of July, delegates from various local committees of correspondence proved that New Jersey did not need assembly approval to proceed on its own. They met in New Brunswick, chose representatives to the Continental Congress, and, even worse, assumed governmental powers, organizing county committees to collect supplies for the relief of Boston. In this case, as in so many others, New Jersey simply followed the lead of its neighbors. Only four colonies used their regular assemblies to elect delegates to the Continental Congress. Elsewhere, committees of correspondence, extralegal assemblies, or conventions did the job. Authority in America no longer derived from the king. "The people" were creating their own governments.

William Franklin urged concessions from both sides. Boston could begin by reimbursing the East India Company for its losses, but Whitehall surely had a role to play as well. While he did not expect Parliament to abdicate its right to legislate for the colonies, it could still take some honorable intermediary steps. In the spring of 1774, he offered some suggestions to Lord Dartmouth. Instead of viewing the prospect of the Continental Congress with dismay, he urged the secretary to look upon the meeting as a golden opportunity. Unlike most English observers, Franklin realized that nearly all the congressional delegates would, like his good friend Joseph Galloway, be seeking a reconciliation with the mother country. While Franklin was convinced that the colonial tendency to rely on extralegal committees instead of legitimate government was wrong-headed, even dangerous, he did not believe that even the most radical American truly wanted independence. The smart thing to do, therefore, would be to coopt the congress by legalizing it and sending Crown representatives to the meeting. The colonial governors, a few delegates from each council and assembly, and a commissioner from England could sit down together, discuss their positions in a cool, deliberate manner, and devise a mutually satisfactory compromise. Everyone would be heard. Everyone would welcome a resolution of the differences dividing England and America. Lack of communication had always plagued imperial relations. If the ministry heeded Franklin's suggestions, this would no longer be the case.

Dartmouth always treated the governor's advice with courtesy, but he never acted on any of it. And the Continental Congress turned out to be just as stiff-necked as the ministry. In the beginning, both William Franklin and Joseph Galloway had harbored cautious hopes for the meeting. Galloway, who headed Pennsylvania's delegation, came to Philadelphia with a plan that he hoped would satisfy all but the most rabid delegates. Franklin knew about Galloway's proposal and may well have had a hand in writing it. Its centerpiece was an interprovincial council elected by the individual assemblies. The council would assume complete control of colonial affairs; it would work in tandem with Parliament on all questions affecting the empire as a whole. The plan, Franklin predicted, would "prove a lasting and beneficial Cement to all the Parts of the British Empire."[31] It left parliamentary supremacy intact while giving the colonies representative government. To be sure, he was not altogether satisfied with Galloway's proposal. A legalist to the end, he disapproved of having the Continental Congress ratify the Plan of Union, as

Galloway's proposal was called. No illegal congress had the right to form a new government. Still, he thought any proposal, even if it was not "perfect," was worth the effort.[32]

The vast majority of the congressional delegates did not agree. While they had come to Philadelphia fully committed to finding a way to reconcile their differences with England, they were not ready to sanction any plan that gave Parliament as much authority as Galloway's proposal did. Indeed, from the beginning, Galloway found himself out of step with the general mood of the congress. The delegates may not have aimed at independence, but after the Coercive Acts they were in no mood to compromise their rights. Everything in Philadelphia, Galloway complained bitterly, was "privately settled by an Interest made out of Doors."[33] The congress met at Carpenter's Hall, despite the governor's generous offer of the more appropriate assembly room in the State House. The delegates elected Philadelphia's Charles Thomson, a staunch American patriot and a political foe of Galloway, as their secretary. While the New York and Pennsylvania delegations tried to pursue a conciliatory approach, most members were much more unbending than Galloway had expected. Under the circumstances, he should not have been surprised when the congress summarily rejected his Plan of Union and expunged it from the record.

The congress defied Franklin's predictions and voted for a colonial boycott on all British trade. More important, it recommended the creation in each colony of a network of local committees, known collectively as the Continental Association, to enforce the boycott. These committees, most of which were created by extralegal congresses, not by legally established assemblies, were in effect taking the law into their own hands. As such, they constituted a step toward independence.

Both Galloway and Franklin tried not to be discouraged. They forwarded copies of the rejected plan to England, where they hoped it would receive a more favorable reading. Unfortunately, the proposal found no more supporters there than it had in Philadelphia. Benjamin had tried to explain the situation in February 1775 when he wrote to Joseph Galloway, claiming that he too wanted a "Constitution. . . . formed and settled for America." Unless Americans' rights and duties were fixed once and for all, he predicted, "Misunderstandings" would continue to arise. He thought, however, that no one in England was willing to contemplate a serious reorganization of the empire.[34] When he obtained a copy of the Galloway plan early in 1775, Franklin turned it over to William Pitt. Pitt thought the plan "ingenious" and hoped to use it as the basis of future negotiations. Still, Franklin warned Galloway that he did not expect the government to give any plan a fair hearing.[35] Moreover, he admitted his own hostility to Galloway's proposal. "When I consider the extream Corruption prevalent among all Orders of Men in this old rotten State," he raged, "and the glorious publick Virtue so predominant in our rising Country, I cannot but apprehend more Mischief than Benefit from a closer Union." While he claimed that he still hoped to avert a war, he thought that continued unity with England would "corrupt and poison" all Americans.[36]

Men like William Franklin and Joseph Galloway simply failed to realize that while there were few on either side of the Atlantic who did not want to resolve the differences dividing England and America, the chances for a compromise were receding almost daily. No one wanted to concede any ground. William Franklin's vision of a responsible, intelligent, and malleable government in London was as unrealistic as the romantic view of American virtue that his father harbored from England.

The governor did more to help the ministry than offer his suggestions for solving the imperial crisis. As early as June 1774, he began systematically to compile and forward all news about events in New Jersey to Whitehall. By September, as the Continental Congress got under way, he started to amass information about colonial disorders everywhere. He sent Dartmouth letters bulging with newspaper clippings describing the activities of the various committees of correspondence. He documented colonial attempts to organize extralegal provincial assemblies. He also enclosed Joseph Galloway's descriptions of the activities of the Continental Congress, whose meetings were held in secret. Franklin was, for all intents and purposes, acting as a self-appointed spy for the English government. He was fully aware of the implications of his activities. Much of his news came from sources who trusted his discretion, men who had no idea that their conversations ended up in Dartmouth's hands. It was just as well that they did not know, Franklin explained candidly, "lest they might be deterred from giving me Information."[37] There were still many colonists who did not realize how committed to serving the king he was, and William obviously intended to keep it that way. There were others, like Joseph Galloway, who willingly supplied the governor with information, and Franklin believed that they deserved protection. Moreover, he feared for his own safety. He remembered all too well how Thomas Hutchinson had suffered when the contents of his private letters had been revealed to the public. The stakes were higher now, and he had no wish to incur the hostility that would surely accompany a public airing of his own letters. Thus he marked nearly every letter he sent to London "secret and confidential."

With each packet he sent, Franklin reiterated what would become a constant theme of all loyalists until the end of the Revolutionary war. The Continental Congress, he maintained, did not speak for most colonists. To the contrary, nearly everyone privately decried the actions of those radicals who had somehow seized the reins of power and were running roughshod over the moderate majority. "Few," he insisted, "have the Courage to declare their Disapprobation publickly, as they well know, if they do not conform, they are in Danger of becoming Objects of popular Resentment."[38] Franklin, like loyalist leaders throughout the continent, did not recognize the depth or breadth of American anger. Moreover, he found it impossible to imagine that honest men might disagree with him. Thus, by definition, he believed that opposition leaders had their own agenda, an agenda that did not serve the interests of the people they so insidiously claimed to represent.

Had Benjamin Franklin known what his son was doing, he would have been devastated. At the beginning of 1775, Benjamin had written to Joseph Galloway. Rumor had it, he warned, that both Galloway and John Jay, a delegate to the Continental Congress from New York, were acting as spies for England. "I do not believe this," he said, "but I thought it a Duty of Friendship to acquaint you with the Report."[39] He would have been more incredulous had he known that his own son was involved in what, from his perspective, was a dishonorable business.

He would have been equally angered by the contents of William's letters. For years he had railed against Americans who claimed that colonial opposition to English policy was the province of a "small Faction."[40] Indeed, he had often written to William arguing that the colonists' "Discontents were really general and their Sentiments concerning their Rights unanimous, and not the Fiction of a few Demagogues, as their Governors us'd to represent them here."[41] He professed to believe that these false depictions of colonial sentiment were largely responsible for the ministry's refusal to heed American demands. So long as English leaders believed that America was divided, that support for Boston was confined to a few well-organized and noisy hotheads, they would stand firm. Franklin was oblivious to the irony of his position. For if his son erred in his estimation of the support American radicals had garnered over the years, his own claims that the vast majority of England's inhabitants supported American demands were just as wrong-headed.

No matter what Franklin may have thought of his son's activities, the governor was clearly—and for the first time in his career completely—in the ministry's good graces. He no longer dreaded letters from London. Even when Dartmouth ignored his advice, he always praised the governor's attempts to contain New Jersey's "democratical" impulses, and he refrained from berating him when his efforts almost necessarily failed. Most important, Dartmouth no longer harbored even a lingering fear that William's ties to his father might sway him from his duty to the king. At long last, William Franklin had earned the ministry's trust, and, having earned it, he would do nothing to destroy it. The elder Franklin sneered at Lord Dartmouth, calling him weak-minded and untrustworthy. His son was grateful for the minister's approbation.

Some historians have argued that William Franklin's clandestine support of the ministry provides the first solid indication that he had made a "decision" to support England against America. Thus, they claim, William Franklin "became" a loyalist sometime in the summer or fall of 1774.[42] But this is a misreading of Franklin's position as well as of the position of most loyal officeholders. Franklin was no more committed to defending the empire in 1774 than he had been when he first became governor. He did not "become" loyal to the Crown in 1774. He had sworn an oath to serve the king in 1762, and he never violated that oath. Unlike his father, he was simply unable to abandon his old habits and to appreciate the possibilities inherent in a new world. Moreover, he saw no reason to turn his back on the tried and true methods of the past. His entire adult life had been shaped by the duties he performed as the king's servant. His sense of identity and purpose made it almost impossible for him to alter his course. So long as the king remained loyal to him, William Franklin, like every other royal governor, would remain loyal to the king.

Even as William was using his resources to gather intelligence for the king, he made his long-awaited move to the sumptuous Proprietary House in Perth Amboy. The move was politically expedient, but personally difficult. He left many good friends in Burlington. More important, it was obvious that Deborah's health was failing. She had never been well since her first stroke in the winter of 1769. Even a casual observer could see that her condition was deteriorating. Her last letters to her husband had been incoherent at best. "I donte go abroade," she told him, and she found "it is so dificall to writ" that she ceased corresponding with anyone but him.[43] Benjamin had ignored the obvious signs of her declining condition. He wrote to her less often, and when he managed to dash off a line or two, he was usually perfunctory. He was busy now, he would say, but would write more extensively later. Somehow, he never did.

William's last visit with Deborah was painful. As she clung to her departing stepson, she predicted that she would not live to see the spring and that unless Benjamin arrived in America before then, she would never see him again. Her prophecy proved accurate. William and Elizabeth had scarcely settled into their new home when a courier galloped up their drive to inform them that Deborah had suffered another stroke on December 14, and had died five days later. William immediately set off for Philadelphia, battling snow and cold as he struggled to reach the city, barely arriving in time for Deborah's funeral. The experience was emotional and, for once, William abandoned his reserve. As he watched his "poor old Mother's" coffin disappear into the icy ground, all of his bitterness and hostility rose to the surface, and he came close to accusing his father of hastening Deborah's death.

Once again, he begged his father to return home and to bring Temple with him. Temple could study law at King's College in New York—where students and faculty were said to be more sympathetic to England than they were at the Pennsylvania Academy. Benjamin could end his life under his son's tender care, for there would always be an apartment for him in Perth Amboy. Perhaps the two Franklins could become partners once more, working together to mediate the differences between England and the colonies. One thing was certain, he said. Benjamin was "look'd upon with an evil Eye" in London, while in America, William had "heard from all Quarters" how "ardently" his father's presence at the Continental Congress had been desired. People thought that where Joseph Galloway had failed in his efforts to reconcile imperial differences, Benjamin Franklin would have succeeded. William was sure that if his father returned home and observed the American scene firsthand, he would be forced to face reality. He could not help but notice the "deep Designs" of the men who had controlled the Continental Congress. "However mad you may think the Measures of the Ministry are," he insisted, "yet I trust you have Candor enough to acknowledge that we are no ways behind hand with them in In[stances] of Madness on this Side the Water." But then he stopped abruptly. He did not want to risk his father's anger. He did not want to unleash another diatribe, another accusation that he had become a "courtier." It was, he said, "a disagreeable Subject, and I'll drop it."[44]

In some ways, Franklin had reason to remain hopeful. While New Jersey was surely caught up in the general antigovernment fervor permeating the colonies, it remained a relatively conservative province. The governor had no hope of influencing the proceedings at the Continental Congress, nor did he have much real influence at Whitehall. Still, he had the ear of a number of New Jersey lawmakers. Some members of his council, and even of the assembly, remained willing to consider proposals for accommodation. No one was more eager to offer such proposals than William Franklin.

In January 1775, despite obvious signs that legitimate government was becoming almost irrelevant throughout America, Governor William Franklin called New Jersey's assembly to Perth Amboy. The legislature had not met for nine months. However, the support bill had long since run out, and if he and his fellow officers wanted their salaries, Franklin had to convene the assembly. This was the first time the lower house had met since its members had forced the governor to accept Stephen Skinner's resignation. It was, more important, the first session since the Continental Congress had asked the colonial governments to endorse a petition that it planned to send to the king. The petition's points were not new. The congress wanted to return to the situation it claimed had existed before 1763, and it wanted the immediate revocation of the Coercive Acts. As if to underscore their moderation, the delegates insisted that they had no desire to limit the royal prerogative. Franklin harbored "some Hopes" that his assembly would not give its stamp of approval to the congressional petition.[45] It was not the substance of the document that bothered him, but he did not want the legislators to endorse the proceedings of an extralegal government. Instead, he preferred that the assembly draft its own separate petition to the king.

Franklin's opening speech was intended to disarm the legislators. He refused to divulge his views of the issues dividing England and America. "It is not," he insisted, "for me to decide on the particular Merits of the Dispute."[46] He did, however, admit his fears that a few misguided enthusiasts were striking at the very rights they pretended to defend. Sounding more like a defender of assembly rights than a supporter of the royal prerogative, he reminded the lawmakers that the Continental Congress had, in fact, usurped their own powers. The various congresses and committees then meeting throughout the province, he argued, had replaced the people's duly constituted representatives. The lawmakers could not, he asserted, "without a manifest breach of your Trust, suffer any Body of Men in this or any of the other Provinces, to usurp and exercise any of the Powers vested in you by the Constitution."[47] The members of the assembly, he lectured, were the legal representatives of the people, and it was up to them, not a self-constituted group of extremists, to defend the rights of those who placed their fortunes in their leaders' hands.

Franklin argued that the legislators should submit their own petition to the king for practical as well as legal reasons. He was convinced that the ministry would listen more attentively to a set of demands emanating from a legally constituted assembly than it would to one drafted by a self-appointed congress. Moreover, he wanted the lawmakers to think for themselves, as he hoped that they would refuse to cater to the fickle whims of the masses. It was, he thought, one of the dangers of a free society that the "*chief Men of a Country*" might "*shew a greater Regard to Popularity than to their own Judgment.*"[48] He begged the legislators to be leaders, not followers, as he reminded them that New Jersey's balanced government could be destroyed from below, as easily as from above. They had, he warned, "two Roads—one evidently leading to Peace, Happiness and a Restoration of the publick Tranquility—the other inevitably conducting you to Anarchy, Misery and the Horrors of a Civil War."[49] He left no doubt which road he wished New Jersey's lawmakers to travel.

The address contained some of Franklin's most cherished beliefs: his faith in the law, his admiration of balanced government, and his belief that the assembly was an essential, if limited, component of that government. It was, interestingly enough, at least in its broad outlines, a view that his father would have found compelling. To be sure, Benjamin had come to believe that balanced government was being destroyed by power-hungry despots at Whitehall, while William saw the danger emanating from the supporters of democracy. Neither man, however, wanted to see the balance destroyed.

Franklin's hopes for the assembly were not fully realized, but neither did he suffer an ignominious defeat. In fact, the assembly agreed to formulate a separate petition to the king, and while the document was a little more pugnacious than the governor would have liked, it was not disrespectful. Still, the legislators decided to ask their original congressional delegates to attend a second Continental Congress that was slated for May. Most important, despite Franklin's pleas, the assembly voted to endorse the congressional petition. It wanted, the governor explained, to preserve an "Appearance of Unanimity throughout the Colonies."[50] Should New Jersey follow an independent course, American unity would be fragmented, and the protest movement might disintegrate.

It was William Franklin's position that disintegrated throughout 1775. He grabbed at what he believed to be his best chance to begin the process of reconciliation that April, when he received a copy of Lord North's proposals to the assemblies. These were the same proposals that his father had disdainfully described as highway robbery, but the governor saw North's plan as essentially conciliatory, especially because it seemed to back away from claiming Parliament's right to tax the colonies. If taxation was the most important issue dividing the empire, then North's gesture surely deserved serious consideration.

Unfortunately for William Franklin, North's timing could not have been worse. On the night of April 18, 1775, General Gage sent some seven hundred British troops into the Massachusetts countryside to seize a cache of arms and supplies that the colonists were amassing. American farmers in the little town of Lexington were waiting for the soldiers when they marched into the village the next morning. Fighting broke out—no one knows who fired the first shot—and in the confusion eight Americans were killed and ten more wounded. The troops marched on to Concord, where they destroyed what military supplies they could find. When they encountered the Concord militia at the North Bridge, another fracas occurred. Two Americans and three Britons were killed in a fight that lasted about five minutes. So far, the British soldiers were holding their own. As they left Concord for Boston, however, their luck changed. American militiamen, secreted behind stone walls, trees, and fences, fired at them as they marched, in full view, down the road. Their retreat became a rout, as the British lost seventy men and suffered even more casualties before they made it back to Boston. As they raised their voices in righteous indignation, Americans were jubilant at what appeared to be an easy victory against a formidable but curiously ineffective foe.

On April 24, word of the battles of Lexington and Concord began to filter into New Jersey. When he heard that English and American blood had been shed in Massachusetts, Franklin was furious, as he lamented "one of the most unlucky Incidents that could have occurred in the present Situation of Affairs."[51] Even moderate Americans were furious at what they considered British aggression against innocent farmers, and they rushed to defend their own provinces from possible assault. Clearly, Gage's troops were an occupying army. They were not in America to defend the colonies. Lexington and Concord had, in the minds of many Americans, transformed the British army into an enemy force.

Still, Franklin called his assembly to Burlington. He no doubt regretted the colony's traditional practice of alternating the venue for the assemblies between the two capital cities. He would have much preferred to meet with the legislators from his home base at Perth Amboy. He regretted, even more, the timing of the meeting. Nevertheless, Dartmouth had ordered all royal governors to present Lord North's proposals to their assemblies. Obedient to the end, Franklin went through the motions. He scheduled the session for May 15, just five days after the Second Continental Congress was to begin meeting in Philadelphia.

Franklin was not optimistic. From his perspective, an already lawless society was drifting ever closer toward anarchy. "Congresses, Conventions and Committees" had replaced all legitimate authority, despite, he kept insisting, the wishes of the vast, but obviously frightened, majority. No one seemed even vaguely interested in the "Dictates of sober Reason." Everywhere people were arming themselves. Bands of militiamen marched through Perth Amboy, obviously relishing the impression they made as they strutted noisily past the governor's mansion. Rumors were rife that the "Lives & properties of every Officer of Government in the King's Colonies" were in danger.[52]

Franklin harbored little hope for his cause when he stood before the assembly on May 16. Still, simply by meeting with the members of the lower house he had achieved a victory of sorts. He was the first colonial governor to discuss the North proposal with his legislators. If by some stroke of luck he managed to convince the assembly to accept North's plan, then he might reverse the trend toward illegal government and start the colonies along the road to reconciliation.

Franklin begged the legislators to give North's proposals a fair hearing. While he admitted that the Crown had not compromised on the issue of parliamentary sovereignty, he thought North's plan went more than halfway. It tacitly abandoned Parliament's claim to the right to tax the colonies. The government would come to each province in "the old accustomed Manner, by Way of Requisition."[53] To be sure, Parliament would ultimately decide how much each colony should contribute, but North had promised to give them all "*every possible* INDULGENCE."[54] The government had, he said, no ulterior motives, no design to destroy American liberties. It merely wanted the colonists to pay their share toward the upkeep of an empire they professed to love. If, he warned, Americans rejected North's offer, it would be they who could be accused of wanting not justice, but independence.

Franklin did his best to defend the North proposal. Not only had he put the best possible gloss on the plan, but he had endeavored to put the legislators on the defensive. He wanted them either to admit that they favored independence or to begin serious discussions aimed at bringing the imperial crisis to an end. Unfortunately, the assembly was not about to compromise. The battles of Lexington and Concord still rankled, and the legislators were in a hostile mood. Thus they refused even to consider the North plan until they received some cue from the Continental Congress. Like Benjamin Franklin, they saw the proposal as taxation decked out in a new costume.

William Franklin was disappointed, if not surprised. "I have done my Duty," he said tersely. He hoped they would at least consider the proposal as a basis for further negotiation. But, he said, referring sarcastically to the assembly's desire to leave any decision concerning the North plan to the congress, it was obvious that the legislators did not think themselves "competent" to arrive at a judgment of their own.[55] If bloodshed came, he warned, they had only themselves to blame. For himself, he insisted that he continued to be dedicated to serving both king and colony. "No Office or Honour in the Power of the Crown to bestow will ever influence me to forget or neglect the Duty I owe my Country," he proclaimed. "Nor the most heinous Rage of the intemperate Zealots induce me to swerve from the Duty I owe His Majesty."[56] No matter how difficult the circumstances became, he was determined to continue serving both masters.

NOTES

[1] WF to William Strahan, 18 June 1771, C. H. Hart, "Letters from William Franklin to William Strahan," *Pennsylvania Magazine of History and Biography* 35 (1911): 448.
[2] Ibid.
[3] BF to WF, 14 July 1773, *PBF* 20:303.
[4] BF to WF, 1 Aug. 1774, ibid. 21:266.
[5] BF to WF, 30 Jan. 1772, ibid. 19:50.
[6] BF to WF, 1 Aug. 1774, ibid. 21:266.
[7] WF to BF, 13 Oct. 1772, ibid. 19:333.
[8] BF to WF, 14 July 1773, ibid. 20:308, 309.
[9] BF to WF, 2 Feb. 1774, ibid. 21:75.
[10] BF to WF, 18 Feb. 1774, ibid., 108.

[11]BF to WF, 7 May [1774], ibid., 212.

[12]Thomas Wharton to Samuel Wharton, 3 May 1774, Wharton Letterbrook, 1773–1784, Historical Society of Pennsylvania, Philadelphia.

[13]WF to BF, 3 May 1774, *PBF* 21:207.

[14]Ibid.

[15]WF to BF, [3 July 1774], ibid., 238.

[16]BF to WF, 6 Oct. 1773, ibid. 20:437.

[17]BF to WF, 7 Sept. [1774], ibid. 21:287.

[18]BF to the Massachusetts House of Correspondence, 2 Feb. 1774, ibid., 76.

[19]BF to Robert Cushing, 22 Mar. 1774, *PBF* 21:152.

[20]BF to Robert Cushing, 3 Sept. 1774, ibid., 280.

[21]BF to Jonathon Williams, Sr., 28 Sept. 1774, ibid. 21:323.

[22]BF to Joseph Galloway, 12 Oct. 1774, ibid., 333.

[23]BF to WF, 22 Mar. 1775, ibid., 547.

[24]Ibid., 576, 577.

[25]Ibid., 582.

[26]Ibid., 583.

[27]Ibid., 594, 595.

[28]WF to Lord Dartmouth, 31 May 1774, F. W. Ricord and William Nelson, eds., *Documents Relating to the Colonial History of the State of New Jersey* (1757–67), 10:459.

[29]Ibid., 458.

[30]WF to Lord Dartmouth, 28 June 1774, ibid., 464.

[31]WF to Lord Dartmouth, 6 Sept. 1774, ibid., 475. For a copy of Galloway's plan, see ibid., 478–92.

[32]WF to Lord Dartmouth, 6 Dec. 1774, ibid., 504.

[33][Joseph Galloway to WF], 5 Sept. 1774, ibid., 477.

[34]BF to Joseph Galloway, 18 Feb. 1774, *PBF* 21:110, 111.

[35]BF to Joseph Galloway, 5[–7] Feb. 1775, ibid., 469.

[36]BF to Joseph Galloway, 25 Feb. 1775, ibid., 509.

[37]WF to Lord Dartmouth, 3 Apr. 1775, Ricord and Nelson, *Documents* 10:570.

[38]WF to Lord Dartmouth, 6 Dec. 1774, ibid., 503.

[39]BF to Joseph Galloway, 25 Feb. 1775, *PBF* 21:508.

[40]BF to Samuel Cooper, 7 July 1773, ibid. 20:268.

[41]BF to WF, 1 Sept. 1773, ibid., 385.

[42]See especially William Sterne Randall, *A Little Revenge: Benjamin Franklin and His Son* (Boston: Little, Brown, 1984), 283.

[43]Deborah Franklin to BF, 29 Oct. 1773, *PBF* 20:449.

[44]WF to BF, 24 Dec. 1774, ibid. 21:402, 404.

[45]WF to Lord Dartmouth, 1 Feb. 1775, Ricord and Nelson, *Documents* 10:537.

[46]*Votes and Proceedings of the General Assembly of the Province of New Jersey* 75A:5.

[47]Ibid.

[48]Ibid.

[49]Ibid., 6.

[50]WF to Lord Dartmouth, 1 Feb. 1775, Ricord and Nelson, *Documents* 10:537.

[51]WF to Lord Dartmouth, 6 May 1775, ibid., 593.

[52]WF to Lord Dartmouth, 6 May 1775, ibid., 591–93.

[53]*Votes and Proceedings* 75B:10.

[54]Ibid., 6.

[55]Ibid., 27.

[56]Ibid., 30.

8

"When in the Course of Human Events"

When Benjamin Franklin sailed for home in the spring of 1775, he was nearly seventy years old. Angry and bitter, he had probably already accepted the reality that few other Americans were willing to face. Independence was inevitable. Only the timing was at issue. In America he began a round of activities that would have exhausted anyone half his age. He knew, he explained, that he was an old man whose most productive years were behind him. What fortune he possessed would have to support him for the rest of his life. He no longer expected to make any contribution to the world of science that would compare with the day he and William had brought the lightning from the skies. He intended to devote what time he had left to preserving his country's liberties. He only hoped that he could persuade his son to join him in his last adventure.

William was waging his own war for the hearts and minds of New Jersey's legislators when his father arrived in America. He was trying to hold his colony together and to fend off—or at least to ignore—all the extralegal committees and congresses that were taking over the country and turning his own world upside down. He was also fighting for his very life, as he began to fear that he would be captured by his enemies and led "like a Bear through the Country."[1] As he saw other governors abandon their posts, fleeing to the safety provided by the king's troops, he occasionally considered following their example. But like his father, William Franklin was a stubborn man. Benjamin had often declared that he would never voluntarily relinquish any position. "I shall never *ask*, never *refuse*, nor ever *resign* an Office," he said.[2] For, as he had once observed to his son, "One may make something of an Injury, nothing of a Resignation."[3] Thus both Franklins stuck to their respective positions, refusing even to sit out the growing controversy on the sidelines. Neither man would shrink from his duty as he saw it. King and country, father and son, were about to go their separate ways.

When Benjamin Franklin arrived in America at the beginning of May, he was both nervous and exhilarated. The mood in the colonies delighted him.

Americans everywhere seemed determined to defend their liberties. Power and money meant nothing to them. This, he opined, marked the difference between "uncorrupted new states, and corrupted old ones." Virtue and frugality permeated the very air the colonists breathed. No one had time for three-course meals anymore. "Simple beef and pudding" satisfied the needs of any good American.[4] "All Parties," he wrote, "are now extinguish'd here. Britain has found means to unite us."[5] While he had promised his English friends that he would make an effort to promote a reconciliation, he thought that the breach between England and America was "irreparable."[6] In fact, he welcomed signs that Americans were preparing for war.

While he was glad to be home and was optimistic—no doubt too optimistic—about colonial unity, he was disoriented, as well. He had not set foot on America's shores for more than a decade. In the last years of her life, Deborah's letters had all too often been filled with descriptions of the funerals of dear friends, and Franklin had worried that if he ever returned to Philadelphia, none of his compatriots would be there to greet him. As soon as he entered the city, church bells chimed and he was thronged by a steady stream of well-wishers. Still, there were many who were not present. A new generation of men had assumed the reins of government in his absence. He was a respected elder statesman—but Philadelphia had changed, and he would need to adapt to those changes under trying circumstances. He would also have to reintroduce himself to his son.

In the early 1770s, Franklin had often considered returning to America, and he had always planned to head straight for New Jersey so that he could "learn thereby more perfectly the state of affairs" in America.[7] But when he actually arrived in the colonies, Franklin traveled immediately to Philadelphia. Now he apparently wanted to hear about the "state of affairs" from men whose views were much different from those of his son.

Still, he was anxious to see William, to introduce him to young Temple, and to make one last effort to persuade him to abandon his misguided loyalty to the king. During his voyage to America, he had spent his time furiously scribbling a long letter to William, describing his last fruitless efforts to negotiate an agreement with England. He hoped that if he could make his son understand how unreasonable the government had been, William might yet resign his governorship and use his talents on behalf of the American colonies. Benjamin also wanted to meet with his longtime friend and protégé Joseph Galloway, imagining that he too might be persuaded to reconsider his position.

Three days after Franklin arrived in America, Benjamin began making plans for the long-awaited reunion with William. But the governor was meeting with his assembly on May 16, and had to postpone any trip to Philadelphia until the session ended. While he waited for his son, Franklin visited Joseph Galloway at Trevose, Galloway's palatial Bucks County estate. Both men surely knew how much their views had diverged. In the past few years, Galloway's letters to London had taken on an increasingly bitter tone. By 1774, he had virtually stopped writing to his old political crony. The Quaker party had begun to collapse as early as 1770, and Galloway's influence had disintegrated with it. As his power diminished, he had complained about his inability to please "an envious and discontented People," insisting that the "Dregs" of society now ran Pennsylvania. "The old Friends of good Order and Government" had been rejected, and Galloway watched helplessly as the "wicked and base Conduct of these mad People" pervaded the colony. Even the proprietors, he said, were preferable to the men who had assumed control of Pennsylvania.[8] Benjamin Franklin, from the safety of England, might wax eloquent about American virtue, but Joseph Galloway, who suffered the "Abuse and Calumny" of his adversaries, knew better.[9] Despite his alienation, Galloway had been appointed as a delegate to both the First and Second Continental Congresses. But the rejection of his Plan of Union had embittered him, and he had resigned his appointment to the Second Congress, announcing his intention to retire from politics altogether. Franklin urged him to reconsider his decision, but to no avail.

William met his father and his son at Trevose sometime toward the end of May or the beginning of June. As he rode into Philadelphia, he was undoubtedly apprehensive. It had been more than a decade since he had seen his father, and Temple was a stranger. Philadelphia itself had taken on a new look. Militia units paraded through the city from morning to night; the noise of drum and fife filled the air. Only the Quakers—and not all of them—disdained the martial fervor enveloping the city in the wake of the battles of Lexington and Concord. As William rode past the State House, whose doors were now barred to anyone but congressional delegates, he must have realized that he was entering alien territory.

No one knows exactly what happened during the first awkward meeting of three generations of Franklin men. Joseph Galloway was the only one who ever mentioned it at all. The glass went about freely that night, as the two elder Franklins and their host reminisced about their shared glories and defeats. But when they talked about their hopes for the future, there must have been considerable constraint. As Benjamin described his last hectic days in London, both Galloway and William Franklin were surely stunned. Gone was the affable statesman they had known for so long, the voice of moderation who could ease any argument with a joke and a smile. This was a more angry and bitter man than they remembered. He had suffered humiliation and defeat at the hands of the king's ministers. He had been disillusioned by the government and had lost all desire for or belief in compromise.

While Franklin emphasized his own role in the abortive peace negotiations that had preceded his return to America, claiming that Whitehall had been unwilling to discuss colonial grievances seriously, both William and Galloway surely suspected that it was Franklin, not the king's ministers, who had refused to negotiate in good faith. Both men must have recognized the depth of their differences with Benjamin. They had personally encountered the instransigence, the double-dealing of colonial radicals, and they knew the elder Franklin was wrong when he said that Americans were willing and "ready to agree upon any equitable Terms."[10]

Franklin's praise of colonial virtue fell on deaf ears. Galloway had suffered the "Insults" and "violent Opposition" of the members of the First Continental Congress when he had stood before them, begging them to consider his Plan of Union.[11] If Franklin had fled England to escape possible imprisonment, Galloway had received anonymous death threats from his political adversaries. While his father depicted the English government as selfish and unbending, William could tell tales of stiff-necked colonials who were more interested in private vendettas and personal aggrandizement than in principle. Benjamin may have seen London at its worst, but William had watched the colonies descend into anarchy. His own colony was being run by illegal congresses and rampaging mobs. He feared for his life and for his property. He knew that England was not perfect, but he still believed that the British system of government was the best and freest in the world. Men of good will, he thought, ran the empire, while America's self-styled patriots hungered for personal power, giving no thought to the destruction they were bringing to their own people.

As the night wore on, it must have become apparent that no one would change his mind. Even so, William and Benjamin did not give up on one another easily. William hoped that in the days and months ahead his father would remain neutral. Benjamin harbored the same aspirations for his son. Neither man would have his wish.

William Franklin rode away from Trevose with fifteen-year-old Temple at his side. Temple was anxious about his anticipated meeting with Elizabeth, who had only recently learned of his existence. William was just as uneasy about the political situation awaiting him at home. He wondered how long he would be able to pretend that a legitimate government existed in New Jersey. An extralegal provincial convention had just met at Trenton and had voted to levy taxes on the colony to pay for the expenses of the militia. Legitimate government, said Franklin, was "nearly laid prostrate," and "all officials from the highest to the lowest [were] only on Sufferance."[12]

As William Franklin struggled to keep his old government from collapsing, his father began to lay the foundations for a new one. There were those, especially at first, who harbored suspicions of Benjamin when he returned to America. Samuel Adams and Richard Henry Lee, who for years had held this father of a royal appointee at arm's length, thought he might even be an English spy. But Franklin soon won over the most wary patriot. Almost immediately on his arrival in Philadelphia, the assembly voted to make him a congressional delegate. On June 30 it also appointed him to the Pennsylvania Committee of Safety. As the committee's president he began helping to raise men and supplies for a possible clash with the king's troops. By July, he was busier than he had been in his entire life. He was up at six each morning and continued a round of meetings that lasted late into the afternoon and sometimes even into the night. He headed Pennsylvania's Constitutional Convention, served on the congressional committee that rejected Lord North's proposals, and at the end of July became postmaster general of a newly created American postal system. He hired his son-in-law, Richard Bache, as his secretary and comptroller, thinking no doubt as he did so that he once would have offered the position to his son.

A year before the signing of the Declaration of Independence, Franklin was ready for America to abandon its imperial connections. In a way, his decision must have been a relief. He had tried so long to play the role of mediator, had been torn between his love for the empire and his devotion to the colonies whose rights he cherished. Even after his experience before the Cockpit he had continued to negotiate with Whitehall. Now that he had made a commitment to independence, he was able to proceed with a single-minded dedication that had eluded him throughout much of his political life.

He and men like him knew that most Americans, even most members of Franklin's own congressional delegation, were not yet ready to sever their ties to England. They would have to move slowly, cautiously, so that they could bring the rest of the country along with them. Thus they followed a curiously zigzag path. Seven days after the Second Continental Congress convened, news arrived that American forces had captured the British fort at Ticonderoga. This act of American aggression upset many members of the congress, for until the assault they could convincingly claim that all their confrontations with the British troops had been defensive, not offensive. Moreover, every military confrontation between England and America made it more difficult for anyone on either side to back down. Still, although no one wanted a war with England, it was time to prepare for the possibility that war might come. On June 15, 1775, the congress asked Virginia delegate George Washington to be the commander-in-chief of what would become the Continental Army. Yet a little over two weeks later, that same congress approved a humble request to the king, quickly dubbed the Olive Branch Petition, begging him to intercede with Parliament on the colonists' behalf. Benjamin Franklin served on the committee that drafted the petition, but he doubted that Whitehall would have "sense enough" to pay any attention to it.[13]

On that, he and his son agreed. William had long insisted that the mother country would not back down in the face of colonial unity, and throughout the spring of 1775 he was comforted by the king's determination to stand firm. By June, Dartmouth had declared America in "open Rebellion," and in July, even as John Dickinson was putting the finishing touches on the Olive Branch Petition, the king declared his intention "to reduce His rebellious Subjects to Obedience."[14] William was especially relieved when London promised to protect all the king's men from possible harm. He was sure that once the colonists realized that the government would not change its course, all but the most radical rabble-rousers would reconsider their own position. Even if they did not, William was confident that the weak and disorganized resistance movement would collapse when it confronted the awful might of the British empire.

In the meantime, however, he still had to deal with an array of personal and political problems. He and his father pretended to remain on good terms, but they seldom wrote to one another and saw each other even less frequently. Benjamin continued to help his son with his all but useless endeavors to wring a profit from the old Indiana company. William had "received the *strongest Assurances* that as soon as the present Great Dispute [was] settled *our Grant shall be perfected*," but it would clearly be many years before the affair would be resolved.[15] William, perhaps from force of habit, still sent copies of his assembly speeches to his father, even though he surely knew that they would only anger him. Benjamin visited Perth Amboy twice during the summer of 1775, but his visits ended in shouting matches so loud that they disturbed the governor's neighbors.

The two men maintained some sense of civility at least in part because of their mutual devotion to Temple. Indeed, they were almost rivals for the boy's affection. William assumed his long-neglected role as father with a vengeance, although Benjamin continued to make most of the major decisions concerning Temple's future. The boy spent a pleasant summer at Perth Amboy, becoming especially fond of his stepmother. In the fall, he returned to his grandfather's care and enrolled at the College of Philadelphia. Benjamin refused even to consider sending Temple to New York's King's College, by then a hotbed of Toryism.

William tried to monitor his son's life after he returned to Philadelphia. Along with all the clothes the careless boy had left behind, he sent more advice than Temple probably cared to receive. He prescribed an ambitious course of study, including Latin, Greek, French, and mathematics. He attended to his son's mental and physical health as well. When a friend told him that Temple appeared "thin and rather melencholly," he was disturbed, although he did not know exactly how to improve his son's mood.[16]

It was easier to attend to Temple's material needs. He could send him a book or two from his own well-stocked library, and it was simple enough to give the free-spending boy enough pocket money to satisfy his seemingly endless needs. But even money soon became a problem, for Temple never seemed to budget his resources wisely. William had always resented his own father's reminders that he seldom lived within his means. Now he found himself offering the same reminders, often with less grace, to Temple.

Still, both William and Elizabeth, who had no children of their own, were happy to have a son on whom to lavish their affection. Moreover, Temple provided his father with his one remaining link to Benjamin Franklin. Even after the two men stopped corresponding, William inquired after Benjamin's health and sent messages of affection to his father in every letter he wrote to his son. Temple also kept his father abreast of Philadelphia's political news. William hesitated to ask Benjamin about politics, so he welcomed Temple's presents of the newspapers and pamphlets making the rounds of Pennsylvania's capital city. While the relationship between Temple and William was often strained, the boy's presence provided one of the few bright spots the Franklins enjoyed in what was becoming a desperate situation.

Everywhere he looked throughout the summer of 1775, William Franklin saw reason to be discouraged. By August, although the congress still claimed that it was searching for a way to end its quarrel with England, Americans were openly gearing up for a war that most of them hoped somehow to avoid. The governor insisted that reconciliation was possible, but privately he prepared for the worst. His only solace was his belief that the vast majority of Americans would reject their self-appointed rebel leaders once they realized that they aimed not at peace but at establishing an independent republic. He knew that there were none in the colonies "who would draw their Swords in Support of Taxation," but he thought there were many who would "fight to preserve the Supremacy of Parliament in other respects" and who would do almost anything to preserve America's "Connexion with Great Britain."[17]

In the meantime it was his duty to rally the spirits of the king's men and, most important, to remain in New Jersey serving as a symbol of continuity, proving that, in his colony at least, the "Appearance" of legitimate government was still alive, if not entirely well.[18] Thus despite his growing fears for his own safety, he refused to abandon his post. Instead, like loyal Americans everywhere, he simply watched helplessly as events careened out of control. While the patriots organized their own forces, creating committees of correspondence and extralegal governments, most loyalist leaders sat passively, waiting for the ministry's directives. Consequently, whatever chance they had of reasserting their own control simply evaporated, as opposition leaders filled the vacuum left by the king's men. New Jersey's patriot faction followed the example set by many other colonies, creating a provincial congress that they hoped would take the place of the duly constituted assembly. The congress soon assumed many of the duties that formerly belonged to the legislature, taking over the militia and collecting tax money for the colony's defense. Franklin realized that for all practical purposes, he and men like him were "little more than Cyphers," more likely to be ignored than attacked.[19]

Throughout the fall, Benjamin and William Franklin, each in his own way, were preparing for war. The Continental Congress appointed Benjamin to committee after committee, as he helped shore up American defenses and began to direct secret efforts to obtain foreign, especially French, support in the event that the colonies finally decided to declare independence. William clung to his position, held his breath, and waited for the next shoe to fall. By September, Benjamin had abandoned even the pretense of seeking reconciliation. He continued to receive frantic letters from bewildered London friends who had viewed his departure from England with high hopes, convinced that he would be able to talk sense into the leaders of the American resistance movement. His friends believed that reconciliation was still possible. They all insisted that the English ministers, not the English people, were responsible for the bellicose statements emanating from the mother country. They also argued that the colonies were partly to blame for the continued impasse, that they were asking for more now than they would have deemed possible just a few months earlier. Franklin's comments, when they came, were curt, even hostile, and he talked more and more of England's "barbarous Tyranny," its "mad Demands" and "mad Measures."[20] "We are," he asserted, "on the high road to mutual enmity, hatred, and detestation." Independence was "inevitable."[21]

In October 1775, Franklin traveled with two other delegates to Cambridge, Massachusetts, to assess the strength of the Continental Army—which was on the verge of collapse—and to return to Philadelphia with recommendations for shoring up the army's resources. After he had fulfilled his duties, he traveled alone to Worcester, Massachusetts, where he picked up his sister Jane, who had fled British-infested Boston to live in relative safety with Franklin's old friend Catherine Greene. For some time, he had been begging Jane to leave the Greene residence, which was already inundated with refugees. At one point, he had suggested that she go to Perth Amboy where she would be safe and comfortable at the governor's mansion. By the fall of 1775, he preferred that Jane reside in Philadelphia.

Despite the rift between father and son, Benjamin and Jane stopped at Perth Amboy on the way to Philadelphia. Jane wanted to see her nephew's "very magnificent" home, and William proudly gave his guests the grand tour.[22] He no doubt avoided his father's eyes as they strolled through the first-floor parlor, which was dominated by the gilt-edged portraits of King George III and Queen Charlotte. Even Jane's presence was probably not enough to ease the tension. Conversation must have been stilted, and everyone was undoubtedly relieved when Benjamin announced that he could not stay the night. Pressing business awaited him in Philadelphia, and he had to be off. When William watched his father's carriage roll away from the house, he had no way of knowing that this was the last time the two men would see each other until the end of the American Revolution.

After his father's depature, William set to work on his preparations for the next session of the New Jersey assembly, which would meet in Burlington in less than a week. He looked forward to the session with a mixture of dread and anticipation. Many of his oldest allies in the colony had deserted him. The loss of William Alexander, Lord Stirling, was especially painful. Alexander had just accepted a commission as colonel of the Somerset militia. To William, the "extraordinary" decision was proof of Alexander's "*Contemptible Meanness* and *dishonesty*."[23] But he had learned not to be surprised at anything misguided Americans might do in these confusing times. Many other members of his council were also defecting to the ranks of the patriot camp. Those who remained carefully hedged their bets.

Indeed, Franklin had begun to accept the unpalatable fact that military force alone would bring America back into the fold. "The leaders of the People," he said, despite their steadfast denials, did not want peace, but their followers were blind to reality. "Were the People even now," he insisted, "left to judge for themselves," there was "no Doubt but that their natural good sense would prevent their engaging in the Support of the present hostile and destructive Measures."[24] For the moment, he had to admit that the king's enemies controlled the agenda for the debate, and he was virtually powerless to change anyone's mind.

Unlike many colonies, New Jersey still had a government of sorts. Moreover, in the fall of 1775, the colony's provincial congress was suffering the effects of a conservative backlash. As they inched toward independence, many in the always cautious colony were, at least momentarily, having second thoughts.[25] Franklin thought that he might be able to persuade New Jersey's lawmakers to abandon their support of the Continental Congress, destroying the appearance of colonial unity and beginning the process of reconciliation. He knew his chances of succeeding were slim, at best. The legislature would be hostile—indeed, when he called its members to Burlington he was not even sure that many of them would show up. But as one of only a handful of governors who could still claim to be even in nominal control of his colony, he had no choice but to make the effort.

Franklin's opening address to the assembly in October 1775 was conciliatory but firm. He refused even to discuss the merits of the issues that divided the empire, while he warned the legislators that if they harbored any illusions that the king would allow them to go their own way without a fight, they were mistaken. He complimented the assembly on the relative calm that pervaded New Jersey, although he admitted his fears that violence in other colonies might spill over into his own. Despite his anxieties, he vowed never to abandon New Jersey, no matter how great the temptation became to do so.

At first, the session went better than Franklin had imagined possible. The house agreed to continue its financial support of the government, thus indicating that some sentiment for upholding legitimate institutions still prevailed. The members also took care of a backlog of routine bills, acting almost as though this was a normal assembly meeting in normal times. They were providing a sense of continuity in an otherwise chaotic world. Even better, petitions from Burlington County began to flood the assembly, begging the legislators to discourage any move toward independence. The assembly even proposed a candidate to replace Benjamin Franklin as its colonial agent. Surely this was proof that the members had no immediate plans to sever ties with the home government. Franklin was most pleased when, on the 28th of November, the assembly voted to appoint a committee to prepare a separate petition to the king, asking the monarch to make every effort to restore the harmony of the empire. The petition was important for two reasons. It indicated that New Jersey legislators were still trying to reconcile the differences between England and America. More important, by acting independently, writing their own petition instead of relying on the petitions of the Continental Congress, they were creating a small fissure in the unified front that had begun to characterize the American resistance movement.

Franklin began to lose control of the session on December 4, after he received word that three members of the Continental Congress were galloping toward Burlington. The congress knew that if New Jersey sent a separate petition to the king, the appearance of colonial unity would be destroyed. And so on December 5, John Dickinson, John Jay of New York, and George Wythe of Virginia pounded on the doors of the New Jersey assembly demanding to be heard.

The three men spoke for less than an hour. They emphasized the absolute necessity of maintaining a united front. England sees us, argued Dickinson, as "a *Rope of sand*," easily divided and afraid to fight. A separate petition would merely confirm that erroneous view. On the other hand, if the colonists stood together, victory would be theirs. There was even a possibility that a display of unity would convince England to back down and to begin serious negotiations to resolve its differences with the colonies.[26]

After the congressional emissaries left the room, New Jersey's lawmakers discussed their next move. In the end, they decided not to send their own petition to the king. William Franklin had lost his most important contest as colonial governor. He had waged a battle with the Continental Congress for the loyalty of his legislature, and he had been defeated.

After December 1775, Franklin's influence in New Jersey was negligible. Militarily and politically the king's supporters were in disarray everywhere. Moderates in Philadelphia continued to maintain that they aimed not at independence but at a redress of colonial grievances. But their protests had taken on a strangely unreal quality. Congress was beginning to discuss the possibility of opening up its trade to the outside world. American forces were marching on Canada. Benjamin Franklin's secret committee of correspondence was preparing to dispatch Silas Deane to France as an unofficial negotiator, and Franklin had made good use of his connections abroad to initiate covert discussions with government officials at the Hague and in Spain. Technically, America still counted itself as a colonial possession. In fact, it was beginning to take on the trappings of an independent country.

On January 9, 1776, Thomas Paine published his pamphlet *Common Sense*. A relative newcomer to America—he had arrived in Philadelphia two years earlier—Paine said aloud what most colonists feared to say even privately. He blamed the king, not Parliament, for tyrannical English policy. He argued that the institution of monarchy was in itself irrational and that governments could be secure and orderly without the much-vaunted balance of interests that the Americans and the English alike assumed was essential for the protection of stability and liberty. He also insisted that Americans should base their demands not on their English heritage but on their status as human beings. The colonists, he said, should claim the rights of man, not the rights of Englishmen. Paine's little pamphlet was a breath of fresh air to colonists teetering on the brink of independence. It gave them the courage to question their loyalty to the king, moving them one very important step toward the rejection of their ties to the empire. What had seemed radical in 1775 had, for many people, become "common sense."

Just four days before Paine's pamphlet hit the streets, William Franklin wrote one of his confidential letters to Lord Dartmouth. His assembly had left Burlington with the government intact—but just barely. Disappointed and more bitter than usual, the governor lashed out at the king's enemies. He still maintained that none but the most infatuated colonists would ever voluntarily cut their ties with England. "All Ranks of People," he said, had assured him of their loyalty. Yet rebel leaders were so skillful that, like lemmings, the vast majority of Americans seemed prepared to follow them over the cliff. Their plot, he feared, would "be carried on by such Degrees, and under such pretenses, as not to be perceived by the People in general till too late for Resistance."[27] William Franklin still could not understand the depth or breadth of colonial discontent.

Franklin sent his letter, bristling with newspaper clippings and documents, through its usual circuitous channels, but his missive never left America's shores. Instead, on January 6, it was intercepted by his old friend—now his sworn enemy—William Alexander. The governor's timing was unfortunate. Just four days earlier, the Continental Congress had issued orders demanding that all suspicious Americans be disarmed and, if necessary, incarcerated if they refused to give their word that they would do nothing to overthrow the patriot government. Armed with the congress's instructions, Alexander had ordered all official mail intercepted. Almost immediately, he stumbled on Franklin's letter. Recognizing its implications, he forwarded it to Philadelphia.

Alexander did not wait for advice from the congress to proceed on his own. Perhaps he feared that Benjamin Franklin's presence in Philadelphia might make it awkward for the delegates to move against the New Jersey governor. Perhaps he thought that Franklin might imitate the example of many of his friends and try to flee the colony. Although William Franklin had always claimed that he would never quit his post voluntarily, Alexander did not intend to take any chances. Thus he summoned his immediate subordinate Lieutenant Colonel William Winds and ordered him to march to Perth Amboy and arrest the governor.[28]

On the night of January 6, at two in the morning, the Franklins were roused by a "violent knocking" at the front door. Elizabeth, whose health had always been poor, was so alarmed that her husband thought she was in danger of "Dying with the Fright."[29] A few moments later, a servant entered the room bearing a note from Colonel Winds asking for Franklin's word that he would not flee the country. Furious, Franklin responded. "I have not the least Intention to quit the Province," he wrote, "nor shall I unless compelled by Violence. Were I to act otherwise it would not be consistent with my Declarations to the Assembly, nor my Regard for the good People of the Province."[30] Despite his assurances, the soldiers did not leave until dawn. Even then, they posted a guard at the front gate.

William was positive that the congress planned to arrest him and move him "to the Interior Part of the Country" where the government could keep an eye on him.[31] If he were removed, of course, the extralegal government in Philadelphia could declare all legitimate authority in New Jersey at an end. Strangely, his spirits were lifted by the threat of physical danger. His own father had experienced a sense of relief upon his return to America when he had finally been able to cast off the cloak of moderation and commit himself to the cause of independence. Now William Franklin was able to do much the same thing. Alexander's attempt to arrest him freed the governor from the need to see all sides of every issue. After January 6, 1776, his adversaries were his enemies.

On the 10th of January, Alexander advised the Continental Congress that he wanted to move Franklin to his own headquarters in Elizabeth, New Jersey, for safekeeping. Not bothering to wait for the congress's permission, he dispatched about one hundred soldiers and a handful of officers to the governor's mansion to arrest William Franklin. Franklin received the news stoically, making the "least Resistance" possible.[32] He would, at the very least, make a dignified exit from Perth Amboy.

Instead, he was granted a reprieve. Chief Justice Frederick Smyth, alarmed by the possible "Ill Consequences" to the colony if the British should decide to punish the colonists for arresting the royal governor, intervened.[33] Colonel Winds agreed to let Franklin remain in his own house while Smyth galloped to Alexander's headquartes to plead Franklin's case in person. Smyth's appeal did the trick, and a few days later Alexander dropped the matter entirely after the congress rebuffed him for his precipitous behavior. For the moment, Governor Franklin remained in nominal charge of New Jersey.

In fact, his position was weaker than ever. He was convinced that the congress allowed him to remain free in hopes that he would flee the colony. "It has long appeared to me," he wrote Lord Germain, the newly appointed secretary for the American Department, that "some of them at least, wanted to have all the King's Governors quit the Colonies, that they might have a Pretence for forming them into separate Republics."[34] If that was their wish, Franklin intended to disappoint them. "My language has constantly been," he declared, "*You may force me, but you shall never frighten me out of the Province.*"[35]

Franklin remained in the colony, but he could no longer pretend to govern it. Many of his closest friends, including Joseph Galloway, had fled the country. A substantial number of his councilors opposed him. Those who did not were afraid to offer him any public support. Even his own family seemed to have abandoned him. No one from Philadelphia wrote a word of commiseration after the attempt to arrest him had failed. William did not expect much sympathy from his father. He only hoped that Benjamin had not argued against him when the congress had discussed his predicament. But surely, he thought, Sally or Temple should have offered some support. Elizabeth lay prostrate. The "least sudden Noise almost throws her into Hysterics," he wrote. She had no "relations or connexions" to comfort her. More than at any time since she had first arrived in America, she felt like a foreigner in an inhospitable land.[36] Even after both Sally and Temple wrote, apologizing profusely and claiming that they knew nothing about the Franklins' ordeal until they had received his letter, William was not appeased. He simply refused to believe that they were the only ones in America who were ignorant of his plight. If they did not know, he refrained from saying, it was because Benjamin Franklin had kept them in the dark.

As the elder Franklin continued working feverishly to move America ever closer to independence, his son chafed at his own helplessness. Bored, worried, and frustrated, he often lashed out at those whose affection he valued most. He engaged in a prolonged quarrel with Temple over his son's spendthrift ways. He spent hours writing in his diary, carefully noting every insult he received in anticipation of the time when he could have his revenge on those who treated him so shabbily. Elizabeth was sick throughout most of the winter. When she was able to write a letter or two, her sense of loss was obvious. "Everything," she told Sally, "is now changed." The "joyous, social evenings" that had once characterized life at the governor's mansion were a thing of the past.[37]

In February 1776, the Continental Congress voted to send Benjamin Franklin along with two other delegates to Canada in an effort to persuade the former French province to join the struggle against England. The mission had little chance for success. Most Canadians had no complaints against British rule, and they had every reason to distrust American motives. Even the efforts of a skilled negotiator such as Franklin and the presence of Charles Carroll, a Catholic, as a member of the delegation would probably prove fruitless. Even so, Pennsylvania moderates viewed the proposed trip with the suspicion it no doubt deserved. It was another indication that America was edging closer to independence. A little over a week after the trip was announced, a delegation from the Pennyslvania assembly met with Franklin, asking for his resignation from the lower house. Franklin readily complied. Ostensibly, the legislators claimed that they wanted him to step down because he had so little time to devote to the interests of his constituents. In fact, the assembly wanted to dissociate itself with someone who was so publicly committed to the destruction of the empire. Franklin saw the assembly's request as evidence that many colonies, including his own, were still dominated by those who would do everything in their power to halt America's snail-like progress toward independence.

William Franklin was even more concerned about his father's plans for the Canadian trip than were the members of the Pennsylvania assembly. He recognized the political implications of the congress's efforts to seek a Canadian alliance. Moreover, he had personal as well as political reasons for his unhappiness with Benjamin's decision to accept this particular congressional assignment. While he may have quit writing to his father, his affection for the man whose support and guidance had always meant so much to him had not diminished. Thus, when he heard about the trip to Canada, William was unabashedly concerned. The trip was much too arduous for a man his father's age. Why, just for once, could he not leave the work of independence to someone else? Moreover, the trip signaled a complete and final break in their relationship. When Benjamin and the other members of the delegation passed through Woodbridge, just north of Perth Amboy, Franklin made no effort to contact a man he must now have counted as one of the enemy. "Nothing," William said, "ever gave me more Pain than his undertaking that journey, nor would anything give me more Pleasure than to hear he had resolved to quit all public Business."[38] But neither William nor Benjamin Franklin was destined to abandon his public duties.

The governor had good reason to fear for his father's well-being on the Canadian expedition. From the beginning, the trip was a disaster. When the emissaries arrived at Montreal in May 1776, they found the American troops there penniless and demoralized. Most Canadians opposed the American war effort, and Franklin predicted that it would not be long before the troops would have to abandon the region entirely. Franklin left the delegation on May 11. He had no sense that further efforts on his part would produce a satisfactory result. Moreover, he was weak and exhausted. By the end of the month he was in New York, growing "daily more feeble."[39] He reached Philadelphia in June, suffering from the gout and not a little depressed. He left town for most of the month to escape the press of business that made it impossible for him to recuperate.

It was just as well that Franklin did not attend many meetings throughout May or June. His absence spared the congress acute embarrassment, and himself considerable anguish, as the Philadelphia government began the process that would result in the arrest and incarceration of William Franklin. On May 10, while Benjamin was still in Montreal, the congress took the first step that would commit America irrevocably to independence, when it resolved that it was "absolutely irreconcilable to reason and good Conscience" for Americans to swear allegiance to "any government under the crown of Great Britain." Five days later, the delegates called for the formation of new governments in those colonies where "no government sufficient to the exigence of their affairs" existed.[40] In essence they were encouraging Americans to abandon their allegiance to the colonial regimes and to create new governments in their place.

William Franklin quickly responded to the challenge issued by the Continental Congress. Throughout the long winter he had brooded quietly as events drifted out of his control. At last he could take some action. The congress had tipped its hand. Its resolves were tantamount to a declaration of independence. If Franklin correctly assessed the views of most people in New Jersey, now was the time for a bold move. He remained convinced that most colonists feared separation from Great Britain as much as they opposed parliamentary taxation. Thanks to the congress, the colonists could no longer pretend that they did not realize that their actions were leading inexorably toward independence. The time was right for Franklin to ask New Jersey's inhabitants to choose between king and congress.

Two weeks after the congressional resolutions, William Franklin ordered his assembly to convene in Perth Amboy on June 20. He had some definite goals in mind. Admiral Richard Howe was due to arrive in the colonies at any moment. He was coming with instructions to make one last effort to resolve the differences dividing England and America. While Franklin knew by now that New Jersey would never sign a separate agreement with the mother country, he hoped to persuade the assembly at least to meet with the admiral and consider whatever proposals he might make. Moreover, he hoped that simply by meeting with his legislators he could give the lie to anyone's thoughts that in New Jersey no legitimate government "sufficient to the exigence of their affairs" existed. Franklin wanted one more chance to duel with his enemies for the loyalty of a colony he had come to think of as home. He never got that chance.

The governor's enemies moved immediately when they heard of his audacious plan to convene the assembly. A new provincial congress, whose members were more radical than the old ones, met in Burlington at the beginning of June. On the 14th, the congress called on all New Jersey legislators to boycott the assembly. The next day, it declared that by trying to convene the legislature Franklin had put himself "in direct contempt and violation of the resolve of the Continental Congress." Thus, he was "an enemy to the liberties of this country," and they decided to take measures to ensure that he would do no further damage to New Jersey's resistance movement.[41] Adding insult to injury, the provincial congress stopped payment of the governor's salary, thus signaling an end to the colony's support of the king's government. The congress had, claimed the outraged governor, illegally usurped not only the king's power but the rights of the assembly as well.

The Continental Congress did not interfere with New Jeresy's efforts to unseat the royal governor, and so the provincial congress forged ahead. On June 15, its members ordered Colonel Nathaniel Heard to arrest William Franklin, telling him to act with "all the delicacy and tenderness which the nature of the business can possibly admit."[42] They knew how important their decision was. "We are," said one delegate, "passing the Rubicon":[43] They could not turn back. Still, most New Jersey leaders hoped that they would not have to incarcerate the governor. If he would give his word not to interfere with their activities, they planned to allow him to retire quietly to Princeton, to Bordentown, or to his own farm on Rancocas Creek. If, however, he continued his stubborn refusal to recognize reality, then Colonel Heard would have to take him into custody. The decision lay squarely with the governor.

On June 17, Colonel Heard, accompanied by Major Jonathan Deare, a Perth Amboy native, arrived at the governor's door and asked William to give his word (or parole) that he would neither flee the colony nor attempt to interfere with the provincial congress. The governor contemptuously refused, demanding as he did so "by what authority" such an "impertinent" order had been issued.[44] Heard was prepared for Franklin's reaction. He produced two documents indicating that he acted under orders of the provincial congress. The governor was not impressed. He did not recognize the congress's authority. Moreover, he could not imagine how anyone could accuse him of attempting to destroy his country's liberties merely because he had tried to convene a duly elected body of the people's representatives. By seeking the advice of the assembly, he was protecting the liberties of New Jersey's inhabitants, while the provincial congress, an illegal body of self-appointed radicals, was usurping the rights of the people. Franklin turned on his heel, slamming the door in Heard's face. He would give no parole to any illegal congress.

Heard, just as undaunted as the governor, posted a guard around the house, while Franklin strode to his library, writing down every word of his conversation with the colonel. He also began to draft a message to the members of his council and the assembly. Acting as both a lawyer and a politician, he pleaded his case before a tribunal whose members he would never see again in his official capacity. He cast himself in the role of an American patriot, as a defender of the rights of Englishmen, especially the rights of representative assemblies. He had convened New Jersey's lawmakers, he insisted, because he thought they would welcome the opportunity to consider the grave issues that lay before them. Indeed, he believed that his failure to call an assembly would have opened him up to the legitimate criticism of king and colony alike. He simply wanted to offer the legislators a chance to discuss their options and defend their rights. Was this the action of a tyrant?

He alone, Franklin claimed, was defending the frame of government that had worked so well for the colony in the past. He had served New Jersey honorably for thirteen years, and he had every desire to continue serving both his country and his king. He had not abandoned either his post or his people. They had abandoned him. Unlike the "pretended patriots" in the provincial congress, whose "pernicious design" was to replace British liberty with "an Independent Republican Tyranny," Franklin wanted to guarantee the integrity of all branches and all interests.[45] He valued New Jersey's stability as well as its liberty, while his enemies were interested only in the liberties of the people. They did not care about balance, order, or stability. As a result, Franklin predicted, their views would lead inevitably to anarchy, followed by democratic tyranny, "the worse and most debasing of all possible Tyrannies."[46] Stubbornly optimistic, he maintained that there was still time for the people of New Jersey to come to their senses, rising up against the men who were destroying their lives. "Depend upon it," he predicted, "you can never place yourselves in a happier situation than in your ancient constitutional dependency on Great Britain. No Independent State ever was or ever can be so happy as we have been, and might still be, under that government."[47] For their own sake, as well as for the people they represented, Franklin hoped that the members of the provincial congress would wake up before it was too late.

As Franklin finished his address to an assembly that no longer existed, he was satisfied that he had presented himself in the best possible light. Laying down his pen, he repeated a vow that had rung like a refrain throughout his long, and generally successful, administration: "*No Office or Honour in the Power of the Crown to bestow, will ever influence me to forget or neglect the Duty I owe my Country, nor the most furious Rage of the most intemperate Zealots induce me to swerve from the Duty I owe His Majesty*."[48] Fine words, indeed. By now, however, William Franklin was no more willing to serve both king and country than was the "most intemperate zealot" against whom he railed.

William and the nearly hysterical Elizabeth sat back and waited for the congress's next move. For three days they saw only their servants and the raucous sentries who guarded every door and window. Meanwhile, the provincial congress struggled with the question of what to do with the stubborn and potentially dangerous governor. Many members worried that if he were allowed to go free, he would try to set himself up as a symbol around which counterrevolutionary elements in the colony might rally. To be sure, loyalists everywhere were in disarray. Those who could afford to do so, men like Joseph Galloway for instance, had already fled the country for the safety of England. The rest seemed to be waiting for English military forces to take the lead in quelling the American rebellion. Still, especially in a moderate colony like New Jersey, the concerns of the provincial congress were not totally chimerical. In April 1776 rebel forces had barely managed to derail New York Governor William Tryon's abortive plot to kidnap General George Washington. It was not beyond the realm of possibility that William Franklin would make a similar effort.

Thus the members of New Jersey's self-proclaimed government asked the Continental Congress for permission to arrest the governor and remove him from New Jersey. The congress, surely relieved that the elder Franklin was out of town when it considered New Jersey's request, responded in the affirmative, merely asking the provincial congress to question Franklin personally, giving him one more chance to accept defeat gracefully, before going forward with its plans.

On June 19, 1776, Heard and Deare ordered the governor to prepare for a journey to Burlington. At 3:30 that afternoon, surrounded by sixteen men armed with guns and bayonets, Franklin's carriage rolled away from the governor's mansion. The effort to arrest the governor in January had been a mere dress rehearsal. This was the real thing.

On his first journey from Perth Amboy to Burlington, Franklin had been a newly appointed governor. His father had sat proudly at his side, and church bells had pealed in jubilation as he rode into town. Now his oath of loyalty to the Crown was the object of mockery, not a badge of honor. Stripped of his dignity, stared at by curious farmers and shopkeepers, subject to the catcalls of unsympathetic onlookers, he tried to ignore his surroundings as he wondered what fate his future held for him.

Franklin's worst fears were soon realized. On the 21st of June, two delegates from the provincial congress arrived at his quarters in Burlington with orders to escort him to congressional headquarters. When Franklin faced his captors, he confronted an assemblage of nervous but determined men. Samuel Tucker, the president of the provincial congress, stood before him. Doctor John Witherspoon, the Presbyterian head of the College of New Jersey, stood to the president's left. Tucker began the session, saying that he had a few questions for "Mr." Franklin. William bristled at Tucker's deliberate omission of his title, and he refused to answer even the most reasonable questions put to him. To respond would have legitimized the proceedings of an illegal assembly. Instead, he defiantly presented a list of his own grievances. He had been falsely accused of being an enemy of his country. Congress had robbed him of his salary and his liberty and was now using an illegitimate tribunal to convict him for crimes he had not committed. "Do as you please," he said, "and make the best of it."[49] With that he fell silent. Like his father at the Cockpit, he took no notice of the proceedings against him.

The provincial congress's verdict was a foregone conclusion. But once Tucker's efforts to question Franklin had failed, no one knew how to proceed. The room fell silent, until John Witherspoon leaped to his feet, launching a vicious personal attack against the still silent governor. His arms flailing wildly, he became more sarcastic, more vituperative the longer he continued. He denigrated William's political beliefs, his fine airs, his claims of gentility, even reminding his audience that the man who stood before him was nothing but a base-born bastard. Having cut the governor down to size, he moved that the provincial congress return William Franklin to his quarters while its members discussed his fate. The motion passed without dissent, and the obdurate governor left the room. With Franklin out of the way, the members of the provincial congress found it easier to dispose of an unpleasant task. Clearly, they said, Franklin was a "virulent enemy to this country," and they asked the Continental Congress to designate a place for the governor's confinement.[50]

When he heard the verdict, Franklin tried to rally public opinion, writing yet another defense of his conduct and smuggling it out of his quarters. But the provincial congress blocked his every move. "Poor men!" cried Franklin.

"They can no more bear the light of truth, it seems, than Owls can endure the light of the sun!"[51] All he asked was a public forum. "This," he insisted, without appreciating the irony of his request, "every honest man must allow I have a right to insist on, if not as a Governor, yet as a native of America, and a freeholder of New Jersey."[52] It was a measure of his fear that he began to demand not the prerogatives of a Crown official but the rights of an English subject.

For the first time, he even wavered, hinting that he might sign a congressional parole. He was, he insisted, not an enemy of the American people. He loved his country. He honored his king. For him, the two were inseparable. "*Pro Rege & Patria* was the Motto I assumed when I first commenced my Political Life," he said, "and I am resolved to retain it till Death shall put an end to my mortal Existence."[53]

Despite Franklin's attempts to ward off the inevitable, the Continental Congress moved with dispatch. By the 25th of June, William had received notice that he would be placed in the custody of Connecticut Governor Jonathan Trumbull. The next day, flushed with fever and, according to his friends, much too sick to travel, he was on his way to Hartford. Before he left Burlington, Franklin wrote to his son. Significantly, he was worried that his incarceration might poison the relationship between Temple and Benjamin. This he wished to avoid at any cost, and he begged his son to be "dutiful and Attentive" to his grandfather and to watch over Elizabeth as well.[54] On July 4, 1776, eight days after he left Burlington, William Franklin rode into Hartford, Connecticut.

Even as the governor had traveled toward the Connecticut capital, the Continental Congress was putting the finishing touches on the Declaration of Independence. On June 7, 1776, Richard Henry Lee, a Virginia delegate, had presented the Congress with a resolution calling for American independence. The congress debated Lee's resolution for the next two days. No one questioned the need for independence. A few, especially members of Pennsylvania's delegation, thought the declaration's timing was wrong. They wanted to postpone the inevitable. Finally, the congress agreed to give the middle colonies time to rally support for Lee's motion, deciding to delay the vote on independence. In the meantime, however, it also appointed a committee to draft a declaration of independence. Benjamin Franklin was one of the members of the committee. He was, however, still suffering from the effects of his trip to Canada, and he played only a minor role in composing the document. He left that task to Thomas Jefferson, the congress's youngest delegate. On July 2, with the delegation of New York abstaining, the Continental Congress voted to separate from England. Two days later, it formally adopted the Declaration of Independence.

Benjamin Franklin was in Philadelphia to vote for a separation from a king and empire he had once venerated. The grand end for which he had been working so tirelessly for so long was about to become a reality. Surprisingly, Franklin's surviving letters do not even discuss his vote on independence or his reaction to what should have been a momentous occasion. Perhaps the final decision was simply an anticlimax. Besides, the decision signaled a beginning, not an end. Independence, once declared, had to be won. And Franklin was already doing what he could to make the declaration a reality. There would be time enough later to think about the implications of the colonists' decision to repudiate their dependent status and embark on new and uncharted seas.

For the moment, there was a state constitution to be written for Pennsylvania, and someone had to make a stab at creating some form of government for the newly independent states. He also had agreed to serve as a member of an unofficial delegation to visit Admiral Richard Howe, who had finally arrived in America and wanted to discuss terms of reconciliation with the colonies whose independence he did not recognize. Franklin thought the trip was a waste of time. He had no interest in pursuing negotiations with a "Warlike Nation" whose "Lust of Dominion" had destroyed the empire. He had, he said, always labored "to preserve from breaking, that fine and noble China Vase the British Empire: for I knew that being once broken, the separate Parts could not retain even their Share of the Strength or Value that existed in the Whole."[55] Now that china vase was shattered. The first British Empire was in the process of disintegration. So, unfortunately, was the long and once valuable relationship between Benjamin and William Franklin.

NOTES

[1]WF to New Jersey Assembly, 23 June 1776, Revolutionary Era MSS, New Jersey Historical Society, Newark.

[2]*Autobiography,* 185.

[3]BF to WF, 18 Feb. 1774, *PBF* 21:108.

[4]BF to [Joseph Priestley], 7 July 1775, ibid. 22:93.

[5]BF to Jonathon Shipley, 15 May 1775, ibid., 42.

[6]BF to [Joseph Priestley], 16 May 1775, ibid., 44.

[7]BF to WF, 5 Jan. 1774, ibid. 21:9.

[8]Joseph Galloway to BF, 12 Oct. 1772, ibid. 19:331.

[9]Joseph Galloway to BF, 27 Sept. 1770, ibid. 17:229.

[10]BF to WF, 22 Mar. 1775, ibid. 21:551.

[11][Joseph Galloway to WF], 26 Mar. 1775, F. W. Ricord and William Nelson, eds., *Documents Relating to the Colonial History of the State of New Jersey* (1757–67) 10:582.

[12]WF to Lord Dartmouth, 5 June 1775, ibid., 604.

[13]BF to [Joseph Priestley], 7 July 1775, *PBF* 22:91.

[14]Lord Dartmouth to WF, 7 June, 5 July 1775, Ricord and Nelson, *Documents* 10:643, 645–47.

[15]WF to BF, 14 Aug. 1775, *PBF* 22:170. It is likely, as some historians have suggested, that Benjamin was willing to help his son because he was trying to protect Temple's interests. Ibid., 325, 326.

[16]WF to William Temple Franklin, 9 Oct. 1775, Franklin Papers 101:6, American Philosophical Society, Philadelphia.

[17]WF to Lord Dartmouth, 2 Aug. 1775, Ricord and Nelson, *Documents* 10:563.

[18]WF to Lord Dartmouth, 5 Sept. 1775, ibid., 658.

[19]Ibid., 659.

[20]BF to David Hartly, 12 Sept. 1775; to Jonathan Williams, Jr., 12 Sept. 1775; to Jonathan Shipley, 13 Sept. 1775, *PBF* 22:196; 198; 199.

[21]BF to David Hartley, 3 Oct. 1775, ibid., 217.

[22]Jane Mecom to Catherine Greene, 24 Nov.[–2 Dec.] 1775, ibid., 272.

[23]WF to Lord Stirling, 15 Sept. 1775, Charles Pettit to Lord Stirling, 7 Sept. 1775, William Alexander Papers 4, New York Historical Society, New York.

[24]WF to Lord Dartmouth, 3 Oct. 1775; Ricord and Nelson, *Documents* 10:663.

[25]See Larry Gerlach, *Prologue to Independence: New Jersey in the Coming of the Revolution* (New Brunswick: Rutgers University Press, 1976), 287–90.

[26]Ricord and Nelson, *Documents* 10:689–91.

[27]WF to Lord Dartmouth, 5 Jan. 1776, ibid., 677, 678.

[28]This description of WF's arrest is taken largely from Sheila Skemp, *William Franklin: Son of a Patriot, Servant of a King* (New York: Oxford University Press, 1990), chap. 11.

[29]WF to Lord Dartmouth, 8 Jan. 1776, Ricord and Nelson, *Documents* 10:699.

[30]Ibid., 699, 700.

[31]Ibid., 700.

[32]WF to Lord Germain, 28 Mar. 1776, ibid., 703.

[33]Ibid., 703.

[34]Ibid.

[35]Ibid., 706.

[36]WF to William Temple Franklin, 22 Jan. 1776, Franklin Papers 101:10.

[37]Elizabeth Franklin to Sarah Bache, New Jersey Historical Society *Proceedings*, 2nd ser., 5 (1877): 128.

[38]WF to William Temple Franklin, 3 June 1776, Franklin Papers, 101:16.

[39]BF to Charles Carroll and Samuel Chase, 27 May 1776, *PBF* 22:440.

[40]Worthington C. Ford, ed., *Journals of the Continental Congress, 1774–1789* (Washington, D.C.: 1904), 4:342, 357, 358.

[41]*Minutes of the Provincial Council of Safety of the State of New Jersey* (Trenton, 1879), 454–57.

[42]Ibid., 457, 458.

[43]Jonathon Dickinson Sergeant to John Adams, 15 June 1776, Paul H. Smith, *Letters of Delegates to Congress, Aug. 1774–1783,* (Washington D.C.: Library of Congress, 1976–), 4:224.

[44]WF to Legislature of New Jersey, 17 June 1776, Ricord and Nelson, *Documents* 10:721.

[45]Ibid., 726.

[46]Ibid.

[47]Ibid.

[48]Ibid., 728.

[49]WF to New Jersey Assembly, 23 June 1776, Revolutionary Era MSS, New Jersey Historical Society.

[50]*Minutes of the Provincial Council,* 470.

[51]WF to New Jersey Assembly, 23 June 1776, Revolutionary Era MSS, New Jersey Historical Society.

[52]WF to New Jersey Assembly, 22 June 1776, Ricord and Nelson, *Documents* 10:730.

[53]WF to New Jersey Assembly, 23 June 1776, Revolutionary MSS, New Jersey Historical Society.

[54]WF to William Temple Franklin, 25 June 1776, Franklin Papers 101:18, American Philosophical Society.

[55]BF to Lord Howe, 20 July 1776, *PBF* 22:520.

EPILOGUE

Benjamin and William Franklin did not meet again until after the Revolution. William remained a prisoner in Connecticut for more than two years, first at Wallingford and then at Middletown. At first, his accommodations were tolerable, and as a gentleman he was allowed to roam the countryside at will. Unfortunately, he used his freedom to render covert aid to the British army, granting pardons to the farmers he met on those not so innocent rides on the outskirts of town. Consequently, at the beginning of May 1777, the defiant prisoner was removed from his lodgings in Middletown and marched forty miles to Litchfield, where he remained in solitary confinement for nearly eight months. There, in his cramped and dirty lodgings, his captors watched him constantly, denying him the use of pen or paper and allowing him almost no contact with the outside world. By this time, most colonial leaders saw Franklin as a threat to their cause.

Benjamin did not lift a hand to secure his son's freedom or even to make his imprisonment more comfortable. Rather, he viewed William's predicament with singular detachment and only reluctantly offered his daughter-in-law any financial support. Indeed, when he sent Elizabeth sixty dollars to help meet her barest expenses, he brusquely reminded her that many others suffered more than she did. By now, he had only two passions. He wanted to win the independence that America had declared in July 1776. And he was determined to keep Temple from embracing the loyalist doctrines that permeated the very air the boy breathed whenever he visited his stepmother at Perth Amboy.

So long as Benjamin remained in America, he could not stop Temple from visiting Elizabeth at her "Tory House."[1] But at the end of September 1776, he found a way to serve both of his passions, when the congress named him as one of three American commissioners to France.[2] Franklin accepted his commission with alacrity, taking sixteen-year-old Temple with him as his personal secretary. He had, he proclaimed, "rescued a valuable young man from the danger of being a Tory, and fixed him in honest republican principles."[3] By October, Temple had left Perth Amboy to join his grandfather in Philadelphia, and by the end of the month Temple, Benjamin, and Sally's son, seven-year-old Benjamin Franklin Bache, were on their way to France.

Benjamin Franklin devoted the war years to the service of his country. His universal reputation as a scientist and political philosopher preceded him to Paris, and he was treated with respect, even awe, by some of France's most renowned luminaries. So long as he remained in France, Franklin played the role of modest republican for all it was worth. Still, he lived a life of opulence that would have surprised, even disappointed, many of the leaders whose cause he so ably represented.[4] In fact, Franklin was perfectly suited to his new role. A seasoned politician who was adept at the gamesmanship that characterized diplomatic activity in the eighteenth century, he enjoyed the intrigue in which he was involved, even while he was a shrewd, indeed tough, bargainer.

For William Franklin, the American Revolution was neither so pleasant nor so rewarding. He was finally released from Litchfield jail in October 1778, at the age of forty-eight. He emerged a bitter man. His wife had died while he was in captivity. Elizabeth had endured both enemy and friendly occupations of Perth Amboy. But when the British army abandoned the East Jersey capital in the spring of 1777, she had fled the advancing American troops and accompanied the army to New York. She survived the journey, but the cumulative effect of her miseries finally took their toll on her delicate constitution. She died, William always insisted, "of a broken heart."[5]

Franklin left Connecticut for the protection of British-controlled New York at the end of October 1778. His property had been confiscated, his salary discontinued, his health nearly broken. He had already paid a heavier price for his loyalty than any other colonial governor. Still, he did not yet join the some eighty thousand loyalists who fled the country.

Instead, Franklin became an unofficial spokesman for all loyal Americans, speaking out against General Henry Clinton's lethargic war effort, seeking help for needy refugees, and interceding on behalf of loyalist prisoners of war. In 1780, he became president of the Board of Associated Loyalists, an American paramilitary outfit that organized and equipped loyalist units and planned guerrilla raids on rebel strongholds. Clinton never trusted the Associated Loyalists. He resented their criticisms of his conduct of the war. Moreover, he had no desire to share power with mere Americans, however loyal they might be. And he always feared that the board would alienate moderate Americans, making his own task more difficult. Thus, he kept the board on a short leash, and it was never as effective as Franklin thought it could be. Still, it was the one loyalist organization that won the official, if reluctant, sanction of the British government.

After the defeat of General Cornwallis at Yorktown in 1781, the war, for all practical purposes, was over. Lord North resigned from the ministry to be replaced by the Earl of Rockingham. Parliament began to press for negotiations that would bring an end to the hostilities between England and its former colonies. William Franklin's Associated Loyalists tried to keep those hostilities alive, ordering the capture and execution of rebel officer Joshua Huddy in a vain effort to disrupt peace negotiations between the British and American forces. Benjamin, from his post in France, worked with John Jay and John Adams to negotiate an end to the war. While Franklin angled for a cession of Canada and an admission of guilt on the part of the British, he had one great aim: American independence. All else was secondary, and this the negotiators achieved. By the end of 1782, the Americans were ready to sign a treaty with the British that recognized their independence. Perhaps not surprisingly, it was Benjamin Franklin who fought hardest against the British request that the new American government compensate the former loyalists for the losses they sustained as a result of the war.

While Benjamin celebrated his and America's victory, his son left his native land in the fall of 1782 for the life of an exile in England, the cloud cast by the execution of Joshua Huddy still hanging over his head. Once in England, he tried to influence the peace negotiations, lobbying especially hard for provisions that would benefit American loyalists. In this, as in so many other efforts in these years, he was basically unsuccessful. Only after the Peace of Paris had been signed did William make an effort to patch up the differences between him and his father. The war was over. He had lost. Now it was time to let bygones be bygones, to "revive that affectionate Intercourse and Connection which till the Commencement of the late Troubles had been the Pride and Happiness of [his] Life." He refused to apologize for his part in the war. "I uniformly acted from a Strong Sense of what I conceived my Duty to my King and Regard to my Country," he said. "If I have been mistaken, I cannot help it. It is an Error of Judgment that the maturist reflection I am capable of cannot rectify, and I verily believe were the same Circumstances to occur Tomorrow, my Conduct would be exactly similar to what it was heretofore." Still, he begged his father for a "personal interview," hoping that now that he had "broken the ice," he and Benjamin might be friends once more.[6]

Benjamin was unmoved. "Nothing," he said, "has hurt me so much and affected me with such keen Sensations as to find myself deserted in my old Age by my only Son; and not only deserted, but to find him taking up Arms against me, in a Cause wherein my good Fame, Fortune and Life were all at Stake."[7] Had William taken a neutral position, he might have forgiven his son. He could not tolerate an active loyalist (see Part Two, Document 8).

The two men saw one another only once after the war. In 1785, as Benjamin was preparing to leave for home, bringing both Temple and Benjamin Bache with him, they met briefly at Southampton. The hurried visit was not cordial. Benjamin persuaded William to sell Temple his New Jersey lands for a paltry two thousand pounds sterling. He also insisted that he turn over some property he owned in New York in lieu of a debt of fifteen hundred pounds he still owed his father. His business with William at an end, Benjamin returned to America. This would be the last time he would cross the Atlantic.

As he reached the age of seventy-nine, Benjamin's contributions to his country were nearly at an end. He was appointed as delegate to the Constitutional Convention held in his own Philadelphia in 1787. His contributions were few, but despite his fading health, he never missed a session. Moreover, his presence at the convention lent it a certain dignity whose importance is impossible to calculate.

In 1788, Franklin retired from public business, living with his daughter until his death in 1790. He died without forgiving his son. Two years before his death, he added a codicil to his will, leaving William some worthless lands in Nova Scotia and the books and papers William already had in his possession. "The part he acted against me in the late War," he explained tersely, "which is of public Notoriety, will account for my leaving him no more of an Estate he endeavored to deprive me of."[8]

William remained in England until his death in 1814. He got some compensation from a parliamentary commission designed to reward those Americans who had suffered losses as a result of their loyalty to the king, but the sum was paltry. To add insult to injury, many English subjects professed to believe that this son of the infamous Benjamin Franklin was not really a loyal Crown servant at all. They claimed that he and his father had been in collusion from the beginning, deliberately supporting opposite sides so that no matter what the outcome of the war, the Franklins would come out on top. Thus William suffered the indignity of having to prove his loyalty to the commission. He always suspected that his relatively small compensation could be explained by the distrust many men harbored for anyone with the last name of Franklin.

In 1788, Franklin married Mary D'Evelyn, an Irish gentlewoman whose companionship helped him fill the many lonely hours that stretched before him. In 1792, Temple returned to England. William's son seemed to have inherited all of his father's and grandfather's charms but none of their virtues. A spendthrift and a dilettante, in 1798 he compounded his difficulties when he fathered an illegitimate daughter, Ellen. Like Benjamin before him, William took care of his son's child, but the strain proved too much. Temple abruptly left for Paris, living with another woman, and all contact between the two men ended. Still, William waited nine years before altering his will, leaving most of his estate to his granddaughter.

In 1811, after a long and painful illness, Mary Franklin died. William was more alone than he had ever been. Joseph Galloway had died in 1803. Sally was gone in 1808. He had no contact with Temple. "I must resign myself," he said, "for the remaining Days of my Existence to that Solitary State which is most repugnant to my Nature."[9] Ironically, his thoughts often turned to his father. His letters were dotted with references to Benjamin Franklin. He began plans for writing a biography of his father. And whenever he looked at Ellen, he was reminded of Benjamin, to whom he insisted she bore a remarkable resemblance.

In 1812, Temple wrote asking for a reconciliation. Unlike his own father, William was pathetically eager for an end to the estrangement with his son. Temple promised to come to England, but somehow he never found the time. William died two years later, without seeing Temple again.

NOTES

[1]BF to William Temple Franklin, 19 Sept. 1776, *PBF* 22:613.

[2]The other two Commissioners were Silas Deane and Arthur Lee.

[3]BF to Richard Bache , 2 June 1779, Albert Henry Smith, *The Writings of Benjamin Franklin* (New York: Macmillan, 1907–09), 7:344, 345.

[4]See Esmond Wright, *Franklin of Philadelphia* (Cambridge, Mass.: Harvard University Press, 1986), 265, 266.

[5]WF to Lord Germain, 10 Nov. 1778, PRO 654 CO5/1002, p. 16, Library of Congress.

[6]WF to BF, 22 July 1784, Franklin Papers MSS, American Philosophical Society, Philadelphia.

[7]BF to WF, 16 Aug. 1784, Smyth, *Writings* 9:252.

[8]BF will codicil, 23 June 1789, Franklin Papers MSS, American Philosophical Society, Philadelphia.

[9]WF to Jonathan Williams, Jr., 28 Oct. 1811, Jonathan Williams Collections, Film 455, American Philosophical Society, Philadelphia.

PART TWO

The Documents

1

WILLIAM FRANKLIN

Letter to Benjamin Franklin

September 7, 1765

In September 1765, Benjamin Franklin was in London, working to attain a royal charter for the colony of Pennsylvania. His son was in Burlington where he was facing his first real test as New Jersey's royal governor. William Coxe, a friend of both Franklins, had just resigned his commission as stamp distributor, and the governor had to deal with the consequences of what he clearly saw as a cowardly and treacherous action. When he described his predicament to his father, William tried to put his colony in the best possible light, as he indicated that Coxe's action was unnecessary and that New Jersey was, in fact, disposed to obey the Stamp Act. The letter is a measure of the helplessness that William Franklin felt as he tried to enforce unpopular policy in New Jersey, even while the ministry gave him little guidance or support. He, like all royal governors, found the task of governing the American colonies to be more and more difficult after 1765.

What motives does William Franklin attribute to the Stamp Act protesters? How does he characterize his own and his colony's actions? What influence did he have in London? In the colonies?

Burlington, Septr. 7, 1765
10 P.M.

Honoured Sir

Having just heard that there is a Vessel to sail for Bristol Tomorrow Morning from Philadelphia, I embrace the Opportunity to send you a Copy of a Letter I this Week receiv'd from Mr. Coxe, with my Answer, and a Letter from our Speaker to the Speaker of Massachusetts Bay. Mr. Coxe never consulted me on his Resignation, but on the contrary told me about 10 Days ago that he should certainly do his utmost to execute the Office; and at that Time he executed before me a Bond[1] sent over to him for the Purpose by the

[1]Stamp distributors had to post a hefty deposit with the ministry to guarantee that they would execute their jobs faithfully.

William Franklin to Benjamin Franklin, September 7, 1765, Public Record Office, London. From Leonard Labaree, ed., *The Papers of Benjamin Franklin* (New Haven: Yale University Press, 1968), 12:260–62.

Secretary of the Stamp Office in England. If he had been threaten'd or insulted on the Occasion, and could not have received Protection from the Government, his Resignation would have been excuseable. But I can't learn that he has received any Threats, or was likely to receive the least Obstruction in the Execution of his Office, so that his Surrender is not only using the Gentleman ill who recommended him to the Office, but the Province in general, as it may subject them to be thought as culpable as the N. England Governments. The Messrs. Smiths here,[2] and indeed most of the Inhabitants, are so angry with him on this Account that they have a Mind to publish something against him in the News-papers by way of Vindication of the Colony. They imagine that Mr. Coxe's Letters will go by this Vessel, and would therefore be glad that you would lay the enclosed Letters before the Treasury, and inform their Lordships that Mr. Coxe is alone to blame for this extraordinary Procedure.

I have as yet received no directions from the Ministry relative to the Stamp Act, but if I should be impowered to appoint an Officer, pro Tempore, for distributing Stamps, upon the Death or Refusal of the one appointed from Home (as is the Case in the Customs) I doubt not but I shall be able to procure one that will execute the Office, with little or no Trouble. I could wish that it might be obtained for Capt. Davenport, but as the Officer is, I understand, to be bound himself in a Bond of £2,000 Sterling besides other Securities, I don't know how that Matter can be managed.

Governor Colden,[3] I'm told, is putting the Fort in a Posture of Defence, has ordered his Son to move in there with all his Effects, and is determined that he shall execute the Stamp Office till one is appointed from Home. He has got some Soldiers from the General, and the Men of War are drawn up before the Town to protect the Stamps when they arrive.

The Boston Writers have basely spirited up the People there to rise and destroy Mr. Oliver's House,[4] on Account of his being the Stamp Officer, &c. But, as is usual with Mobs when they once feel their own Power, they have gone much beyond what was desired by those who first raised them, and destroy'd the Houses, and plundered the Effects of several even of those who were against the Stamp Act, particularly Mr. Hutchenson the Lieut. Govr. But I must refer you to the Papers which I enclose, for further Particulars.

The Behaviour of these Mobs has intimidated most of the Stamp Officers, and occasioned them to resign. But Mr. Hughes[5] was with me last Sunday,

[2]The Smith brothers, all of whom were from Burlington, were John, a leading defender of the Quakers; Samuel, a New Jersey historian; and Richard, a clerk of the New Jersey assembly.

[3]Cadwallader Colden, governor of New York during the Stamp Act controversy.

[4]Andrew Oliver, a member of the Massachusetts council and the designated stamp distributor for the colony.

[5]John Hughes, stamp distributor for Pennsylvania and a good friend of Benjamin and William Franklin.

and seemed determin'd to hold out to the last. It is said the Presbyterians of N. England have wrote to all their Brethren throughout the Continent, to endeavor to stir up the Inhabitants of each Colony to act as they have done, in hopes of thereby making it appear to the Ministry too difficult a Matter to call them to account for their late outrageous Conduct.

Mr. Hughes, and your Friends at Philadelphia will I suppose write to you by this Conveyance, which makes it less necessary for me to say any thing of their Politics, and indeed, I have only Time to add Betsy's Duty, and that of Honoured Sir Your affectionate Son

Wm: Franklin

2

BENJAMIN FRANKLIN

Letter to William Franklin

November 9, 1765

On November 1, 1765, the Stamp Act was slated to go into effect. Eight days later, Benjamin Franklin met with Lord Dartmouth, who had recently assumed the duties of president of the Board of Trade. Naturally, the two men discussed the Stamp Act. Franklin was not reluctant to admit his opposition to the act, but his objections were couched in practical terms, as he emphasized the difficulty Parliament would have in enforcing it. He did his best to avoid discussions that emphasized constitutional principle. Admittedly, this was the wisest tactic for him to take, for the ministry had made it clear that it would not entertain any arguments that called parliamentary sovereignty into question.

What tactics for repealing the Stamp Act does Franklin suggest? What practical obstacles to enforcing the Stamp Act does England face? What is Franklin's attitude toward England and the empire in 1765? Why would Parliament find it difficult to respond to American protests by repealing the Stamp Act?

Benjamin Franklin to William Franklin, November 9, 1765, Historical Society of Pennsylvania. From Leonard Labaree, ed., *The Papers of Benjamin Franklin* (New Haven: Yale University Press, 1968), 12:361–65.

. . . I had a long Audience on Wednesday with Lord Dartmouth. He was highly recommended to me by Lords Grantham and Bessborough, as a young Man of excellent Understanding and the most amiable Dispositions. They seem'd extremely intent on bringing us together. I had been to pay my Respects to his Lordship on his Appointment to preside at the Board of Trade; but during the Summer he has been much out of Town, so that I had not till now the Opportunity of conversing with him. I found him all they said of him. He even exceeded the Expectations they had raised in me. If he continues in that Department, I foresee much Happiness from it to American Affairs. He enquired kindly after you, and spoke of you handsomely.

I gave it him as my Opinion, that the general Execution of the Stamp Act would be impracticable without occasioning more Mischief than it was worth, by totally alienating the Affections of the Americans from this Country, and thereby lessening its Commerce. I therefore wish'd that Advantage might be taken of the Address expected over (if express'd, as I hop'd it would be, in humble and dutiful Terms) to suspend the Execution of the Act for a Term of Years, till the Colonies should be more clear of Debt, and better able to bear it, and then drop it on some other decent Pretence, without ever bringing the Question of Right to a Decision. And I strongly recommended either a thorough Union with America, or that Government here would proceed in the old Method of Requisition, by which I was confident more would be obtained in the Way of voluntary Grant, than could probably be got by compulsory Taxes laid by Parliament. That particular Colonies might at Times be backward, but at other Times, when in better Temper, they would make up for that Backwardness, so that on the whole it would be nearly equal. That to send Armies and Fleets to enforce the Act, would not, in my Opinion, answer any good End; That the Inhabitants would probably take every Method to encourage the Soldiers to desert, to which the high Price of Labour would contribute, and the Chance of being never apprehended in so extensive a Country, where the Want of Hands, as well as the Desire of wasting the Strength of an Army come to oppress, would encline every one to conceal Deserters, so that the Officers would probably soon be left alone. That Fleets might indeed easily obstruct their Trade, but withal must ruin great Part of the Trade of Britain; as the Properties of American and British or London Merchants were mix'd in the same Vessels, and no Remittances could be receiv'd here; besides the Danger, by mutual Violences, Excesses and Severities, of creating a deep-rooted Aversion between the two Countries, and laying the Foundation of a future total Separation. I added, that notwithstanding the present Discontents, there still remain'd so much Respect in America for this Country, that Wisdom would do more towards reducing Things to order, than all our Force; And that, if the Address expected from the Congress of the Colonies should be unhappily such as could not be made the Foundation of a Suspension of the Act, in that Case three or four wise and good Men, Personages of some Rank and Dignity, should be sent over to America, with a Royal Commission to enquire into Grievances, hear Complaints, learn the true State of Affairs, giving Expectations of Redress where they found the People really aggriev'd, and endeavouring to convince and reclaim them by Reason, where they found them in the Wrong. That such an Instance of the Considerateness, Moderation and Justice of this Country towards its remote Subjects would contribute more towards securing and perpetuating the Dominion, than all its Force, and be much cheaper. A great deal more I said on our American Affairs; too much to write. His Lordship heard all with great Attention and Patience. As to the Address expected from the Congress, he doubted some Difficulty would arise about receiving it, as it was an irregular Meeting, unauthoriz'd by any American Constitution. I said, I hoped Government here would not be too nice on that Head;[1] That the Mode was indeed new, but to the People there it seem'd necessary, their separate Petitions last Year being rejected. And to refuse hearing Complaints and Redressing Grievances, from Punctilios about Form, had always an ill Effect, and gave great Handle to those turbulent factious Spirits who are ever ready to blow the Coals of Dissension. He thank'd me politely for the Visit, and desired to see me often.

It is true that Inconveniences may arise to Government here by a Repeal of the Act, as it will be deem'd a tacit giving up the Sovereignty of Parliament: And yet I think the Inconveniences of persisting much greater, as I have said above. The present Ministry are truely perplex'd how to act on the Occasion: as, if they relax, their Predecessors will reproach them with giving up the Honour, Dignity, and Power of this Nation. And yet even they, I am told, think they have carry'd Things too far; So that if it were indeed true that I had plann'd the Act (as you say it is reported with you) I believe we should soon hear some of them exculpating themselves by saying I had misled them. I need not tell you that I had not the least Concern in it. It was all cut and dry'd, and every Resolve fram'd at the Treasury ready for the House, before I arriv'd in England, or knew any thing of the Matter; so that if they had given me a Pension on that Account (as is said by some, I am told) it would have been very dishonest in me to accept of it. . . .

I think there is no Doubt, but that tho' the Stamp Act should be repeal'd some Mulct[2] or Punishment will be inflicted on the Colonies, that have suffered the Houses of Officers, &c. to be pull'd down; especially if their respective Assemblies do not immediately make Reparation.

[1]Too legalistic about that point.
[2]Fine or penalty.

3

JOHN DICKINSON

From *"Letters from a Farmer in Pennsylvania to the Inhabitants of the British Colonies"*

1767, 1768

In 1767, Lord Charles Townshend proposed, and Parliament enacted, legislation known as the Townshend Acts, which placed duties on such English imports as paper, paint, lead, glass, and tea. Townshend planned to use the revenues earned from the acts to help defray the expense of defending England's overseas empire and to pay the salaries of governors and other Crown officers in the colonies. The colonists insisted that, like the Sugar and Stamp Acts, the Townshend Acts were another example of taxation without representation and that as such they denied Americans their rights as English citizens. When American leaders dealt with the problems created by the Townshend Acts, they walked a fine line. They wanted to resist implementation of the acts; yet they did not want to encourage the riots that, in many colonies, had gotten out of hand during the Stamp Act controversy.

Pennsylvanian John Dickinson tried to rise to the occasion with his "Letters from a Farmer," printed in many newspapers throughout the colonies in the winter of 1767–68. Letter II offered a spirited but reasoned attack on the Townshend Acts, as it tried to draw a line between regulating trade, which Parliament had a right to do, and taxing the colonies, which he thought was unconstitutional.

What is John Dickinson's view of America's role in the British Empire? If you were a member of Parliament, how would you react to Dickinson's efforts to define your duties and rights? How does he argue that the Stamp Act marked a fundamental change in British policy? Is he right?

Letter II

My dear Countrymen,

There is another late Act of Parliament, which appears to me to be unconstitutional and as destructive to the liberty of these colonies, as that

---

John Dickinson, "Letters from a Farmer in Pennsylvania to the Inhabitants of the British Colonies," in Samuel E. Morison, ed., *Sources and Documents Illustrating the American Revolution, 1764–1788,* 2nd ed. (Oxford: Clarendon Press, 1929), mentioned in my last letter; that is, the Act for granting the duties on paper, glass, etc.

The Parliament unquestionably possesses a legal authority to regulate the trade of Great Britain and all her colonies. Such an authority is essential to the relation between a mother country and her colonies; and necessary for the common good of all. He, who considers these provinces as States distinct from the British Empire, has very slender notions of justice, or of their interests. We are but parts of a whole; and therefore there must exist a power somewhere to preside, and preserve the connexion in due order. This power is lodged in the Parliament; and we are as much dependent on Great Britain as a perfectly free people can be on another.

I have looked over every statute relating to these colonies, from their first settlement to this time; and I find every one of them founded on this principle till the Stamp Act administration. All before are calculated to regulate trade and preserve or promote a mutually beneficial intercourse between the several constituent parts of the Empire; and though many of them imposed duties on trade, yet those duties were always imposed with design to restrain the commerce of one part, that was injurious to another, and thus to promote the general welfare. The raising a revenue thereby was never intended. Thus the king, by his judges in his courts of justice, imposes fines which all together amount to a very considerable sum and contribute to the support of government: but this is merely a consequence arising from restrictions that only meant to keep peace and prevent confusion; and surely a man would argue very loosely, who should conclude from hence that the king has a right to levy money in general upon his subjects. Never did the British Parliament, till the period above mentioned, think of imposing duties in America *for the purpose of raising a revenue*. Mr. Grenville first introduced this language, in the preamble to the 4 Geo. III, c. 15, which has these words: "And whereas it is just and necessary that a revenue be raised in Your Majesty's said dominions in America, for defraying the expences of defending, protecting, and securing the same: We, Your Majesty's most dutiful and loyal subjects, the Commons of Great Britain, in Parliament assembled, being desirous to make some provision in this present session of Parliament, towards raising the said revenue in America, have resolved to give and grant unto Your Majesty the several rates and duties herein after mentioned," etc.[1]

A few months after came the Stamp Act, which reciting this, proceeds in the same strange mode of expression, thus: "And whereas it is just and necessary that provision be made for raising a further revenue within Your Majesty's dominions in America, towards defraying the said expences, we

[1]The Sugar or Revenue Act of 1764.

Your Majesty's most dutiful and loyal subjects, the Commons of Great Britain, etc., give and grant," etc., as before.

The last Act, granting duties upon paper, etc., carefully pursues these modern precedents.[2] The preamble is, "Whereas it is expedient that a revenue should be raised in Your Majesty's dominions in America, for making a more certain and adequate provision for defraying the charge of the administration of justice, and the support of civil government in such provinces, where it shall be found necessary; and towards the further defraying the expences of defending, protecting, and securing the said dominions, we Your Majesty's most dutiful and loyal subjects, the Commons of Great Britain, etc., give and grant," etc., as before.

Here we may observe an authority expressly claimed and exerted to impose duties on these colonies; not for the regulation of trade; not for the preservation or promotion of a mutually beneficial intercourse between the several constituent parts of the Empire, heretofore the sole objects of parliamentary institutions; but for the single purpose of levying money upon us.

This I call an innovation; and a most dangerous innovation. It may perhaps be objected that Great Britain has a right to lay what duties she pleases upon her exports, and it makes no difference to us whether they are paid here or there. To this I answer: these colonies require many things for their use, which the laws of Great Britain prohibit them from getting anywhere but from her. Such are paper and glass. That we may legally be bound to pay any general duties on these commodities relative to the regulation of trade, is granted; but we being obliged by the laws to take from Great Britain any special duties imposed on their exportation to us only, with intention to raise a revenue from us only, are as much taxes upon us as those imposed by the Stamp Act.

What is the difference in substance and right whether the same sum is raised upon us by the rates mentioned in the Stamp Act, on the use of paper, or by these duties on the importation of it? It is only the edition of a former book, shifting a sentence from the end to the beginning.

Suppose the duties were made payable in Great Britain.

It signifies nothing to us, whether they are to be paid here or there. Had the Stamp Act directed that all the paper should be landed at Florida, and the duties paid there before it was brought to the British colonies, would the Act have raised less money upon us, or have been less destructive of our rights? By no means: for as we were under a necessity of using the paper, we should have been under the necessity of paying the duties. Thus, in the present case, a like necessity will subject us, if this Act continues in force, to the payment of the duties now imposed.

[2]The Townshend Acts.

Why was the Stamp Act then so pernicious to freedom? It did not enact, that every man in the colonies should buy a certain quantity of paper—No: It only directed that no instrument of writing should be valid in law if not made on stamped paper.

The makers of that Act knew full well that the confusions that would arise from the disuse of writings would compel the colonies to use the stamped paper, and therefore to pay the taxes imposed. For this reason the Stamp Act was said to be a law that would execute itself. For the very same reason, the last Act of Parliament, if it is granted to have any force here, will execute itself, and will be attended with the very same consequences to American liberty.

Some persons perhaps may say that this Act lays us under no necessity to pay the duties imposed, because we may ourselves manufacture the articles on which they are laid; whereas by the Stamp Act no instrument of writing could be good, unless made on British paper, and that too stamped. . . .

Here then, my dear countrymen, ROUSE yourselves, and behold the ruin hanging over your heads. If you ONCE admit that Great Britain may lay duties upon her exportations to us, *for the purpose of levying money on us only,* she then will have nothing to do but to lay those duties on the articles which she prohibits us to manufacture—and the tragedy of American liberty is finished. We have been prohibited from procuring manufactures, in all cases, anywhere but from Great Britain (excepting linens, which we are permitted to import directly from Ireland). We have been prohibited in some cases from manufacturing for ourselves, and may be prohibited in others. We are therefore exactly in the situation of a city besieged, which is surrounded by the works of the besiegers in every part but one. If that is closed up, no step can be taken, but to surrender at discretion. If Great Britain can order us to come to her for necessaries we want, and can order us to pay what taxes she pleases before we take them away, or when we land them here, we are as abject slaves as France and Poland can show in wooden shoes and with uncombed hair.

Perhaps the nature of the necessities of dependent states, caused by the policy of a governing one, for her own benefit, may be elucidated by a fact mentioned in history. When the Carthaginians were possessed of the island of Sardinia, they made a decree, that the Sardinians should not raise corn, nor get it any other way than from the Carthaginians. Then, by imposing any duties they would upon it, they drained from the miserable Sardinians any sums they pleased; and whenever that oppressed people made the least movement to assert their liberty, their tyrants starved them to death or submission. This may be called the most perfect kind of political necessity.

4

WILLIAM FRANKLIN

Letter to Lord Hillsborough

November 23, 1768

After Parliament had passed the Mutiny or Quartering Act in 1765, the relationship between Governor William Franklin and Lord Hillsborough, the president of the Board of Trade and the secretary of the American Department, reached its nadir. Two issues divided the adversaries. In the winter of 1768, the Massachusetts legislature sent a circular letter to the colonies calling for united action against the Townshend Acts. Hillsborough ordered all governors to prohibit their assemblies from replying to the Bay Colony initiative, but his instructions arrived in New Jersey after the assembly had already written to the Massachusetts lawmakers. Hillsborough accused Franklin of poor judgment and perhaps even of disloyalty for allowing his assembly to respond.

The second issue was that, like many colonial governors, Franklin was hard put to persuade his assembly to supply the king's troops stationed in New Jersey in ways that conformed with the strict letter of the law. When Franklin refused to veto two technically unacceptable supply bills, Hillsborough censured his conduct. Stung by the secretary's rebuke and concerned that for whatever reason New Jersey had been unfairly singled out for the minister's reproach, he wrote a freewheeling defense of his own and his colony's conduct. Not content with explaining his decision to approve the supply bills, he discussed every grievance he had endured as New Jersey's royal governor—from his inadequate salary to his disagreements with British imperial policy.

What does Franklin's letter reveal about the obstacles facing colonial governors in these years? To whom does he assign most of the blame for his own difficulties—the English ministers or his assembly? How does Franklin use pragmatic appeals rather than arguments on the basis of principle to persuade Hillsborough to alter his course? How do you think that the New Jersey assembly would have reacted to Franklin's letter, if its members had had a chance to read it?

William Franklin to Lord Hillsborough, November 23, 1768, Public Record Office, American and West Indies, vol. 172 (162). From Frederick W. Ricord and William Nelson, eds., *Documents Relating to the Colonial History of the State of New Jersey, 1767–1776* (Newark: Daily Advertiser's Printing House, 1886), 10:64–95.

To the Rt Hon[ble] the Earl of Hillsborough

Burlington New Jersey Nov[r]. 23[d] 1768

My Lord,

The Animadversions and Censures which your Lordship, in your Letter No. 13, has thought proper to make upon my Conduct during the last Session of the Assembly of this Colony, give me much Concern; but my Uneasiness would be far greater were I not conscious that they are unmerited, and that it is in my Power to prove them so to every impartial Person. As such, I flatter myself I may address your Lordship, as you have, with the greatest Appearance of Candor and Impartiality, been kindly pleas'd to say, "that you should be happy, by my Explanation of the Motives of my Conduct, to find that there has not been so just Grounds for those Animadversions as you have too much Foundation to apprehend." This Explanation, my Lord, I shall therefore give you fully and freely, as it is a Duty I owe to your Lordship's Station, and to my own Character.

The first Matter mentioned by your Lordship is, That "His Majesty is concerned to find by the printed Votes of the House of Representatives, (transmitted by me) that they have thought fit, by their Resolutions and Proceedings, if not openly to deny at least to draw into Question the Power and Authority of Parliament to enact Laws binding upon the Colonies in all Cases whatever." As this relates to the Assembly only, whose Sentiments or Conduct I am no ways concerned to vindicate, and as I have myself neither openly nor privately deny'd or call'd in question the Power of Parliament, it is not necessary for me to urge any thing in my own Behalf on this Head. I shall therefore only observe to your Lordship, that the Right of Parliament to lay Taxes on the Colonies is not questioned by the Assembly of New-Jersey alone, but also by every other House of Representatives on the Continent. Your Lordship, however, says "The King is the more surpriz'd at such a Conduct in his Assembly of *New-Jersey,* when His Majesty considers the Example set them by the Assemblies of the neighbouring Colonies of *New-York* and *Pensylvania,* who appear to have entertained a *very just sense* of the unwarrantable Measure recommended by the Assembly of Massachusets Bay." But I do assure you my Lord, that whoever gave the King such Information respecting the Assemblies of New-York and Pensylvania, has been greatly mistaken. . . .

[The governor goes on to describe the reaction to the Massachusetts circular letter in New York and Pennsylvania, in an effort to show that the actions of the New Jersey assembly were "not singular" but in fact were similar to those of other colonies—Ed.]

My Motive in giving your Lordship so particular an account of the Transactions of the Assemblies of New York and Pennsylvania, is not to palliate or justify the Conduct of the Assembly of New Jersey, but merely to shew that they have not been singular on the occasion, and that even the Colonies which his Majesty thought had set them an Example to the contrary, had acted in a manner nearly similar. Indeed I think it my Duty to assure your Lordship, while I am on this Subject, that it is my firm Opinion, That there is scarce an Assembly man in America, but what either believes that the Parliament has not a Right to impose Taxes for the Purposes of a Revenue in America, or thinks that it is contrary to Justice, Equity and Sound Policy to exercise that Right, under the present Circumstances of the Colonies, supposing it ever so unquestionable.

The Disputes between Great Britain and her Colonies on this Head are of the utmost Importance to the British Interest, and tho' they have now subsisted for several years seem not the nearer being settled. The Parliament, it is true, did by an Act passed in the 6th year of his present Majesty,[1] declare that they had full Power & Authority to make Laws binding upon the Colonies in all Cases, whatever; and this Act, tho' it was far from satisfying the Minds of the Colonists as to the Point of Right, yet they in general quietly acquiesc'd in it, upon a Supposition that the Parliament would be contented with having made that Declaration of their Power, and never attempt to exercise it more in raising a Revenue within the Colonies. But when an Act passed last year "for granting certain Duties in the Colonies & Plantations in America,"[2] it immediately rekindled the Flame that had subsided from the Time of the Stamp Act, and has occasioned as general Dissatisfaction and Uneasiness as ever prevailed among any People. A Military Force has been sent over, which I believe, will have the good Effect to prevent such scandalous Riots, and Attacks on the Officers of Government, as had before prevail'd in the Town of Boston, and probably be a Means of hindring (for some Time at least) any public Opposition being given to the Execution of Acts of Parliament. But this does not remove the principal Difficulty. Mens Minds are sour'd, a sullen Discontent prevails, and, in my Opinion, no Force on Earth is sufficient to make the Assemblies acknowledge, by any Act of theirs, that the Parliament has a Right to impose Taxes on America. And tho' the People may, for a while, avoid publickly opposing Duties and Taxes laid on them by Great Britain, yet I apprehend that, as long as this Temper continues, they will do all in their Power, in their private Capacities, to prevent the consumption of British Manufactures in the Colonies, that the Mother Country may thereby lose more in her Commerce than she can possibly gain by way of Revenue. . . .

[Franklin goes on to defend himself, at some length, from various specific

[1]The Declaratory Act of 1766.
[2]The Townshend Acts.

attacks on his and New Jersey's conduct that had emanated from Lord Hillsborough.—Ed.]

But nothing contain'd in your Lordship's Letter has more astonish'd me, than that Part where you mention that "you have receiv'd the King's Commands to "Signify to me His Majesty's Disapprobation of my Conduct in assenting to the Act [passed in June 1767] for making Provision for Quartering His Majesty's Troops, notwithstanding a Law of the same Nature, passed in 1766, had been before rejected by His Majesty in Council, for the same Reasons." I have that Confidence in the Goodness & Justice of my Royal Master, which persuades me to believe that this could not have happened, had the Matter been rightly represented to His Majesty. It is possible that your Lordship may be unacquainted with the Circumstances of that Transaction, as it was previous to your Appointment to the American Department. I must therefore beg leave to state them fully to your Lordship, that you may be the better enabled to judge whether my Conduct in this respect has really merited the Censure it has receiv'd. The *first* Act of Assembly for Supplying the King's Troops quartered within this Province with Necessaries was passed in *June* 1766, the Year after the Act of Parliament for that Purpose. When I transmitted it to the then Secretary of State I wrote to him concerning it, as follows, *"In the Act for Supplying the several Barracks erected in this Colony with Furniture, and other Necessaries for accommodating the King's Troops in, or marching through this Colony,* they have, instead of Specifying the several Articles required to be furnished by the late Act of Parliament, impowered the Barrack Masters to provide *Firewood, Bedding, Blankets, & such other Necessaries as have been heretofore usually furnished to the several Barracks within this Colony*. I did all I could to prevail on them to insert the *very Words* of the *Act of Parliament,* and to impower the Barrack Master to furnish, at the expence of the Province, the *same Articles* as were therein required. But it was to no Purpose. They said they had always furnish'd every Thing which was necessary; that the Officers & Soldiers who had been quarter'd here never complain'd, but on the contrary many of them acknowledg'd they were better accommodated here than they had ever been at Barracks in Europe: They added, that they look'd upon the Act of Parliament for quartering Soldiers in America, to be virtually as much an Act for laying Taxes on the Inhabitants as the Stamp Act, and that it was more partial as the Troops were kept in a few of the Colonies. I was therefore oblig'd to take the Act as it was tendered, or to let His Majesty's Troops remain unprovided with Necessaries. I have, however, the Pleasure of finding the Regiment station'd in this Province perfectly Satisfy'd with their Quarters. No Complaints whatever have been made to me, and I believe there are but few if any Articles of Consequence required by the Act of Parliament but what they are furnished with here." . . .

[Franklin describes, in considerable detail, his dealings with the New Jersey assembly over the issue of the Mutiny Act. In the process, he tries to defend both his and the assembly's actions.—Ed.]

His Lordship had indeed wrote to me on the 18th of *July,* that "His Majesty was displeas'd at the *Assembly* for having avoided a complete Obedience to an Act of the British Parliament," &c but his Lordship did not give me the least Intimation in this Letter that *my Conduct* in Passing it was in any wise disapprov'd, nor acquaint me whether the New Jersey Law of 1766 was or was not disallowed, and if he had, it was then too late to prevent the Law of 1767.—Had I understood before the Passing of this Law that the one passed in 1766 was repealed, and that His Majesty disapprov'd of *my Conduct* in having *assented* to it, or had I receiv'd any Intimation from the King's Ministers that I must not, on any Consideration whatever, give my Assent to a Law for that Purpose, unless it was a complete Obedience in every respect to the Act of Parliament, I should not on any Account have acted contrary. But as I receiv'd no Commands or Intimations of the kind, I was induced to think that I was left to act, as I had done before, in the best Manner I could for His Majesty's Service, & the Publick Good; and that if it should not be in my Power, after using my utmost Endeavors, to obtain these Purposes exactly in the Manner required, I was then to obtain them in the best way I could, and not for mere Modes to Sacrifice Essentials. This, I know, has hitherto been the Rule of Conduct with several other Governors, as well as myself; and many Instances may be given where Governors in order to carry His Majesty's Measures into Execution, and to serve the Public, have been obliged to deviate from the strict Letter of the King's Instructions. But no Instance do I remember of the Govr being blam'd for such a Deviation, especially where the principal End of the Instruction was obtain'd: And tho' the Deviation in the present Case is from a Mode prescribed by an Act of Parliament, yet I humbly conceive, the same Occasion, (the King's Service and the Publick Interest,) will justify this as well as the other. I do not mean, however, that Governors have, or ought to have a Power of Dispensing with Acts of Parliament, but only that they may be at Liberty, where Circumstances render it necessary, to consent to some small Deviation from the *Mode,* provided the *principal End* of the Act is obtain'd, and the Deviation is not contrary or repugnant to *that*. . . .

[Franklin continues to defend his willingness to accept the New Jersey assembly's supply bill, pointing out that he had very little leverage in the colony. He had virtually no patronage power, and his own salary was very small. This meant that he had a difficult time earning the proper deference from members of his own assembly.—Ed.]

I beg your Lordship's Pardon for the Length of this Letter. I could have made it shorter, but that I was unwilling to omit any Circumstance which might explain the Motives of my Conduct, or have a Tendency to remove His Majesty's Displeasure,—than which Nothing could affect me more sensibly, as I have long valued myself on a strict Performance of my Duty, and the strongest Attachment to my Sovereign. I hope that I have not, in the Course of my Defence, dropt any Expression which can any way offend your Lordship. I am sure it was not my Intention. I have the highest respect for your Lordship's Character, and greatly wish to stand well in your Lordship's Opinion. If I succeed in Removing His Majesty's Displeasure, and your Lordship's Prejudices against my Conduct, I shall be happy. But whatever may be the Event, my Sentiments of Duty and Loyalty will remain the same, and I shall chearfully Submit to the Pleasure of that King whom it has hitherto been my chief Glory to serve faithfully.

I have the Honor to be, with the greatest Respect,

My Lord, Your Lordship's
most obedient & most humble Servant
W.m Franklin

5

BENJAMIN FRANKLIN

"Causes of the American Discontents before 1768"

January 1768

Parliament's decision to pass the Townshend Acts in 1767 caused Benjamin Franklin to rethink his attitude toward Anglo-American relationships, even as it put him in the limelight, forcing him to defend the colonial position more vigorously and more publicly than he had done throughout the Stamp Act controversy. The following excerpt from an essay published in The London Chronicle in January 1768 goes over well-worn ground as it summarizes the imperial debate over the Stamp Act, the Mutiny or Quartering Act, and the Townshend Acts. At the same time, it reveals Franklin's evolving perspective on imperial issues. In it, Franklin casts himself as an "impartial historian" who

Benjamin Franklin, "Causes of the American Discontents Before 1768," January 1768, *The London Chronicle,* 5–7 January 1768. From William B. Wilcox, ed., *The Papers of Benjamin Franklin* (New Haven: Yale University Press, 1972), 15:3–13.

is simply explaining—but not necessarily advocating—the colonial position. By 1768, he was emphasizing the constitutional, not just the practical, reasons behind colonial opposition to parliamentary taxation.

Why did Americans object to the ministry's decision to pay the salaries of royal officeholders? What is the nature of the relationship between England and America that Franklin envisions? How has that relationship begun to change? What evidence does the essay provide that might make some readers believe there was indeed a ministerial conspiracy to destroy American liberty?

To the Printer of *The London Chronicle*

The Waves never rise but when the Winds blow.—Prov.

Sir,

As the cause of the present ill humour in America, and of the resolutions taken there to purchase less of our manufactures, does not seem to be generally understood, it may afford some satisfaction to your Readers, if you give them the following short historical state of facts.

From the time that the Colonies were first considered as capable of granting aids to the Crown, down to the end of the last war, it is said, that the constant mode of obtaining those aids was by *Requisition* made from the Crown through its Governors to the several Assemblies, in circular letters from the Secretary of State in his Majesty's name, setting forth the occasion, requiring them to take the matter into consideration; and expressing a reliance on their prudence, duty and affection to his Majesty's Government, that they would grant such sums, or raise such numbers of men, as were suitable to their respective circumstances.

The Colonies being accustomed to this method, have from time to time granted money to the Crown, or raised troops for its service, in proportion to their abilities; and during all the last war beyond their abilities, so that considerable sums were return'd them yearly by Parliament, as they had exceeded their proportion.

Had this happy method of Requisition been continued, (a method that left the King's subjects in those remote countries the pleasure of showing their zeal and loyalty, and of imagining that they recommended themselves to their Sovereign by the liberality of their voluntary grants) there is no doubt but all the money that could reasonably be expected to be rais'd from them in any manner, might have been obtained, without the least heart-burning, offence, or breach of the harmony, of affections and interests, that so long subsisted between the two countries.

It has been thought wisdom in a Government exercising sovereignty over different kinds of people, to have some regard to prevailing and established opinions among the people to be governed, wherever such opinions might in their effects obstruct or promote publick measures. If they tend to obstruct publick service, they are to be changed, if possible, before we attempt to act against them; and they can only be changed by reason and persuasion. But if publick business can be carried on without thwarting those opinions, if they can be, on the contrary, made subservient to it, they are not unnecessarily to be thwarted, how absurd soever such popular opinions may be in their natures. This had been the wisdom of our Government with respect to raising money in the Colonies. It was well known, that the Colonies universally were of opinion, that no money could be levied from English subjects, but by their own consent given by themselves or their chosen Representatives: That therefore whatever money was to be raised from the people in the Colonies, must first be granted by their Assemblies, as the money raised in Britain is first to be granted by the House of Commons: That this right of granting their own money, was essential to English liberty: And that if any man, or body of men, in which they had no Representative of their chusing, could tax them at pleasure, they could not be said to have any property, any thing they could call their own. But as these opinions did not hinder their granting money voluntarily and amply whenever the Crown by its servants came into their Assemblies (as it does into its Parliaments of Britain or Ireland) and demanded aids; therefore that method was chosen rather than the hateful one of arbitrary taxes.

I do not undertake here to support these opinions of the Americans; they have been refuted by a late Act of Parliament,[1] declaring its own power; which very Parliament, however, shew'd wisely so much tender regard to those inveterate prejudices, as to repeal a tax that had militated against them. And those prejudices are still so fixed and rooted in the Americans, that, it has been supposed, not a single man among them has been convinced of his error, even by that Act of Parliament.

The person then who first projected to lay aside the accustomed method of Requisition,[2] and to raise money on America by Stamps, seems not to have acted wisely, in deviating from that method (which the Colonists looked upon as constitutional) and thwarting unnecessarily the fixed prejudices of so great a number of the King's subjects. It was not, however, for want of knowledge that what he was about to do would give them great offence; he appears to have been very sensible of this, and apprehensive that it might occasion some disorders, to prevent or suppress which, he projected another Bill, that was

[1]The Declaratory Act of 1766.
[2]Lord Grenville.

brought in the same Session with the Stamp Act, whereby it was to be made lawful for military Officers in the Colonies to quarter their soldiers in private houses. This seem'd intended to awe the people into a compliance with the other Act. Great opposition however being raised here against the Bill by the Agents from the Colonies, and the Merchants trading thither, the Colonists declaring, that under such a power in the Army, no one could look on his house as his own, or think he had a home, when soldiers might be thrust into it and mix'd with his family at the pleasure of an officer, that part of the Bill was dropt; but there still remained a clause, when it passed into a Law, to oblige the several Assemblies to provide quarters for the soldiers, furnishing them with firing, bedding, candles, small beer or rum, and sundry other articles, at the expence of the several Provinces. And this Act continued in force when the Stamp Act was repealed, though if obligatory on the Assemblies, it equally militated against the American principle abovementioned, *that money is not to be raised on English subjects without their consent.*

The Colonies nevertheless being put into high good humour by the repeal of the Stamp Act, chose to avoid fresh dispute upon the other, it being temporary and soon to expire, never, as they hoped, to revive again; and in the meantime they, by various ways in different Colonies, provided for the quartering of the troops, either by acts of their own Assemblies, without taking notice of the A[cts] of P[arliamen]t, or by some variety or small diminution, as of salt and vinegar, in the supplies required by the Act, that what they did might appear a voluntary act of their own, and not done in obedience to an A[ct] of P[arliamen]t which, according to their ideas of their rights, they thought hard to obey.

It might have been well if the matter had thus passed without notice; but a G[overno]r[3] having written home an angry and aggravating letter upon this conduct in the Assembly of his Province, the outed P[rojecto]r of the Stamp Act[4] and his adherents then in the opposition, raised such a clamour against America, as being in rebellion, and against those who had been for the repeal of the Stamp Act, as having thereby been encouragers of this supposed rebellion, that it was thought necessary to inforce the Quartering Act by another Act of Parliament, taking away from the Province of New York, which had been the most explicit in its refusal, all the powers of legislation, till it should have complied with that act. The news of which greatly alarmed the people every where in America, as (it has been said) the language of such an act seemed to them to be, Obey implicitly laws made by the Parliament of Great Britain to raise money on you without your consent, or you shall enjoy no rights or privileges at all.

[3]Probably Sir Henry Moore, governor of New York.
[4]Lord Grenville.

At the same time a Person lately in high office,[5] projected the levying more money from America, by new duties on various articles of our own manufacture, as glass, paper, painters colours, &c. appointing a new Board of Customs, and sending over a set of Commissioners with large salaries to be established at Boston, who were to have the care of collecting those duties; which were by the act expressly mentioned to be intended for the payment of the salaries of Governors, Judges, and other Officers of the Crown in America; it being a pretty general opinion here, that those Officers ought not to depend on the people there for any part of their support.

It is not my intention to combat this opinion. But perhaps it may be some satisfaction to your Readers to know what ideas the Americans have on the subject. They say then as to Governors, that they are not like Princes whose posterity have an inheritance in the government of a nation, and therefore an interest in its prosperity; they are generally strangers to the Provinces they are sent to govern, have no estate, natural connection, or relation there, to give them an affection for the country; that they come only to make money as fast as they can; are sometimes men of vicious characters and broken fortunes, sent by a Minister merely to get them out of the way; that as they intend staying in the country no longer than their government continues, and purpose to leave no family behind them, they are apt to be regardless of the good will of the people, and care not what is said or thought of them after they are gone. Their situation at the same time gives them many opportunities of being vexatious, and they are often so, notwithstanding their dependance on the Assemblies for all that part of their support that does not arise from fees established by law; but would probably be much more so, if they were to be supported by money drawn from the people without their consent or good will, which is the professed design of this new act. That if by means of these forced duties Government is to be supported in America, without the intervention of the Assemblies, their Assemblies will soon be looked upon as useless, and a Governor will not call them, as having nothing to hope from their meeting, and perhaps something to fear from their enquiries into and remonstrances against this Mal-administration. That thus the people will be deprived of their most essential rights. That it being, as at present, a Governor's interest to cultivate the good will by promoting the welfare of the people he governs, can be attended with no prejudice to the Mother Country, since all the laws he may be prevailed on to give his assent to are subject to revision here, and if reported against by the Board of Trade, are immediately repealed by the Crown; nor dare he pass any law contrary to his instructions, as he holds his office during the pleasure of the Crown, and his Securities are liable for the penalties of their bonds if he contravenes those instructions. This is what they say as to

[5]Lord Townshend.

Governors. As to *Judges* they alledge, that being appointed from hence, and holding their commissions *not* during *good behaviour,* as in Britain, but during *pleasure,* all the weight of interest or influence would be thrown into one of the scales, (which ought to be held even) if the salaries are also to be paid out of duties raised upon the people without their consent, and independent of their Assemblies approbation or disapprobation of the Judges behaviour. That it is true, Judges should be free from all influence; and therefore, whenever Government here will grant commissions to able and honest Judges during good behaviour, the Assemblies will settle permanent and ample salaries on them during their commissions: But at present they have no other means of getting rid of an ignorant or an unjust Judge (and some of scandalous characters have, they say, been sometimes sent them) but by starving him out.

I do not suppose these reasonings of theirs will appear here to have much weight. I do not produce them with an expectation of convincing your readers. I relate them merely in pursuance of the task I have impos'd on myself, to be an impartial historian of American facts and opinions.

The colonists being thus greatly alarmed, as I said before, by the news of the Act for abolishing the Legislature of New-York, and the imposition of these new duties professedly for such disagreeable purposes; (accompanied by a new set of revenue officers with large appointments, which gave strong suspicions that more business of the same kind was soon to be provided for them, that they might earn these salaries;) began seriously to consider their situation, and to revolve afresh in their minds grievances which from their respect and love for this country, they had long borne and seemed almost willing to forget. They reflected how lightly the interest of all America had been estimated here, when the interest of a few inhabitants of Great Britain happened to have the smallest competition with it. . . . It is time then to take care of ourselves by the best means in our power. Let us unite in solemn resolutions and engagements with and to each other, that we will give these new officers as little trouble as possible, by not consuming the British manufactures on which they are to levy the duties. Let us agree to consume no more of their expensive gewgaws.[6] Let us live frugally, and let us industriously manufacture what we can for ourselves: Thus we shall be able honourably to discharge the debts we already owe them, and after that we may be able to keep some money in our country, not only for the uses of our internal commerce, but for the service of our gracious Sovereign, whenever he shall have occasion for it, and think proper to require it of us in the old *constitutional* manner. For notwithstanding the reproaches thrown out against us in their

[6]A term often used by Benjamin Franklin to describe frivolous items that Americans imported into the colonies.

public papers and pamphlets, notwithstanding we have been reviled in their Senate as *Rebels* and *Traitors,* we are truly a loyal people. Scotland has had its rebellions, and England its plots against the present Royal Family; but America is untainted with those crimes; there is in it scarce a man, there is not a single native of our country, who is not firmly attached to his King by principle and by affection. But a new kind of loyalty seems to be required of us, a loyalty to P[arliamen]t; a loyalty, that is to extend, it is said, to a surrender of all our properties, whenever a H[ouse] of C[ommons], in which there is not a single member of our chusing, shall think fit to grant them away without our consent; and to a patient suffering the loss of our privileges as Englishmen, if we cannot submit to make such surrender. We were separated too far from Britain by the Ocean, but we were united to it by respect and love, so that we could at any time freely have spent our lives and little fortunes in its cause: But this unhappy new system of politics tends to dissolve those bands of union, and to sever us for ever.

These are the wild ravings of the at present half distracted Americans. To be sure, no reasonable man in England can approve of such sentiments, and, as I said before, I do not pretend to support or justify them: But I sincerely wish, for the sake of the manufactures and commerce of Great Britain, and for the sake of the strength which a firm union with our growing colonies would give us, that these people had never been thus needlessly driven out of their senses. I am, your's, &c.

6

WILLIAM FRANKLIN

Speech to the New Jersey Assembly

January 13, 1775

In January 1775, Governor William Franklin convened his assembly at Perth Amboy. He hoped to convince its members to ignore the efforts of the Continental Congress to present a united front to England. Rather, he wanted the legislators to act on their own, to submit a separate petition to the Crown for the redress of any grievances that they may have harbored against England. Significantly, he couched his pleas in terms that any American patriot would

William Franklin, speech to the New Jersey Legislature, January 13, 1775, *Votes and Proceedings of the General Assembly of the Colony of New Jersey* (Burlington: Isaac Collins, 1775), 5–7.

have had a hard time condemning, as he begged the lawmakers to defend their legal right to represent their constituents' interests and to prevent an illegal congress from usurping their constitutional rights. The address represented Franklin's respect for the law, his belief in balanced government, and his support for the time-honored rights of colonial assemblies.

If you were a New Jersey legislator in January 1775, how would you react to Franklin's plea to petition the British government for redress of American grievances? How would you respond to his claim that the assembly is responsible for upsetting the balance of the British government?

Gentlemen of the Council, and Gentlemen of the Assembly,

It would argue not only a great Want of Duty to His Majesty, but of Regard to the good People of this Province, were I, on this Occasion, to pass over in Silence the late alarming Transactions in this and the neighbouring Colonies, or not endeavour to prevail on you to exert yourselves in preventing those Mischiefs to this Country, which, without your timely Interposition, will, in all Probability, be the Consequence.

It is not for me to decide on the particular Merits of the Dispute between Great-Britain and her Colonies, nor do I mean to censure those who conceive themselves aggrieved for aiming at a Redress of their Grievances. It is a Duty they owe themselves, their Country, and their Posterity. All that I would wish to guard you against, is the giving any Countenance or Encouragement to that destructive Mode of Proceeding which has been unhappily adopted in Part by some of the Inhabitants in this Colony, and has been carried so far in others as totally to subvert their former Constitution. It has already struck at the Authority of one of the Branches of the Legislature in a particular Manner. And, if you, Gentlemen of the Assembly, should give your Approbation to Transactions of this Nature, you will do as much as lies in your Power to destroy that Form of Government of which you are an important Part, and which it is your Duty by all lawful Means to preserve. To you your Constituents have intrusted a peculiar Guardianship of their Rights and Privileges. You are their legal Representatives, and you cannot, without a manifest Breach of your Trust, suffer any Body of Men, in this or any of the other Provinces, to usurp and exercise any of the Powers vested in you by the Constitution. It behoves you particularly, who must be constitutionally supposed to speak the Sense of the People at large, to be extremely cautious in consenting to any Act whereby you may engage them as Parties in, and make them answerable for Measures which may have a Tendency to involve them in Difficulties far greater than those they aim to avoid.

Besides, there is not, Gentlemen, the least Necessity, consequently there will not be the least Excuse for your running any such Risks on the present Occasion. If you are really disposed to represent to the King any Inconveniences you conceive yourselves to lie under, or to make any Propositions on the present State of *America,* I can assure you, from the best Authority, that such Representations or Propositions will be properly attended to, and certainly have greater Weight coming from each Colony in it's separate Capacity, than in a Channel, of the Propriety and Legality of which there may be much Doubt.

You have now pointed out to you, Gentlemen, two Roads—one evidently leading to Peace, Happiness, and a Restoration of the publick Tranquility—the other inevitably conducting you to Anarchy, Misery, and all the Horrors of a Civil War. Your Wisdom, your Prudence, your Regard for the true Interests of the People, will be best known when you have shewn to which Road you give the Preference. If to the former, you will probably afford Satisfaction to the moderate, the sober, and the discreet Part of your Constituents. If to the latter, you will, perhaps for a Time, give Pleasure to the warm, the rash, and the inconsiderate among them, who, I would willingly hope, violent as is the Temper of the present Times, are not even now the Majority. But it may be well for you to remember, should any Calamity hereafter befal them from your Compliance with their Inclinations, instead of pursuing, as you ought, the Dictates of your own Judgment, that the Consequences of their returning to a proper Sense of their Conduct, may prove deservedly to yourselves.

I shall say no more at present on this disagreeable Subject, but only to repeat an Observation I made to a former Assembly on a similar Occasion. "Every Breach of the Constitution, whether it proceeds from the Crown or the People, is, in its Effects, equally destructive to the Rights of both. It is the Duty, therefore, of those who are intrusted with Government, to be equally careful in guarding against Encroachments from the one as the other. But *It is* (says one of the wisest of Men) *a most infallible Symptom of the dangerous State of Liberty, when the chief Men of a free Country shew a greater Regard to Popularity than to their own Judgment.*"

W^M. Franklin

7

WILLIAM FRANKLIN

Letter to Lord Dartmouth

May 6, 1775

In the spring of 1775, William Franklin received a copy of Lord North's last effort to accommodate colonial anger over imperial policy. Unfortunately, the secretary's proposals arrived just as the battles of Lexington and Concord were being fought. Thus, as the governor explained to Lord Dartmouth, it would be more difficult than ever to persuade his assembly to listen to North's offer. Indeed, as Franklin's description of the colonies indicates, he was himself close to despair as he saw events spinning out of control everywhere.

How does Franklin explain the fact that so many Americans, even avowed "Tories," were joining extralegal organizations? What is Franklin's attitude toward English policy? What fears does he express for his own safety?

To the Right Honble the Earl of Dartmouth

Perth Amboy, May 6th 1775

My Lord,

A few Days ago I was honoured with your Lordship's several Dispatches of the 22^d^ of February and 3^d^ of March.

The Resolution of the House of Commons on the 20th of February, declaratory of the Sense of Parliament upon the Subject of Taxation, especially as explained by your Lordship's Circular Dispatch, afforded me very particular Pleasure, as it gave me Strong Hopes that it would be productive of a thorough Reconciliation between the two Countries. This likewise was the Sentiment of such of His Majesty's Council in this Province as I had an Opportunity of communicating it to, who immediately advised the Calling of the General Assembly, that no Time might be lost in accomplishing so desirable a Purpose. But an Event has since occurred which has, in some Degree, checked those flattering Hopes, and given me Reason to apprehend that an amicable Accom-

---

William Franklin, letter to Lord Dartmouth, May 6, 1775, Public Record Office, American and West Indies, vol. 177 (195), from Frederick W. Ricord and William Nelson, eds., *Documents Relating to the Colonial History of the State of New Jersey, 1767–1776* (Newark: Daily Advertiser's Printing House, 1886), 10:590–97.

modation will be with Difficulty, if at all, effected at this Time. The Accounts we have from Massachusetts Bay respecting the Proceedings of the King's Troops, and the late Engagement between them and the Inhabitants of that Province, have occasioned such an Alarm and excited so much Uneasiness among the People throughout this and the other Colonies, that there is Danger of their committing some outrageous Violences before the present Heats can subside. They are arming themselves, forming into Companies, and taking uncommon Pains to perfect themselves in Military Discipline. Every Day new Alarms are spread, which have a Tendency to keep the Minds of the People in a continual Ferment, make them suspicious, and prevent their paying any Attention to the Dictates of sober Reason and common Sense. A great Number of the Inhabitants of Freehold in Monmouth County were persuaded to believe that Hostilities were ordered to be commenced against all the Colonies, and that a Man of War was lying in the Bay near Sandy-hook with a Design to send up a Boat in the Night to carry off the Money in the Treasury, and the Records in the Secretary's Office at Amboy. In Consequence of this Report, some of the Committee of Freehold with upwards of 30 of the Militia, arm'd with Firelocks, set out on Wednesday Afternoon last, and travelled through Brunswick to Woodbridge within 3 Miles of this place, where they got about Midnight, and would have come down immediately here, in order to carry off the Treasury & Records, had they not been persuaded by some of the Woodbridge Committee to desist from their Enterprize till they could call a Meeting of the neighbouring Committees in the Morning. These Committees when they met disapproved of the Measure, & prevailed on those inconsiderate People to return Home, which they did, marching through Amboy by my Door, with Colours Drum & Fife.

All legal Authority and Government seems to be drawing to an End here, and that of Congresses, Conventions, and Committees establishing in their Place. The People are everywhere entering into Associations similar to that of New York, whereby they engage to "adopt and endeavour carry into Execution *whatever Measures* may be recommended by the *Continental Congress,* or resolved upon by the *Provincial Convention,* and that they will *in all Things follow* the Advice of their *General Committees,*" &c. This Association has been entered into by many of what are here called Tories, and Friends to Government, as well as by the other Party; they being in a Manner compelled thereto through Apprehensions for their personal Safety, and as it seemed the only Expedient, in such an Exigency, for the preservation of Peace & good Order and the Security of private Property.

It is highly probable that General Gage must have had very strong Reasons, or he would not have sent out the Party to Concord, and risk'd the commencing Hostilities, at a Time when all His Majesty's Governors on the Continent had

Directions, and were consequently taking Measures to promote an amicable Settlement of the present unhappy Difference. It was, however, expected that previous to the Commencement of any military Operations, the Assembly of Massachuset's Bay would have been called, and that the Governor would have laid before them the Resolution of the House of Commons, declarative of their Sentiments respecting the future Taxation of the Colonies, and explained them in the manner mentioned in your lordship's Circular Dispatch of the 3d of March: And that no hostile Measure of any kind would have been taken that could have had a Chance of bringing on an Engagement with the Troops, until after their Refusal to acquiesce with the Propositions held out in that Resolution, or that they had been warned, by a Proclamation, of the ill Consequences that would infallibly attend their Contumacy. The General's Motives for not pursuing such a Plan of Conduct will, I doubt not, from his distinguished Character, and well-known Prudence, be found strictly justifiable and proper; yet it is greatly to be regretted that the late Skirmish happened at the Time it did, as it has, in its Consequences, proved one of the most unlucky Incidents that could have occurred in the present Situation of Affairs. It will not only be a Means of retarding, if not entirely defeating the Wishes & Measures of His Majesty for a happy Reconciliation; but will endanger the Lives & properties of every Officer of Government in the King's Colonies to the Southward of New England who may refuse to acquiesce in their Proceedings. It has, indeed, been repeatedly declared that they were determined to make Reprisals, and that in case Genl Gage should seize upon or punish any of the people of that Country, they would seize upon the King's Officers & Friends of Government, throughout the Colonies, and treat them in the same Manner. Nor have I the least Doubt but such would be the Consequence, if military Operations were carried on, and a Number of the Inhabitants are killed or taken Prisoners: For in none of the Capitals of those Southern Colonies have they, as yet, either Troops, Forts or Men of War, that can afford them any Protection. A matter which surely ought to be particularly attended to, and provided for, before any Hostilities are commenced.

Altho' there seems at present but little Hopes that the Terms proposed by the House of Commons, & approved of by His Majesty will be immediately agreed to by the several Assemblies, yet I cannot but think that when they come to be explained and rightly understood by the People, there will be a Disposition to comply with them, or some others of a similar Nature. The Assemblies will probably avoid coming singly to any Determination before they know the Sentiments of the general Congress to be held this Month at Philadelphia. I have just heard that the Lieut Governor & Council of New York have determined not to lay the propositions before the Assembly of that Province, thinking Men's Minds are at present too much heated & inflamed to consider the Matter with that Calmness & Attention which the Importance of it requires. And I am likewise informed that the Govr. of Pensylvania has communicated them to the Assembly of that Province, who have declined acceding to them, & have declared that they "cannot think the Terms pointed out afford a just and reasonable Ground for a final Accommodation between G. Britain & the Colonies;" intimating besides, "that all Aids from them should be their own free & voluntary Gifts, not taken by Force, nor extorted by Fears,—that the Plan held forth may be classed under one of these Descriptions—and that if they had no *other* Objection to it they could not honorably adopt it without the Advice & Consent of the other Colonies."

It is not unlikely that I shall receive a somewhat similar Answer from the Assembly of this Province; and, indeed, I am inclined to think that every other Assembly will wait to take their Tone from the general Congress; and that therefore, unless the Plan is satisfactorily explained to them, we shall be as wide from the final Settlement of the Disputes as ever. But as they are not a legally authorised Body, and the Governors cannot take any direct Notice of them, there seems no other Method so proper for obtaining their Sentiments on the Plan, and thereby bringing the Matter to a Speedy Decision, as to communicate it as soon as possible to the several Assemblies, and give them an Opportunity of informing the Congress of the Nature of it, and of consulting them on the Occasion.—I formerly (in my Dispatch No. ——) Suggested the Expediency of having a duely authorized Congress of Persons to be chosen by the several Assemblies, which should be impowered to meet and consult with such Persons as His Majesty should commission for the Purpose, and it still appears to me to be a Measure necessary to expedite the final Settlement of this troublesome & destructive Contest. For, I am convinced that Matters are now carried so far that the Americans in general are disposed to run the Risk of a total Ruin rather than suffer a Taxation by any but their own immediate Representatives and that there is not the least Reason to expect they will ever, in this Instance, consent to acknowledge the Right, even if they should be obliged to submit to the Power of Parliament. The Plan now offered to them is happily a Waving of the Exercise of that Right on Conditions corresponding with their own former Declarations, and which I cannot therefore but hope the reasonable Part of them will think it the Duty of this Country to adopt.

What renders the Situation of American Governors more difficult and dangerous in these Times of Disorder than it would otherwise would be, is the publication of their Correspondence with His Majesty's Ministers. If they neglect to transmit a circumstantial Account of the principal Transactions in their Provinces, they will be guilty of a Breach of their Duty, and necessarily & deservedly incur His Majesty's Displeasure. But let their Detail be ever so strictly conformable to the Truth, and the Facts even supported by the Accounts published in the Newspapers by the Leaders of the People themselves, yet, if it does not altogether quadrate with the Ideas which these Men may afterwards choose to have entertained of their Conduct, the Governors are sure to be held up as Enemies to their Country, and every undue Means are taken to make them the Objects of the People's Resentment. I am led to mention this Matter to your Lordship, particularly at this Time, from the following Paragraph published in Holt's last New York Journal, viz.t—"By the Copies of Letters lately laid before the Parliament (printed in London) from the Governors of the several British Colonies, relative to the late unconstitutional and tyrannical Acts of Parliament, it appears that Gov.r Eden of Maryland was the *only* one who honestly & ingenuously represented the Case, with his Opinion thereon, to the Ministry; which Conduct & Opinion will do him lasting Honour. In general, the Governors & other Ministerial people, outstrip their Instructions and anticipate the Wishes of their Patrons even in their most blameable Designs. Had it not been owing to the Encouragement, & even Temptation thus given to the Ministry, in their last treasonable & most horrible Design of Destroying the English Constitution, and enslaving the Colonies, it is more than probable they would have desisted from the black Attempt."—Your Lordship may easily judge of the pernicious Tendency of such publications at such a critical juncture as the present. There is no defending ourselves against the Consequences, and we must patiently submit. But if the two Houses of Parliament have a Right to call for State Papers to be laid before them, as being the great Council of the Nation, it seems astonishing they should not, from Motives of Policy, keep those kind of Communications perfectly secret, as all other national Councils do. The Evil is not merely the exposing an Officer to the Resentment of an ungovernable Populace but the furnishing the Enemies of the Nation with such Intelligence of the State of Affairs as must often be of great Detriment to the Publick. I must beg therefore that the *secret* Intelligence I sent your Lordship by the last Packet may be destroyed, as should it be copied & transmitted here, it would probably prove the Destruction of a very worthy Gentleman, and one of the warmest Friends to Government in this Country.[1]

I have the Honor to be, with the greatest Respect & Regard,

My Lord, Your Lordship's most obedient
& most humble Servant
W.M Franklin

[1]Franklin is probably referring to information concerning Joseph Galloway's Plan of Union and to his accounts of the proceedings of the Continental Congress, all of whose sessions were held in secret.

8

BENJAMIN FRANKLIN

Letter to William Franklin

August 16, 1784

On July 22, 1784, William Franklin wrote a letter to his father from London, where he had gone into exile after it became clear that England would recognize American independence. Benjamin was in France, where he had helped negotiate the Peace of Paris, effectively ending the war between England and its former American colonies. The two men had not seen each other in nearly a decade. William wrote to his father in hopes of renewing their old relationship. Benjamin, however, while he claimed to find his son's letter "agreeable," was not quite ready to forgive and forget.

How do you think that William Franklin reacted when he received this letter? Why might Benjamin have been more willing to forgive Joseph Galloway than he was his own son?

Passy, Aug. 16, 1784

Dear Son,

I received your Letter of the 22d past, and am glad to find that you desire to revive the affectionate Intercourse, that formerly existed between us. It will be very agreeable to me; indeed nothing has ever hurt me so much and affected me with such keen Sensations, as to find myself deserted in my old Age by my only Son; and not only deserted, but to find him taking up Arms against me, in a Cause, wherein my good Fame, Fortune and Life were all at Stake. You conceived, you say, that your Duty to your King and Regard for your Country requir'd this. I ought not to blame you for differing in Sentiment with me in Public Affairs. We are Men, all subject to Errors. Our Opinions are not in our own Power; they are form'd and govern'd much by Circumstances, that are often as inexplicable as they are irresistible. Your Situation was such that few would have censured your remaining Neuter, *tho' there are Natural Duties which precede political ones, and cannot be extinguish'd by them.*

This is a disagreable Subject. I drop it. And we will endeavour, as you

---

Benjamin Franklin, letter to William Franklin, August 16, 1784. From Albert H. Smyth, ed., *The Writings of Benjamin Franklin* (New York: Macmillan, 1906), 9:252–54.

propose mutually to forget what has happened relating to it, as well as we can. I send your Son over to pay his Duty to you.[1] You will find him much improv'd. He is greatly esteem'd and belov'd in this Country, and will make his Way anywhere. It is my Desire, that he should study the Law, as a necessary Part of Knowledge for a public Man, and profitable if he should have occasion to practise it. I would have you therefore put into his hands those Law-books you have, viz. Blackstone, Coke, Bacon, Viner, &c. He will inform you, that he received the Letter sent him by Mr. Galloway, and the Paper it enclosed, safe.

On my leaving America, I deposited with that Friend[2] for you, a Chest of Papers, among which was a Manuscript of nine or ten Volumes, relating to Manufactures, Agriculture, Commerce, Finance, etc., which cost me in England about 70 Guineas; eight Quire Books, containing the Rough Drafts of all my Letters while I liv'd in London. These are missing. I hope you have got them, if not, they are lost. Mr. Vaughan[3] has publish'd in London a Volume of what he calls my Political Works. He proposes a second Edition; but, as the first was very incompleat, and you had many Things that were omitted, (for I used to send you sometimes the Rough Drafts, and sometimes the printed Pieces I wrote in London,) I have directed him to apply to you for what may be in your Power to furnish him with, or to delay his Publication till I can be at home again, if that may ever happen.

I did intend returning this year; but the Congress, instead of giving me Leave to do so, have sent me another Commission, which will keep me here at least a Year longer; and perhaps I may then be too old and feeble to bear the Voyage. I am here among a People that love and respect me, a most amiable Nation to live with; and perhaps I may conclude to die among them; for my Friends in America are dying off, one after another, and I have been so long abroad, that I should now be almost a Stranger in my own Country.

I shall be glad to see you when convenient, but would not have you come here at present. You may confide to your son the Family Affairs you wished to confer upon with me, for he is discreet. And I trust, that you will prudently avoid introducing him to Company, that it may be improper for him to be seen with. I shall hear from you by him and any letters to me afterwards, will come safe under Cover directed to Mr. Ferdinand Grand, Banker at Paris. Wishing you Health, and more Happiness than it seems you have lately experienced, I remain your affectionate father,

B. Franklin

[1]William Temple Franklin.
[2]Joseph Galloway.
[3]Benjamin Vaughan, friend and former publisher of Benjamin Franklin.

A Franklin Chronology (1706–1814)

1706

January 17: Birth of Benjamin Franklin in Boston.

1723

Fall: Benjamin Franklin arrives in Philadelphia.

1724

November: Benjamin Franklin's first trip to London (till 1726).

1728

Benjamin Franklin sets up print shop on Market Street, Philadelphia.

1730

September: Benjamin Franklin marries Deborah Reed. Birth of William Franklin.

1732

October: Birth of Francis Folger Franklin.

1736

November: Death of Francis Folger Franklin.

1743

October: Birth of Sarah Franklin.

1743–48

King George's War.

1746

Winter: William Franklin joins king's army as an ensign.

1748

July–October: William Franklin joins Conrad Weisner's expedition to the Ohio territory.

1750

William Franklin begins studying law with Joseph Galloway.

1752

February: Benjamin Franklin publishes *Experiments and Observations on Electricity* describing his kite experiment.

1753

August: Benjamin Franklin appointed co-deputy postmaster general of North America, with William Hunter.

1754

June: Benjamin and William Franklin travel to Albany for Albany Conference.

1755–63

French and Indian War.

1755

April: Benjamin and William Franklin visit General Edward Braddock at his headquaters in Maryland.

July: Braddock defeated by French and Indian forces.

1756

December–January: The Franklins help restore order on the Pennsylvania frontier.

1757–62

Benjamin Franklin travels to London as agent of Pennsylvania assembly. William Franklin accompanies him to complete his legal studies.

1758

November: William Franklin called to the bar.

1759 or 1760

Birth of William Temple Franklin.

1762

August: Benjamin Franklin sails for America.

September: William Franklin marries Elizabeth Downes. William Franklin commissioned as royal governor of New Jersey.

November: William and Elizabeth Franklin return to America.

1763

March: William Franklin takes oath of office as governor of New Jersey.

Spring: Pontiac's Rebellion waged on Pennsylvania frontier.

October: Proclamation of 1763 divides British America into two parts and prohibits settlement west of the Appalachians.

1764

March: Sugar or Revenue Act develops new duties on imports to maintain English troops in America.

Fall: Benjamin Franklin loses reelection bid to Pennsylvania assembly.

November: Benjamin Franklin returns to England to seek royal charter for Pennsylvania.

1765

February: Stamp Act imposes taxes on newspapers and other documents.

October: Stamp Act Congress held in New York.

November: Privy Council tables Pennsylvania's request for a royal charter.

1766

February: Benjamin Franklin testifies before Parliament about effect of English policies on Americans.

March: Repeal of Stamp Act. Declaratory Act asserts Parliament's right to legislate for the colonies.

1767

May: Townshend Acts impose duties on imports such as paper, lead, paint, and tea.

December: John Dickinson begins his "Farmer's Letters."

1768

January: Lord Hillsborough becomes secretary of American Department.

February: Massachusetts assembly distributes circular letter about resisting the Townshend Acts.

April: Benjamin Franklin appointed London agent for Georgia's assembly.

Midsummer: Two British regiments sent to Boston to maintain order and help customs commissioners.

July: East Jersey treasury robbery.

1769

December: Benjamin Franklin appointed agent for New Jersey's assembly.

1770

March 5: Boston Massacre.

March: Repeal of most Townshend duties—with the exception of the duty on tea. East Jersey citizens riot quelled over court reform and land disputes.

October: Bejamin Franklin appointed London agent of Massachusetts legislature.

1771

January: Benjamin Franklin's quarrel with Lord Hillsborough over his credentials as agent.

Spring: Governor Hutchinson refuses to accept salary from Massachusetts assembly.

August: Benjamin Franklin begins writing *Autobiography*.

1772

August: Lord Hillsborough resigns from Board of Trade and American Department, replaced by Lord Dartmouth.

July: Massachusetts assembly petitions king, demanding the right to continue paying the governor's salary.

November: Massachusetts resolutions questioning both Parliament's and the king's authority in the colony.

December: Benjamin Franklin sends Hutchinson-Oliver letters to Massachusetts Speaker Thomas Cushing.

1773

May: Tea Act becomes law, reinstating the Townshend duty on tea.

June: Massachusetts assembly asks king to remove Governor Hutchinson and Lieutenant Governor Oliver from office.

December 16: Boston Tea Party protests Tea Act tax.

1774

January: Benjamin Franklin's public humiliation at the Privy Council hearing on the petitions to remove Hutchinson and Oliver from Massachusetts. Benjamin Franklin removed from his position as postmaster general.

February: Stephen Skinner resigns as East Jersey treasurer.

March: Boston Port Act closes Boston Harbor in response to the Boston Tea Party.

May–June: Coercive Acts require colonies to quarter English troops and expand governors' powers.

September: First Continental Congress begins meeting. Galloway's Plan of Union rejected, tabled, and expunged by Continental Congress.

Fall: William Franklin moves to Perth Amboy.

October: Continental Congress issues Declaration of Rights and Resolves and adopts the Suffolk Resolves, in resistance to the Coercive Acts.

November: Benjamin Franklin writes "Hints for a Desirable Union."

December: Deborah Franklin dies.

1775

February: Lord North introduces plan of reconciliation.

April: Battles of Lexington and Concord.

May: New Jersey assembly rejects North's plan. Benjamin Franklin arrives in Philadelphia; becomes Pennsylvania delegate at Second Continental Congress.

May or June: Three generations of Franklins meet at Trevose, Joseph Galloway's estate.

June: George Washington named commander-in-chief of continental Army.

July: Benjamin Franklin becomes postmaster general of new American postal system. Olive Branch Petition asks king to intercede with Parliament on colonies' behalf.

1776

January: Thomas Paine publishes *Common Sense*. William Franklin's letter to Dartmouth intercepted by William Alexander. First attempt to arrest William Franklin.

February: Benjamin Franklin part of ambassadorial delegation to Canada.

June 19: Arrest of William Franklin. Richard Henry Lee offers resolution in Continental Congress calling for American independence.

July 4: Congress unanimously adopts Declaration of Independence.

September: Benjamin Franklin becomes commissioner to France, taking William Temple Franklin and Benjamin Franklin Bache with him to Paris.

1778

October: William Franklin released from prison.

1779

December: William Franklin becomes president of Board of Associated Loyalists.

1781

October: Lord Cornwallis surrenders at Yorktown.

1782

August: William Franklin leaves for London.

1783

April: Congress ratifies Peace of Paris ending the War for Independence.

1785

July: Benjamin and William Franklin meet for the last time at Southhampton.

1788

William Franklin marries Mary D'Evelyn.

1790

April: Benjamin Franklin dies.

1814

November: William Franklin dies.

Selected Bibliography

Students interested in a general overview of the revolutionary era will suffer from an embarrassment of riches. For students who want to find out more about the variety of ways that historians have approached the Revolution, a number of good anthologies exist. George Athan Billias, ed., *The American Revolution: How Revolutionary Was It?* 4th ed. (New York: Holt, Reinhart, and Winston, 1990), is a good place to begin. Students may also wish to consult Ray A. Billington, ed., *The Reinterpretation of Early American History* (San Marino: Huntington Library, 1966); or Richard D. Brown, ed., *Major Problems in the Era of the American Revolution, 1760–1791* (Lexington, Mass.: D. C. Heath, 1992).

A few works helped inform the general framework of this book. They include Bernard Bailyn, *Ideological Origins of the American Revolution* (Cambridge: Harvard University Press, 1967) and *Origins of American Politics* (New York: Knopf, 1968); Pauline Maier, *From Resistance to Revolution: Colonial Radicals and the Development of American Opposition to Britain, 1765–1776* (New York: Knopf, 1972; Gordon Wood, *The Creation of the American Republic, 1776–87* (Chapel Hill: University of North Carolina Press, 1969) and *Radicalism of the American Revolution* (New York: Knopf, 1992); Gary B. Nash, *The Urban Crucible: Social Change, Political Consciousness and the Origins of the American Revolution* (Cambridge: Harvard University Press, 1979).

For a general understanding of the Revolution from the loyalist perspective, see William Nelson, *The American Tory* (Boston: Beacon Press, 1968); Wallace Brown, *The King's Friends: The Composition and Motives of the American Loyalist Claimants* (Providence: Brown University Press, 1965), and *The Good Americans* (New York: William Morrow, 1969); and Robert M. Calhoon, *The Loyalists in Revolutionary America, 1760–81* (New York: Harcourt Brace Jovanovich, 1973).

Fine biographies of individual loyalists include Bernard Bailyn, *The Ordeal of Thomas Hutchinson* (Cambridge: Harvard University Press, 1974); Carol Berkin, *Jonathan Sewall: Odyssey of an American Loyalist* (New York: Columbia University Press, 1974); and John Ferling, *The Loyalist Mind: Joseph Galloway and the American Revolution* (University Park: Pennsylvania State University Press, 1977). Pauline Maier's *The Old Revolutionaries: Political Lives in the Age of Samuel Adams* (New York: Knopf, 1980) provides excellent interpretive biographies of five patriot leaders.

Studies of Benjamin Franklin abound. The most thorough treatment of Franklin remains Carl Van Doren's *Benjamin Franklin* (New York: Viking, 1938). Much more readable studies include Esmond Wright, *Franklin of Philadelphia* (Cambridge: Harvard University Press, 1986), Thomas J. Fleming, *The Man Who Dared the Lightning: A New Look at Benjamin Franklin* (New York: William Morrow, 1971), and Claude-Anne Lopez and Eugenia Herbert, *The Private Franklin: The Man and His Family* (New York: Norton, 1975). There are only a few readily accessible studies of William Franklin. They include Willard S. Randall, *A Little Revenge: Benjamin Franklin and His Son* (Boston: Little, Brown, 1984); Larry Gerlach, *William Franklin: New Jersey's Last Royal Governor* (Trenton: New Jersey Historical Commission, 1975), and Sheila L. Skemp, *William Franklin: Son of a Patriot, Servant of a King* (New York: Oxford University Press, 1990).

Pennsylvania politics in the revolutionary era are confusing at best. Gary Nash's *Urban Crucible* is useful in helping sort out some of the ins and outs of the era, as are Benjamin H. Newcomb, *Franklin and Galloway: A Political Partnership* (New Haven: Yale University Press, 1972); William S. Hanna, *Benjamin Franklin and Pennsylvania Politics* (Stanford: Stanford University Press, 1964), and James H. Hutson, *Pennsylvania Politics, 1746–1770: The Movement for Royal Government and Its Consequences* (Princeton: Princeton University Press, 1972). For New Jersey politics, the best overview of the period is Larry Gerlach's *Prologue to Independence: New Jersey in the Coming of the Revolution* (New Brunswick: Rutgers University Press, 1976). Students might also wish to consult John E. Pomfret, *Colonial New Jersey: A History* (New York: Charles Scribner's Sons, 1973). John Shy's *Toward Lexington: The Role of the British Army in the Coming of the Revolution* (Princeton: Princeton University Press, 1965) will help students put William Franklin's quarrels over the Mutiny Act in perspective.

England and America faced a series of crises between 1763 and 1776. Edmund S. and Helen M. Morgan's *The Stamp Act Crisis: Prologue to Revolution* (Chapel Hill: University of North Carolina Press, 1953) provides an interpretive analysis of one of the most important early debates between the colonies and the mother country. For a discussion of the Townshend Acts, see "The Townshend Acts of 1767," *William and Mary Quarterly*, 3rd ser., 27 (1970): 90–121. Benjamin W. Labaree, *The Boston Tea Party* (Boston: Northeastern University Press, 1979), remains the best single account of that incident. Eric Foner's *Tom Paine and Revolutionary America* (New York: Oxford University Press, 1976) is the most recent attempt to explain Paine's role in moving America toward independence. Garry Wills's *Inventing America: Jefferson's Declaration of Independence* (Garden City, N.Y.: Doubleday, 1978) analyzes the meaning and importance of the Declaration. For an English perspective on the events leading to the Revolution, see Robert W. Tucker and David C. Hendrickson, *The Fall of the First British Empire: Origins of the War of American Independence* (Baltimore: Johns Hopkins University Press, 1982).

Benjamin Franklin was deeply involved in the diplomatic side of the American Revolution. For this aspect of the revolutionary story, see Jonathan R. Dull, *A Diplomatic History of the American Revolution* (New Haven: Yale University Press,

1985) and *Franklin the Diplomat: The French Mission* (Philadelphia: American Philosophical Society, 1982); or Gerald Stourzh, *Benjamin Franklin and American Foreign Policy*, 2nd ed. (Chicago: University of Chicago Press, 1969). For help in understanding the military problems William Franklin faced after he left captivity, see Don Higginbotham, *The War of American Independence: Military Attitudes, Policies, and Practice, 1763–1789* (New York: Macmillan, 1971); Piers Mackesy, *The War for America, 1775–1783* (Cambridge: Harvard University Press, 1964); John Shy, *A People Numerous and Armed: Reflections on the Military Struggle for American Independence* (New York: Oxford University Press, 1976); and William P. Willcox, *Portrait of a General: Sir Henry Clinton in the War of Independence* (New York: Knopf, 1964).

Index